CW00552878

OXFORD MID-CENTURY STUDIES

The Oxford Mid-Century Studies series publishes monographs in several disciplinary and creative areas in order to create a thick description of culture in the thirty-year period around the Second World War. With a focus on the 1930s through the 1960s, the series concentrates on fiction, poetry, film, photography, theatre, as well as art, architecture, design, and other media. The mid-century is an age of shifting groups and movements, from existentialism through abstract expressionism to confessional, serial, electronic, and pop art styles. The series charts such intellectual movements, even as it aids and abets the very best scholarly thinking about the power of art in a world under new techno-political compulsions, whether nuclear-apocalyptic, cold-war-propagandized, transnational, neo-imperial, super-powered, or postcolonial.

IAN WATT

THE NOVEL AND THE WARTIME CRITIC

MARINA MACKAY

UNIVERSITY PRESS

OXFORD
UNIVERSITY PRESS

Great Clarendon Street, Oxford, OX2 6DP,
United Kingdom

Oxford University Press is a department of the University of Oxford.
It furthers the University's objective of excellence in research, scholarship,
and education by publishing worldwide. Oxford is a registered trade mark of
Oxford University Press in the UK and in certain other countries

First Edition published in 2018
Impression: 1

Published in the United States of America by Oxford University Press
198 Madison Avenue, New York, NY 10016, United States of America

British Library Cataloguing in Publication Data
Data available

Library of Congress Control Number: 2018906174

ISBN 978–0–19–882499–2

Printed and bound by
CPI Group (UK) Ltd, Croydon, CR0 4YY

Acknowledgements

Material from the first chapters originally appeared in 'The Wartime Rise of *The Rise of the Novel*', *Representations*, 119 (Summer 2012), 119–43, © 2012 by the Regents of the University of California. I am grateful to the *Representations* editorial board, and especially Kent Puckett, for encouragement before this book was ever thought of. And it is only a book now thanks to Jacqueline Norton at Oxford University Press, Series Editors Allan Hepburn, Adam Piette, and Lyndsey Stonebridge, and the anonymous readers for the Press: my sincere thanks to them all for their help and encouragement.

I could not be more grateful to Feeny Watt for allowing me to quote from her father's remarkable archive, as well as for reading a late draft of this book in its entirety. Ian Watt's family—his children Feeny and George, and his granddaughter Alison Reed—have been more generous and supportive than any author could hope for.

Most of the unpublished material quoted in what follows is deposited in Stanford University's Special Collections, and I am glad to have the chance to thank the unstintingly helpful Stanford archivists for help both on site and long distance. Thanks also to Bridget Gillies of the University of East Anglia Special Collections, who did so much of my work there for me, and to Miranda Rectenwald and her colleagues in the Special Collections of Washington University in St Louis, who made it possible for me to hear Watt's voice for the first time by digitizing a fragile recording of a lecture Watt delivered there decades earlier. Finally, I am grateful to research staff at The National Archives for their speedy recovery of a document that I doubted had survived.

Any book must accrue many more debts than its author knows, but it is a pleasure to acknowledge mine to Nicoletta Asciuto, Miriam Bailin, Ros Ballaster, Guinn Batten, John Bender, Lara Bovilsky, Matthew Campbell, Bliss Carnochan, Robert Caserio, Mark Damazer, Lara Ehrenfried, Harris Feinsod, Jason Harding, Dillon Johnston, Peter Kalliney, Michelle Kelly, Benjamin Kohlmann, Susan Jones, Joseph

Loewenstein, Deidre Lynch, Peter D. McDonald, Donald MacKay, Peter Mackay, Kate McLoughlin, Sandra Macpherson, Ashley Maher, Laura Marcus, William Maxwell, Leo Mellor, Steven Meyer, Emilie Morin, Ankhi Mukherjee, John Nash, Seamus Perry, Gill Plain, Rachel Potter, Petra Rau, Alastair Renfrew, Rod Rosenquist, Ray Ryan, Victor Sage, Corinne Saunders, Wolfram Schmidgen, Claire Seiler, Vincent Sherry, James Smith, Richard Sugg, Matthew Taunton, Julia Walker, Patricia Waugh, Clare Westall, Mark Wollaeger, and Steven Zwicker.

I owe special debts to the two colleagues closest at the end: David Dwan, for reading my work with his characteristic kindness and imagination, and Abigail Williams, for unfailing inspiration, backbone, and laughter. Finally, it was thanks to Dan Grausam that I even considered writing this book, thousands of miles away from here and in what already feels another lifetime. It would be impossible to write about lives shaped by contingency and not wonder at the luckier accidents of our own.

Contents

Introduction

'Looking back, then,' Ian Watt told an audience in 1978, 'I can see beneath what I hope is the unassuming surface of *The Rise of the Novel* the troubled undercurrents of a fairly representative set of the main intellectual tendencies of its period of gestation—1938 to 1956'.[1] Watt outlines these influences: 'two great but very different traditions of thought: first, of the empirical, historical, and moral elements of my Cambridge training; second, of the many other theoretical elements in the European tradition—formalism and phenomenology in a minor way, and Marxism, Freud, and the Frankfurt School in somewhat larger part'.[2] Watt's intellectual debts are easily identified because he declared them so readily. He studied at Cambridge in the late 1930s with the Leavises and I. A. Richards. He became friends with Theodor Adorno shortly after the Second World War, while he was taking graduate seminars in anthropology and sociology at UCLA ('the Frankfurt School... was then located in the area round the Pacific Palisades').[3] On the same Commonwealth Fellowship, he studied social theory at Harvard with Talcott Parsons, where he first encountered the work of Max Weber (which 'made me very aware of the dubiousness of many of the unchallenged assumptions I had more or less unconsciously picked up').[4] An intellectual orientation emerges as the effect of serial accidents rather than the work of individual design, or, as Watt put it, 'academic writing, in its small way, is also subject to the processes of history'.[5]

1. Ian Watt, 'Flat-Footed and Fly-Blown: The Realities of Realism', *Stanford Humanities Review*, 8/1 (2000), 58.
2. Watt, 'Flat-Footed', 58.
3. Watt, 'Flat-Footed', 55.
4. Watt, 'Flat-Footed', 56.
5. Ian Watt, 'Serious Reflections on *The Rise of the Novel*', in Ian Watt, *The Literal Imagination: Selected Essays*, ed. Bruce Thompson (Palo Alto: Society for the Promotion of Science and Scholarship and the Stanford Humanities Center, 2002), 1.

Like Watt's own book, *Ian Watt: The Novel and the Wartime Critic* is about 'the troubled undercurrents' of 1938 to 1956, and about the ways in which criticism was 'subject to the processes of history' in those years. Whereas Watt was forthcoming about his intellectual debts, he said little about the other historical forces that affected his thinking, but the progress of the project that became *The Rise of the Novel* was dramatically interrupted for seven years by the Second World War, and, above all, by one of the most shatteringly traumatic of war experiences, when Watt was taken prisoner at the fall of Singapore and became one of Japan's many thousands of brutalized prisoners on the Burma–Thailand Railway. My book is about how that world helped to shape his hugely influential scholarly work, and, more broadly, about the extent to which the historiography of the novel is bound to the historical events of the mid-century.

In one sense, Watt's was a shared experience of injury and deprivation; in another, it was a profoundly individual one, and 'individual experience', as he reminds us early in *The Rise of the Novel*, 'is always unique, and therefore new'.[6] I turn to the detail of Watt's biography in the first chapter, but the next few pages outline the wider critical contexts for my argument. Most important among them is the recent attention given to the distinctiveness of mid-century thought, already the subject of major works focusing on the intellectual life of the United States around the Second World War. In his impressive *The Age of the Crisis of Man* (2015), Mark Greif defines the decades between the mid-1930s and mid-1970s as a period when 'man' was 'the figure everyone insisted must be addressed, recognized, helped, rescued, made the center, the measure, the "root," and released for "what was in" him'.[7] Mid-century thinkers sought a new humanism adequate to their times, 'human respect giving its grounds entirely to itself, without God, natural law, positive fiat, or even anything identifiable about the human person'; they asked, 'what could be left of the Enlightenment without the idea of progress?'[8] Amanda Anderson presents a compatible account of this period in *Bleak Liberalism* (2016), where she finds at mid-century the

6. Ian Watt, *The Rise of the Novel: Studies in Defoe, Richardson and Fielding* (Berkeley and Los Angeles: University of California Press, 2001), 13. Subsequent references are to this edition and are cited parenthetically as *RN* followed by page numbers.
7. Mark Greif, *The Age of the Crisis of Man: Thought and Fiction in America, 1933–1973* (Princeton: Princeton University Press, 2015), 8.
8. Greif, *The Age of the Crisis of Man*, 23, 24.

strongest evidence that liberalism accommodates 'sober and even stark views of historical development, political dynamics, and human and social psychology'.[9] As she explains, 'it in fact sounds odd to anyone steeped in that period of history to assert that liberalism is bleak—odd because it is so obviously true', but what is most distinctive about the mid-century moral context is 'the interplay between a tragic ethos and a pragmatic politics, whereby the political commitment is somehow deepened by the subtending existential stance'.[10] The story I tell here supports Greif's and Anderson's sense of a liberal humanism finding its impetus rather than its contradiction in perceptions of human vulnerability and limitation.

I share their interest in the mid-century as unfinished business. They show how our contemporary political and moral paradigms are bound to historical perspectives that are both slipping from living memory and yet too recent to have been examined with the sustained attention that would allow us to recognize the origins of our own ideas. The mid-century is perhaps uniquely important for literary critics as the transatlantic high-water mark for the cultural influence, even prestige, of English as a discipline, and Greif offers a fascinating account of how mid-century criticism fell into line with the prevailing discourse of 'the crisis of man', creating a canon to which living novelists such as William Faulkner and Ernest Hemingway retrofitted themselves in real time.[11]

From that point of view, Greif's book is also part of an important turn towards historicizing post-war criticism. The project of historicizing theory began some time ago. Back in 1993, Tobin Siebers argued that the theoretical assumptions underpinning post-war American criticism were 'a product of the cold war, and the repeated emphasis by the New Critics on objectivity, ambiguity, paradox, the impossibility, and double meaning are part of the cold war climate'.[12] For Siebers, the deconstructive modes that breathed new life into the New Critical attention to the text in itself were no less historically determined, even as history was among the things poststructuralism seemed to be escaping. In the introduction to his 2004 collection *Historicizing Theory*, Peter

9. Amanda Anderson, *Bleak Liberalism* (Chicago: University of Chicago Press, 2016), 2.
10. Anderson, *Bleak Liberalism*, 24, 28.
11. Greif, *The Age of the Crisis of Man*, 103–41.
12. Tobin Siebers, *Cold War Criticism and the Politics of Skepticism* (New York: Oxford University Press, 1993), 30.

Herman argued for the need to historicize theory outside of 'the old History of Ideas approach, which views texts almost exclusively in relation to previous texts and only rarely in relation to the political or social events surrounding and informing them'.[13] Thus, for example, his volume includes Karen Raber's fascinating reading of Michel Foucault in relation to the French experience of the Second World War; a teenager when the war broke out, Foucault had seen at first hand a fatally compliant populace during the period of the German Occupation and Vichy regime.[14] Rupert Read has likewise made the case for reading Wittgenstein's *Philosophical Investigations* as 'a war book': written between the enforcing of the Nuremberg Laws and the final year of the Second World War, the *Philosophical Investigations* 'aims to midwife its readers' acknowledging—really acknowledging—the humanity of all human beings, and not merely of a favored subset'.[15]

With literary criticism rather than theory in mind, Simon During and Joseph North have recently offered important accounts of English between its institutionalization as an academic subject and the changes wrought by theory, addressing the divorce between contemporary literary studies and its formerly public-facing cultural life. During offers an avowedly elegiac account of the pre-theory moment in *Against Democracy* (2012), when he writes of the collapse of the culturally interventionist (in Britain, Leavisite in a broad sense) critical project: 'The divorce of language from experience was now shaped as academic orthodoxy. Paradoxically, the linguistic turn helped hobble literary criticism: it broke its connection to wider social critique and to larger social purposes.'[16] Like North in *Literary Criticism: A Concise Political History* (2017), During believes that the discipline might gain from knowing where, historically, it began. They disagree on the political roots of literary criticism—During emphasizes conservative origins (pre-eminently T. S. Eliot) whereas North recuperates left-liberal progenitors (Richards, William Empson)—but they both stress how

13. Peter C. Herman, 'Introduction: The Resistance to Historicizing Theory', in Peter C. Herman (ed.), *Historicizing Theory* (Albany, NY: State University of New York Press, 2004), 1.
14. Karen Raber, 'Michel Foucault and the Specter of War', in Herman (ed.), *Historicizing Theory*, 49–67.
15. Rupert Read, 'Wittgenstein's *Philosophical Investigations* as a War Book', *New Literary History*, 41/3 (Summer 2010), 593.
16. Simon During, *Against Democracy: Literary Experience in the Era of Emancipations* (New York: Fordham University Press, 2012), 74.

mid-century literary criticism understood its own potentially transformative social purposes. In North's summary, the 'largely lost project' of literary criticism was 'an institutional program of aesthetic education—an attempt to enrich the culture directly by cultivating new ranges of sensibility, new modes of subjectivity, new capacities for experience—using literature as a means'.[17] This was Watt's intellectual world, and one reason why he is an instructive figure is that his career corresponds precisely to the rise and fall of 'criticism' as During and North understand it, bridging the institutionalization of English in interwar Cambridge and the entrenchment of theory in the English departments of the elite American universities in which he spent most of his career.

Around the same time as Watt was using his own work, as I mentioned earlier, in the kind of academic talk that he termed 'solicited transgression in the self-congratulation line', among the responsibilities of his eminence was the expectation that he would voice more directly his views on the state of the discipline.[18] In 1971, he crossed swords with his interwar English mentors, the Leavises, when he reviewed *Dickens: The Novelist* on the BBC. Their book was part of the flurry of publications marking the centenary of Dickens's death, and Watt reflected on how the Leavises' apparent change of heart accorded with the upward trajectory of Dickens's reputation more generally. Watt broadly agreed with their revised judgements but deplored their accompanying denigration of the work of American scholars, which the Leavises dismissed here as 'wrong-headed, ill-informed in ways we have demonstrated, and essentially ignorant and misleading':

> This corrective purpose is remorselessly pursued, as one critic after another is dispatched in a parenthesis or buried in a footnote.
>
> Why bother, one wonders? Can one imagine the Dove of the Annunciation turning into a rancorous jackdaw that thinks it worth his while to hoard what he hates? How can any fallible human being be quite so sure that everyone else is wrong? Wasn't Edmund Wilson's influential essay an important tribute? And didn't Wilson himself later apologise for some of its shortcomings? For that matter, didn't another American, Lionel Trilling, make many of [F. R.] Leavis's points on *Little Dorrit*, including the analogy with Blake, nearly twenty

17. Joseph North, *Literary Criticism: A Concise Political History* (Cambridge, MA: Harvard University Press, 2017), 14, 6.
18. Watt, 'Flat-Footed', 53.

years ago, and conclude that Dickens was 'one of the two greatest novelists of England'? Was it an American who wrote in 1932 that 'Dickens stands primarily for a set of crude emotional exercises', or was it Q. D. Leavis? And wasn't it F. R. Leavis who in 1948 excluded Dickens from the Great Tradition because 'his genius was that of a great entertainer'. I can think of only one analogy to this combination of relentless condemnation of others and obliviousness to one's own proneness to error. The Pope, like other human beings, has changed his public pronouncements in the course of history: but he alone has asserted that all of them were equally infallible.[19]

But, to borrow Watt's question, 'Why bother?' His voluminous professional correspondence leaves the impression of someone with considerable ironic detachment and an aversion to academic drama. It was not even as if he had any special investment in Dickens, about whose fiction he was fairly lukewarm. As far as the Leavises themselves were concerned, he had always declared his most unfashionable debts to them. But their attack on American scholarship *as such* clearly exasperated him enough to feel it was worth correction, even if he knew that his review would draw a furious response from the Leavises (it did).[20]

However, it was also in the 1970s that Watt watched his own humanist mode provoke (in his word) 'antipathy'.[21] A fluent French speaker—son of a Frenchwoman and a Scottish teacher of French, he had studied at the Sorbonne in the late 1930s—Watt had followed with unease the inroads of structuralism into Anglophone criticism: a critical dead-end, he thought, with those 'deep universal structures' that he satirized as its 'timeless verities'.[22] What followed structuralism he considered potentially more damaging, an ominous flight from philosophical method. Even leaving aside 'the appalling logical inadequacy of such writers as Lacan', he wrote, the main institutional outcome of poststructuralism had been a mass of theory textbooks in the style of 'do-it-yourself kits

19. Ian Watt, 'The Leavises on Dickens', *Listener*, 11 March 1971, 300.
20. The main features of Q. D. Leavis's response are rudeness (Watt is accused of 'spite' and 'blatant dishonesty'), self-aggrandizement (it is not Cambridge undergraduates but 'pupils of mine' who take a distinguished Dickens lecturer to task), and scattershot grievances against Cambridge and the profession at large ('I have been *persona non grata* to the Cambridge English Faculty as regards appointments for 40 years'; unnamed careerists have continually 'plagiarised' their work 'for academic advancement'; 'we have been forever persecuted'). 'Letters: The Leavises on Dickens', *Listener*, 8 April 1971, 451.
21. Tzetan Todorov, *Literature and its Theorists: A Personal View of Twentieth-Century Criticism*, trans. Catherine Porter (Ithaca, NY: Cornell University Press, 1987), 119.
22. Watt, 'Flat-Footed', 66, 63.

which promise the user a magic transformation into being what he most wants—to be a philosopher without doing philosophy'.[23]

Watt had his own reasons to be concerned by the increasing institutional power of critical theory in the late 1970s. When the manuscript of *Conrad in the Nineteenth Century* (1979) was 'in effect, turned down' because a reader for the University of California Press deplored its theoretical eclecticism, Watt wrote to the Press that 'I don't think anyone is entitled to assert as a general principle that every book of criticism should contain "a forthright statement or explanation of the rationale of its critical method"'.[24] Disliking programmatic intellectual positions, the critic who defended American criticism against the Leavises now mobilized the urbanity of British critical traditions: 'This critical reticence may just be a reflection of the English notion of polite manners in public discourse; but there are surely some positive advantages.'[25] (Famously, Leavis had refused René Wellek's challenge in 1937 to explain the theory underpinning his judgements.[26]) Not everything, Watt felt, needs to be spelled out. This was how he explained his refusal to add a methodological preface:

> The full critical justification of my Conrad enterprise which the Editorial Committee asks me to add to my preface would not be particularly difficult to do (examples are available in most doctoral dissertations); but, through its necessary abstractness, over-simplification, and implied self-importance, it would remove the book from the particular literary sphere where I think it belongs; and if I began the book with such a statement, I would immediately bore, offend, or deter many of my readers, since I would in effect be saying, 'This is where I stand on the various principles which we critics have been quarrelling about over the centuries. Pay very close attention because it's the price of admission to the book that follows.'[27]

The book was eventually accepted without the theoretical positioning on which its publication had initially been conditional, but the dispute is an important reminder that Watt was closing out his career against

23. Watt, 'Flat-Footed', 66.
24. Ian Watt, 'Realism and Modern Criticism of the Novel', *Stanford Humanities Review*, 8/1 (2000), 80.
25. Todorov, *Literature and its Theorists*, 119.
26. Ian MacKillop gives a brief, balanced summary of the Leavis/Wellek encounter in *F. R. Leavis: A Life in Criticism* (London: Penguin, 1995), 171–2.
27. Todorov, *Literature and its Theorists*, 120.

the polarizing backdrop not simply of contesting theories about literature but of pro-'theory'/anti-'theory' positions altogether.

Pressed by Todorov on his refusal 'to affirm a general critical position', Watt explained that 'the reluctance to state one's premises is partly because of my empiricism, or my skepticism about philosophical methods in general; but also because of my particular belief in the function of critical writing. It is relatively humble.'[28] The growing expectation in this period of more complex methodological commitments meant that, on the one hand, Watt's work could be cast as lightweight and lacking rigour, the charge encoded most politely in the default term 'empirical'; on the other hand, Watt could be used as quite a hefty stick to beat critics dazzled (so this competing story goes) by their faddish embrace of all things theoretical, or, as his former colleague Joseph Frank put it in 2000, 'the hit-parade of lit-crit ideologies that have strutted across the cultural scene in the past twenty years or so'.[29] If Watt's views about literature were a product of a particular historical moment, so was the subsequent debate that too stridently attacked or defended critics' right to proceed without elaborating all the underlying implications of these views.

Although no literary critic thinks to aspire to the virtues of the work she discusses—the wish not to sell them short goes without saying—this book is inevitably vulnerable to similar methodological challenges to those directed at Watt: an inattention to precursors; a tendency to shore up a contestable or outmoded canon; a totalizing view of the relationships between writing and life, and between historical experience and intellectual orientations. Charged with similar positivist offences, Watt provided an Olympian non-response: 'a yawn followed by a plea of *nolo contendere*'.[30] The legal metaphor—Watt's refusal to supply the literary-critical equivalent of either legal defence or allocution ('I do not wish to contend' avoids both)—underscores his sense

28. Todorov, *Literature and its Theorists*, 115, 119.
29. Joseph Frank, 'Foreword', *Stanford Humanities Review*, 8/1 (2000), ix. See also Joseph Frank, 'The Consequence of Ian Watt: A Call for Papers on Diminished Reputations', *Common Knowledge*, 13/2–3 (2007), 497–511. Frederick Crews's foreword to a posthumous collection of Watt's essays characterizes Watt's work as 'the most telling, if implicit, critique of an academic practice that by now is humanistic in name only. Would it be too much to hope that, when the dust has mercifully settled over poststructuralism and postmodernism, critics will rediscover the kind of engagement from which Ian Watt never swerved?' (*The Literal Imagination*, xiii).
30. Todorov, *Literature and its Theorists*, 115.

that recitations of one's own principles may be little more than conventional rhetorical exercises ('examples are available in most doctoral dissertations').

Further-reaching questions of reticence bring me to the main topic of this book, which is about what was also not said at the time. Some of it might have gone without saying when events were so painfully proximate, but most of it could never have been said by the people most directly affected. The core of this book is a war experience about which Watt wrote relatively little and only self-effacingly, and never with reference to his academic life. Chapter 1 reconstructs that war experience from capture to demobilization, showing how it is coded in the whole body of his criticism, not least as a preoccupation with the tacitness of critical sympathy and the advantages of autobiographical silence.

Chapter 2 turns to Watt's landmark *The Rise of the Novel* and reads Daniel Defoe in relation to the culture of the Second World War's prison camps. Watt famously argued in his discussions of *Robinson Crusoe* and *Moll Flanders* that the novel was brought about by and reciprocally advanced the rise of individualism, a claim that has been scrutinized by many subsequent scholars of the early novel. This chapter reads Watt's claims in relation to the radical individualisms recorded in the mid-century literature of imprisonment, focusing on that body of writing's most recurrent of stock figures, the feared and admired racketeer who survives, even thrives, in conditions of almost universal privation. Moll Flanders exemplifies 'the psychology of a special kind of business entrepreneur', Watt argued, and the English economist R. A. Radford ('an ex-prisoner of some three months' standing') wrote in his 1945 essay 'The Economic Organisation of a P. O. W. Camp' of how, 'through his economic activity, the exchange of goods and services, his [the prisoner's] standard of material comfort is considerably enhanced'.[31] The prisoner-entrepreneur is a figure of fascination in the fiction and memoirs of this period, appearing in the work of major writers from Primo Levi to J. G. Ballard, as well as in the many now-forgotten memoirs also discussed in this chapter. Supporting my claim that the individualists who populate Watt's reading

31. Ian Watt, 'The Recent Critical Fortunes of Moll Flanders', *Eighteenth-Century Studies*, 1/1 (Autumn 1967), 112. R. A. Radford, 'The Economic Organisation of a P. O. W. Camp', *Economica*, 12/48 (November 1945), 189.

of Defoe are figures from the prison camp is the fact that the camp entrepreneur is a central, and surprisingly sympathetic, figure in the unpublished and unknown short stories Watt wrote at the same time as he was redrafting what would become *The Rise of the Novel*.

I turn then to Samuel Richardson. Chapter 3 addresses Watt's similarly influential claims about the rise of the novel as the rise of realism by asking why he singled out *Pamela* as the prime instance of the commercialization of private fantasy that he took to be the dominant and most pernicious characteristic of the modern culture industry. This chapter reads his caustic treatment of Richardson's mass-market fairytale alongside his published writings on the wishful misrepresentation of the Japanese prison camps in *The Bridge on the River Kwai* ('The big prizes to the whopping liars' was his summary verdict on that movie's enthusiastic reception[32]). I argue that the exasperated handling of *Pamela* in *The Rise of the Novel* is an attack less on the courtship novel than on the cultural environment of which Watt took Richardson's style and success to be early symptoms. Individualism becomes the ego's imaginary omnipotence over intractable circumstances, and the supposed 'formal realism' of eighteenth-century romantic fiction and Hollywood cinema proves to be mere 'pseudo-realism' working to nurture intoxicating delusions of autonomy. But there is also, I suggest, a competing version of Richardson in *The Rise of the Novel*, when Watt's identification with the fatally imprisoned protagonist of *Clarissa*—no one knew better than the former prisoner of war what it meant to have no options left—indicates a more fraught understanding of selfhood than we usually associate, thanks ironically to the influence of Watt's own book, with the traditional view of individualism and the novel.

Chapter 4 tries to account for the problem many have identified in *The Rise of the Novel*: that Watt's argument cannot accommodate Henry Fielding, neither a realist at the level of narrative form nor concerned with individualism except as a threat to social stability. Indeed, the conventional view that *The Rise of the Novel* sold Fielding short emerged before the book was even published, when Watt's then-employer, the University of California, declined to award Watt a doctorate because of the perceived weakness of the Fielding material in the manuscript of

32. Watt's comment appears on a newspaper clipping about the film's large television viewing figures. Stanford University Special Collections, SC401-ACCN 1990–131, Box 56, Folder 'Kwai: Observer and Life'.

The Rise of the Novel, which Watt submitted at Berkeley in lieu of a conventional Ph.D. thesis. Yet he always professed the importance of Fielding, within and outside the book, and this chapter takes equally seriously Watt's declared admiration for Fielding and the relatively cold-blooded and abbreviated quality of his treatment of him. I suggest here that the 'realism of assessment' he identifies with Fielding expresses a commitment to shared social and moral standards capable of defending the inner as well as the collective life from total collapse at times of crisis—a wholly calculated lowering of the psychological temperature. This chapter reads Watt's Fielding alongside the decisively anti-individualist thrust of prison-camp writing as it describes pivotal moments when prisoners felt themselves slipping down into social as well as environmental degradation; it suggests that Fielding, as a champion of civic order, spoke for Watt to the disciplined collectivity that, all witnesses report, made their survival possible in the end.

It would be impossible to overstate the importance of collective discipline in these beleaguered camps. Third on the critic (and war veteran) Samuel Hynes's inventory of ways in which Second World War prisoners could maximize their chances of survival—right after, first, getting captured in Europe rather than the Far East, and, second, being an officer rather than another rank—is working to 'construct a prison society; model it on the army or on an English public school'.[33] The joking manner notwithstanding, Hynes knew that reconstructed prison-camp societies had saved thousands of lives, in a development that helps to explain the attraction for Watt of Fielding's sociable conservatism. As this chapter also shows, Watt's other major monograph, *Conrad in the Nineteenth Century*, focuses above all on the conflicts between individualism and group identity: 'It is largely Conrad's tragic awareness of the reciprocal but conflicting demands of the individual and of society which makes his fiction seem so modern today,' Watt wrote.[34] The Conrad book addresses the deeply problematic nature of solidarity at moments of crisis, as when Conrad's narrators overwrite the collapse of order with more affirmative and normative versions of what ought to have happened, or when Conrad registers the psychic

33. Samuel Hynes, *The Soldiers' Tale: Bearing Witness to Modern War* (London: Penguin, 1997), 257.

34. Ian Watt, *Conrad in the Nineteenth Century* (Berkeley and Los Angeles: University of California Press, 1979), 358–9. Subsequent references are to this edition and are cited parenthetically as *C.*, followed by page numbers.

costs of a social conformity in which he otherwise wanted to believe: 'if he felt a deeper and more conscious commitment to solidarity, he also felt a deeper and more conscious resentment of its obligations' (*C.* 336).

Chapter 5 takes up a question that Watt asked when he announced the timeliness of Conrad at mid-century:

> For since the Second World War, the experience of a whole generation has brought it close to Conrad's personal position; partly because world history has played over so many of his themes in deafening tones; and partly because our habituation to alienation, reinforced by the vision of the other great modern writers, has inevitably brought us back to the dominating question in Conrad: alienation, yes, but how do we get out of it?[35]

Conrad's effort to salvage community from the ruins of older systems of value is made to anticipate no less than the 'experience of a whole generation'—Watt's own. This chapter explores the overlap between Watt's priorities and the fiction of his time, and particularly the path out of the perceived alienations of modernism offered by forms of realism in the years after the war. This chapter argues that Watt's key-words of individualism, empiricism, and realism became central to both the novel and novel criticism at mid-century because they were useful terms for trying to come to terms with the 1940s for those who suffered some of the worst experiences that even that abysmal decade could offer. Asking searching questions about the function of the novel, this period attempted to recover realism as a means for moral reckoning and social rehabilitation.

Chapter 6 focuses on the institutional dimension of Watt's work as a post-war humanist, for his military and scholarly careers intersect in his attention to the ways in which literature and literary criticism not only express social attitudes but bring societies into being in the form of disciplines and institutions. This chapter describes how, as a 24-year-old prisoner, Watt cut his teeth on academic administration as one of the founders of a prison camp 'English department', indicating his faith (actually warranted, it turned out there) that even in catastrophic circumstances the organized humanities fulfilled powerful needs. This was the forerunner to an administrative career in which he would ultimately become the founding director of the Stanford Humanities Center, and a member of the 1974 working party that led to the creation of the

35. Ian Watt, 'Joseph Conrad: Alienation and Commitment', *Essays on Conrad*, ed. Frank Kermode (Cambridge: Cambridge University Press, 2000), 13.

National Humanities Center. Looking at Watt's post-war understanding of institutions of literature, exemplified in this chapter by the vision of 'English' that he had to formulate in order to create from scratch the founding humanities department at the new University of East Anglia, we find an argument for forms of sociability, creativity, and historicity in literary studies that looks back to the catastrophic circumstances of the camps.

1

Lt Ian Watt, POW

'This book is about Allied prisoners of war taken by the Japanese in World War II. With those POWs, the cliché that every human life has a book in it takes on the force of a real truth: the life of any one of them is worth a book.'

Gavan Daws, *Prisoners of the Japanese* (1994)[1]

'Because what you have to remember, Charley boy, is that you're one of the lucky ones. You're back.'

Henry Green, *Back* (1946)[2]

The idea that there is a book in every former prisoner of the Japanese during the Second World War has a special aptness in relation to the life discussed here. No one could have understood better the book-worthiness of a life story than one of Daws's interviewees, the influential post-war critic Ian Watt. For Watt, the early novel's use of quasi-autobiographical forms was 'as defiant an assertion of the primacy of individual experience in the novel as Descartes's *cogito ergo sum* was in philosophy' (*RN* 15). But, before he was a critic, Watt was a soldier, a prisoner of war, and a slave labourer. This book argues that his wartime world decisively influenced post-war ideas about the novel.

'Defoe is a welcome and portentous figure,' Watt announced in *The Rise of the Novel: Studies in Defoe, Richardson and Fielding* (1957), his classic work on the emergence of the novel in eighteenth-century England:

Welcome because he seems long ago to have called the great bluff of the novel—its suggestion that personal relations really are the be-all and end-all of

1. Gavan Daws, *Prisoners of the Japanese: POWs of World War II in the Pacific* (New York: William Morrow, 1994), 17.
2. Henry Green, *Back* (Champaign, IL: Dalkey Archive Press, 2009), 74.

life; portentous because he, and only he, among the great writers of the past, has presented the struggle for survival in the bleak perspectives which recent history has brought back to a commanding position on the human stage. (*RN* 133–4)

All readers of Defoe recognize that 'struggle for survival'. As early as *The Storm* (1704), his non-fictional account of a natural disaster, Defoe signalled what would prove to be a career-long fascination with the relative degrees of selfishness and altruism with which individuals respond to catastrophes that materialize out of blue skies. His interest in reflex responses to emergency informs the memorably volatile careers of all his protagonists: Robinson Crusoe, Moll Flanders, Bob Singleton, and Colonel Jack are prisoners of unpredictable fortune, while the deracinated courtesan Roxana takes desperate measures to erase her disavowed past when social survival requires the death of her importunate daughter. The unforeseen disaster is a shared one when H. F. traps himself in diseased-ravaged London in *Journal of the Plague Year*, in yet another Defoe narrative in which those 'personal relations' Watt identifies as only seemingly indispensable to the novel are both a luxury and a liability. To find yourself close, in any sense, to other people is to put your own life at risk.

Years before he wrote the books that would become permanently important for Britain's literary history—thanks, above all, to the canonical story of early English prose fiction invariably summed up in Watt's phrase 'the rise of the novel'—the entrepreneur and political journalist Defoe had learned at first hand how difficult the fight for survival could be. John Richetti sums up Defoe's business affairs as 'a series of spectacular failures', and Defoe was repeatedly imprisoned for seditious libel as well as debt, with his incendiary satire *The Shortest Way with the Dissenters* notoriously earning him three stints in the pillory in the summer of 1703.[3] As a lesson about the precariousness of human life, the pillory could hardly be bettered: a life-endangering disgrace that subjected its immobilized victim to whatever missile bystanders felt moved to deliver. The eighteenth-century pillory was 'a wise old institution, that inflicted a punishment of which no one could foresee the extent', Charles Dickens satirically recalled in *A Tale of Two Cities*, his classic novel about people finding themselves on the wrong side of historical events—as Defoe was, and as was Watt.[4]

3. John Richetti, *The Life of Daniel Defoe* (Malden, MA: Blackwell, 2005), 4.
4. Charles Dickens, *A Tale of Two Cities* (London: Penguin, 2003), 63.

For, if bankruptcy, prison, and the pillory taught Defoe about the 'struggle for survival' of which Watt wrote, Watt also knew much more than most people about it. He knew more than most, too, about what he called 'the bleak perspectives which recent history has brought back to a commanding position on the human stage'. Little could have qualified him better to speak from these perspectives than his experience as a prisoner of war in the Far East for the three and a half years between February 1942 and August 1945, one of over 140,000 Allied prisoners of the Japanese. Like most who went through that experience, the young officer Watt knew at close quarters disease, torture, beatings, disability, malnutrition, exhaustion, and terror, in an imprisonment that resembles not only an unforeseen reversal of the kind that punctuates the eventful lives of Defoe's characters, but also a mid-century throwback to the depths of misery Defoe knew during his own imprisonments. Central to John Bender's ground-breaking treatment of eighteenth-century carceral culture in relation to the emergent novel is the 'seeming randomness' of the 'chaotic' older prisons, and Maximillian Novak points out that Defoe spent a total of five months in Newgate at a time when the disease endemic to England's squalid gaols 'killed off more inmates than the gallows'.[5] There was never anything abstract for Defoe about Moll Flanders's memories of Newgate: 'no Colours can represent the Place to the Life; nor any Soul conceive aright of it, but those who have been Sufferers there.'[6] Nor was there anything impersonal for Watt about the problems of imprisonment and survival that he would make central to his reading of Defoe when he returned after his own harrowing incarceration to the coolly academic topic of why the English novel emerged when it did.

Although the landmark work that eventually came from this research in 1957 remains the most widely known book on its subject, it is striking that Watt's standing as a critic was always at least as high among peers who were not themselves eighteenth-century specialists as among those who were. Across the post-war period, commentators as distant from that field and as different from each other as Irving Howe (writing in the 1950s), Tzvetan Todorov (writing in the 1980s), and Edward Said (writing in the 2000s) all characterized Watt as a literally exemplary

5. John Bender, *Imagining the Penitentiary: Fiction and the Architecture of Mind in Eighteenth-Century England* (Chicago: University of Chicago Press, 1987), 1, 11. Maximillian E. Novak, *Daniel Defoe: Master of Fictions* (Oxford: Oxford University Press, 2001), 210, 702.
6. Daniel Defoe, *Moll Flanders* (Oxford: Oxford University Press, 2009), 276.

humanities scholar for the power of his insights into how literature touches on human experience, or what Said called Watt's worldliness.[7] Of course within eighteenth-century studies, *The Rise of the Novel* retains its unique, perhaps uniquely aggravating, canonical stature even after more than sixty years of challenges attesting to the book's significance. In a generous appraisal of Watt's legacy at the end of the twentieth century, Richetti described it as 'a book that has drawn hosts of envious detractors because of its success', while Lennard J. Davis parodied critics' tendency to make Watt their straw man:

> Gone is the myth of *the* novel, a discrete form, a knowable practice, that arose at a specific time for a specific purpose. We run Ian Watt from pillar to postmodern. He made some really big mistakes—he thought there was 'a' novel; he thought it had a beginning; he assumed it was a narrative fiction that displaced previous narrative fictions and had a 'rise' located in metropole England. In doing so, he was naive, sexist, racist, Anglophilic, logocentric, essentialist, positivist, vulgarly materialistic, and probably homophobic. But nobody is perfect.[8]

'To scholars of the eighteenth-century novel, it may seem "a truth universally acknowledged" that "narrative realism" and "the rise of the novel" are outmoded categories,' writes Rachel Carnell in the opening sentence of a 2006 study that goes on to revive these distinctively Watt concepts.[9] Few critical works in any literary-historical field have continued so long after their publication to provoke serious, if exasperated, engagement from other specialists rather than the conscientious citation and thought-inhibited piety appropriate to the period piece. *The Rise of the Novel* continues to be amplified, supplemented, or attacked—it

7. In Howe's laudatory review, *The Rise of the Novel* is 'that rare thing: a model of excellence', a major departure from what Howe considered 'the sectarian dogmatism' of recent years (Irving Howe, 'Criticism at its Best', *Partisan Review*, 25 (1958), 150, 145). Todorov singles out Watt for anti-programmatic, humanist 'masterpieces of literary criticism' (Todorov, *Literature and its Theorists*, 106). Said reviewed Watt's *Conrad in the Nineteenth Century* as 'nothing short of a masterpiece': 'one could call Mr Watt's style of criticism Johnsonian: it is generous, and it endows its material with perspective and humanity'; 'Watt's study of Conrad is worldly in the best sense of that term, and because of that worldliness it is one of the great critical works produced since the 1950s' (Edward W. Said, 'Conrad in the Nineteenth Century', *New York Times*, 9 March 1980, 1, 23, 23).
8. John Richetti, 'The Legacy of Ian Watt's *The Rise of the Novel*', in Leo Damrosch (ed.), *The Profession of Eighteenth-Century Literature: Reflections on an Institution* (Madison: University of Wisconsin Press, 1992), 96. Lennard J. Davis, 'Who Put the "The" in "the Novel"? Identity Politics and Disability in Novel Studies', *NOVEL: A Forum on Fiction*, 31/3 (Summer 1998), 317–18.
9. Rachel Carnell, *Partisan Politics, Narrative Realism, and the Rise of the British Novel* (Basingstoke: Palgrave, 2006), 1.

must somehow be reckoned with—by every critic concerned with the novel's emergence, that vast field of enquiry for which Watt's very title, with or without sceptical quotation marks, remains the usual shorthand designation.[10] The continued currency of the phrase even after all this time is suggested by Nicholas Seager's 2012 survey of the field in a series of overviews of 'essential criticism': Seager's book is titled simply *The Rise of the Novel*.

'The Rise of the Novel is one of the best-known, most commonly taught, and enduringly satisfying concepts in literary criticism,' Seager opens, and Watt's book is its 'classic formulation'.[11] '"The rise of the

10. In increasing distance from Watt: Michael McKeon, *Origins of the English Novel, 1600–1740* (Baltimore: Johns Hopkins University Press, 1987), is a sophisticated amplification that insists on a dialectical rather than teleological account of forces that produced the novel; J. Paul Hunter, *Before Novels: The Cultural Contexts of Eighteenth-Century Fiction* (New York: Norton, 1990), addresses the prehistory of the novel, and includes a generous prefatory tribute to Watt's accomplishment (xx); Nancy Armstrong, *Desire and Domestic Fiction: A Political History of the Novel* (Oxford: Oxford University Press, 1987) and *How Novels Think: The Limits of Individualism from 1719–1900* (New York: Columbia University Press, 2005), follows Watt in identifying novelistic subjectivity with liberal subjectivity, while focusing respectively on the feminization of subjectivity and the function of the realist novel in delimiting personhood; Lennard J. Davis, *Factual Fictions: The Origins of the English Novel* (New York: Columbia University Press, 1983), focuses on the relationship between the novel and the ambiguities of 'news' in the long eighteenth century; Homer Obed Brown, *Institutions of the English Novel: From Defoe to Scott* (Philadelphia: University of Pennsylvania Press, 1997), objects to what he takes to be Watt's treatment of the eighteenth-century novel as if it were merely waiting to be discovered prior to its early nineteenth-century institutionalization; William Beatty Warner, *Licensing Entertainment: The Elevation of Novel Reading in Britain, 1684–1750* (Berkeley and Los Angeles: University of California Press, 1998), approaches the eighteenth-century novel not as privileged individual works but as one among numerous forms of media culture; Margaret Anne Doody, *The True Story of the Novel* (New Brunswick: Rutgers University Press, 1996), rejects almost all Watt's premises, attributing the emergence of the novel instead to the multicultural worlds of the classical Mediterranean. When I say that 'the rise of the novel' is established shorthand, I refer to such major contributions to that field as Jane Spencer, *The Rise of the Woman Novelist* (Oxford: Oxford University Press, 1986); Cathy Davidson, *Revolution and the Word: The Rise of the Novel in America* (New York: Oxford University Press, 1986); Frances Ferguson, 'Rape and the Rise of the Novel', *Representations*, 20 (Autumn 1988), 88–112; Firdous Azim, *The Colonial Rise of the Novel* (London: Routledge, 1993); Josephine Donovan, *Women and the Rise of the Novel, 1405–1726* (Basingstoke: Macmillan, 1999); Leah Price, *The Anthology and the Rise of the Novel* (Cambridge: Cambridge University Press, 2000); Carnell, *Partisan Politics, Narrative Realism, and the Rise of the British Novel*; and Laura Doyle, *Freedom's Empire: Race and the Rise of the Novel in Atlantic Modernity* (Durham, NC: Duke University Press, 2008). In fact, the 'rise of the novel' formula appears as early as Charlotte E. Morgan, *The Rise of the Novel of Manners: A Study of English Prose Fiction between 1600 and 1740* (New York: Columbia University Press, 1911).
11. Nicholas Seager, *The Rise of the Novel* (Basingstoke: Macmillan, 2012), 1.

novel" is one of the most widely circulated narratives of English studies,' William Beatty Warner writes: it is among 'the grand narratives of British literary studies'.[12] In a retrospective afterword to his own important revisionist work, Davis alludes to the resilience of *The Rise of the Novel* when he concedes that, although he had 'tried to drive a stake into the heart of that study', 'Watt's work still lives'—as if its tenacious hold over novel studies makes *The Rise of the Novel* something akin to either a deathless revenant or one of Richardson's invulnerable heroines ('The affair is over. Clarissa lives.').[13] As Ros Ballaster points out in another influential departure from Watt, Davies's own book, with its closing chapters on Defoe, Richardson, and Fielding, reveals indelible traces of Watt's thought even at the level of organization.[14] J. Paul Hunter was probably not exaggerating when he wrote that 'Everyone... who has written about the beginnings of the English novel has been engaged in rewriting Watt and, in so doing, renewing him'.[15] But notwithstanding all that has been written in augmentation or demolition of Watt's claims about the emergence of the novel, no one has asked why he should have arrived at them in the first place: a story less about the mid-eighteenth century than of the mid-twentieth.

My first aim, then, is to uncover the formative impact of Watt's devastating war experience on *The Rise of the Novel*, and to suggest why we might take seriously the origins of classic mid-century intellectual paradigms in the historical contexts that helped to make them possible. Like *The Rise of the Novel*, the first section of this book is in three main parts: on Watt's fraught and historically symptomatic versions of Defoe, Richardson, and Fielding respectively. It reads Watt's literary interests in individualist enterprise (Defoe) and interiority (Richardson) and ostensibly more conservative forms of solidarity (Fielding) in relation to the literature of the Second World War prison camps. The final chapters of the book look outward in order to describe what a war-inflected criticism can tell us, first, about the renewed centrality of novelistic realism at mid-century—'realism' being absolutely the keyword of the Watt tradition of thinking about the novel, as well as of

12. Warner, *Licensing Entertainment*, 1.
13. Davis, *Factual Fictions*, xiv. Samuel Richardson, *Clarissa* (Penguin: London, 2004), 883.
14. Ros Ballaster, *Seductive Forms: Women's Amatory Fiction from 1684 to 1740* (Oxford: Clarendon Press, 1992), 13.
15. Hunter, *Before Novels*, xx.

mid-century fiction and criticism at large—and, second, about the contingent human factor in this period's institutions of humanities scholarship.

Departures

Homer O. Brown was surely being deliberately provocative about Watt's transatlantic influence when he emphatically counted him among 'American academics' in his anti-Watt thesis, *Institutions of the English Novel* (1997).[16] Even on more distant acquaintance than Brown's, it would be difficult to think of Watt as anything other than English—English in a virtually paradigmatic way, almost, as a former army officer of canonical literary tastes and the empirical disposition of the kind that Chris Baldick found running through British literary criticism from Matthew Arnold through the first half of the twentieth century.[17] As it happens, Watt was a trueborn Englishman only with the satirical inflection that Defoe had given the phrase in his famous Williamite lines on the nation's mongrel formation, where 'A True-Born Englishman's a contradiction, | In speech an irony, in fact a fiction'.[18]

Watt's full name, Ian Pierre Watt, points in this direction, with a French middle name that he appears seldom to have used after the 1950s and the unmistakably Scottish first and last names under which he published. He was certainly English in that he was born on 9 March 1917 in the Lake District village of Windermere, and grew up near Dover, one of three children of a Scottish father, Thomas Watt, a Stirling-born teacher of French, and a French mother, Renée Guitton, from Roxana's hometown of Poitiers. So, on the one hand, he was certainly English—born a little south of the Border and brought up a little west of the Channel—and, on the other hand, not English at all by identification, according to his former Stanford colleague Thomas Moser, who remembered Watt dryly correcting anyone who referred to him as such ('Not a drop of Anglo-Saxon blood!').[19]

16. Brown, *Institutions of the English Novel*, xiii.
17. Chris Baldick, *The Social Mission of English Criticism, 1848–1932* (Oxford: Clarendon Press, 1987), 203–5.
18. Daniel Defoe, *The True-Born Englishman and Other Writings*, ed. P. N. Furbank and W. R. Owens (London: Penguin, 2011), 36.
19. Thomas C. Moser, 'Some Reminiscences', *Stanford Humanities Review*, 8/1 (2000), 41.

In any case, he spent little time after the age of 21 in the country of his birth. By the time the war broke out Watt had left Cambridge for Paris to take up a postgraduate scholarship at the Sorbonne, and within two years of the war's ending he had married a native of Los Angeles, Ruth Mellinkoff, and spent most of his academic career in California, first rising through the professorial ranks at the University of California, Berkeley (1952–62), before serving at Stanford from 1964 until his retirement. His long expatriation was interrupted only briefly by two years in England, where he returned in 1962 to set up the School of English Studies at the embryonic University of East Anglia in Norwich, which admitted its first student intake a year later, and where Watt served on the university's first executive committee. Institutional memory at UEA, inclining towards the piquant as institutional memory does, has Watt returning to California after only two years because the pet snake he kept in his office suffered from Norwich's cool winters; more soberly, he gave 'family reasons' as his official motivation and, as he and Ruth Watt explained to Margaret Drabble when she was researching her biography of the novelist Angus Wilson (whom Watt had appointed as a Senior Lecturer), the family appears to have found sleepy Norwich a difficult place to settle in.[20] A return to the United Kingdom that was intended to be permanent—and Watt's American wife had believed it permanent at the very moment they sailed from New York—had lasted only two years. But it is easy to understand why the home country might not have felt like home.

For, spare and self-effacing though they often are, Watt's autobiographical comments typically speak the same language of homelessness and displacement as we find in his critical writing: in his reading of the rise of the novel as a reflection of modern social flux, and then his study of the émigré Joseph Conrad, and finally in his unfinished book on what he saw as the cultural distortions of modern individualism. For example, in an autobiographical reminiscence he wrote in 1984 for the Stanford Alumni magazine—in which, somewhat ironically, he was

20. The snake story appears in print in Lorna Sage's obituary for Watt's successor in the Dean's office. 'Obituary: Professor Nicholas Brooke', *Independent*, 10 November 1998. (The snake belonged to Watt's son.) Margaret Drabble interviewed Ian and Ruth Watt in 1992: 'the Watts did in the event find Norwich uncongenial: their American-reared children found the schools old-fashioned, with too much sport and religion' (Margaret Drabble, *Angus Wilson: A Biography* (London: Secker & Warburg, 1995), 315). The reference to Watt's departure for 'family reasons' appears in the Annual Report of the Vice-Chancellor, 1963–4, University of East Anglia Special Collections.

asked to represent 'England' for a feature on foreign-born members of the faculty—he began by describing his realization on coming home from the war that his mother had a French accent. 'Naturally, since she was French,' he conceded: 'And then I remembered that, while I was a prisoner, several people had surprised me by saying that there was something funny about the way I talked. Did I have a touch of French too? Was I a stranger in my own country?'[21] Asked to write about being an alien resident of California in 1984, then, he writes instead about feeling completely foreign on his return to Britain after his imprisonment in the Far East almost forty years earlier. The essay describes meeting old friends upon his repatriation, who 'hadn't really changed, but I had; and they didn't know it, but I did', and concludes with Watt explaining that he can bear to visit his childhood town now only as a tourist.[22] The foreignness of his speech and his feeling of foreignness at returning to England after the war become one; they both produce 'that sense of speaking falsetto to all these people from the past'.[23] Watt recalled elsewhere how he and other former prisoners clustered together immediately after the war, because 'one could only talk with people who understood one's language, and that meant people who had shared one's history'.[24]

Many former prisoners used these linguistic metaphors to describe their feeling of post-war displacement. In his acclaimed memoir *The Railway Man* (1995), Scottish veteran Eric Lomax recalled the impossibility of making his experience understood at home: 'I am sure that tens of thousands of returning soldiers walked bewildered into the same incomprehension. It was as though we were now speaking a different language to our own people.'[25] Of course, even an ostensibly less traumatic war experience than Watt's or Lomax's could have been transformative in this respect; the anecdote with which Raymond Williams opened *Keywords* (1976) describes a meeting with another veteran on their return to Cambridge in 1945, when both men agreed that it was as if the people of 'this new and strange world around them' were

21. Ian Watt, 'Dover, November 1945', Stanford University Special Collections, SC401-ACCN 1994–106, Box 23, Folder 1.
22. Watt, 'Dover, November 1945'. 23. Watt, 'Dover, November 1945'.
24. Ian Watt, 'The Liberty of the Prison: Reflections of a Prisoner of War', *Yale Review*, 44 (1956), 529.
25. Eric Lomax, *The Railway Man* (New York: Norton, 1995), 209.

speaking a different language from those who had served.[26] Williams had ended the war as a tank commander leading his men into Germany, where they liberated the Sandbostel concentration and prisoner-of-war camp (Stalag X-B) early in May 1945.[27] Asked by an interviewer if the war had affected him, Williams' reply was unequivocal: 'It was appalling. I don't think anybody really ever gets over it.'[28]

'I'd never thought I was the man of action type myself—and the people I know don't seem to be either,' an autobiographical surrogate reflects early in one of the unpublished war stories that Watt drafted shortly after his demobilization: 'But what happened made me think again, and even now, back home, though I've read several books about it, I'm still wondering if I really am or not.'[29] For many among this generation of literary critics—students turned soldiers, soldiers turned scholars like Watt and Williams—the Second World War had dramatically overturned distinctions between the 'man of letters' and the 'man of action'.

When the war broke out in September 1939, Watt volunteered immediately and was called up three months later. In April 1940 he joined the 7th Battalion of the Royal West Kent Regiment as a second lieutenant. By this time the so-called Phony War of the winter of 1939–40 was well and truly over, and the coming weeks would bring the fall of France and the Low Countries, as well as the forced evacuation of the British Expeditionary Force at Dunkirk. But the conflict that had been underway for years in the Far East had officially become a full-scale war between Japan and China in 1937, and it was in this distant theatre that Watt's military career would play out, a future assured when he was posted as an officer to the 5th Battalion of the Suffolk Regiment. Within three months of promotion to the rank of lieutenant in November 1941, Watt was a severely wounded prisoner of war.

The 5th Suffolks left England in the winter of 1941 as part of the doomed 18th Division, which travelled 20,000 miles from the Suffolks' regimental home in East Anglia to the Far East, a journey that took

26. Raymond Williams, *Keywords: A Vocabulary of Culture and Society* (London: Fontana, 1976), 9.
27. Fred Inglis, *Raymond Williams* (London: Routledge, 1995), 100–1.
28. Raymond Williams, *Politics and Letters: Interviews with New Left Review* (London: New Left Books, 1979), 57.
29. Ian Watt, 'A Chap in Dark Glasses', Stanford University Special Collections, SC401-ACCN 1990-131, Box 56, Folder 'POW Stuff'.

them across the North Atlantic to Canada, down the North American coast to the Caribbean, across the South Atlantic to South Africa, from South Africa to India, and from India to Singapore. Their objective was the defence of Singapore, an island colony of less than 300 square miles, attached by what proved to be a disastrously vulnerable causeway to the southern tip of Malaya. Diminutive Singapore was an outpost of empire distinctive for its propagandistic as well as its strategic importance, and both were critical at this potentially pivotal moment. The authors of one major history of the Second World War describe its significance in a dramatic way when they explain that Singapore was considered 'one of the two keystones upon which the survival of the Empire depended (the other being neither Suez nor Gibraltar but nothing less than the security of the United Kingdom itself)'.[30] This was the impregnable 'Fortress Singapore' of the imperial propaganda. As things turned out, it might more accurately have been named 'illusion isle', as the Australian Rohan Rivett called it in his memoir of imprisonment as a non-combatant swept up with the Allied personnel at the fall of Singapore, or, alternatively, 'the naked island' of his compatriot and fellow prisoner Russell Braddon's title.[31]

Singapore fell after mere days of fighting: 'a few days that, whatever we might do later, would be with us for the rest of our lives,' Watt called them in another of his unpublished war stories from the late 1940s.[32] The decision to surrender Singapore on 15 February 1942—the 5th Suffolks had arrived in Singapore only on 29 January—was perhaps the most humiliating of Britain's wartime reversals, particularly when it became known that British and Commonwealth forces had outnumbered the victorious Japanese by a ratio of over two to one. In his celebrated history-cum-memoir of the Second World War, Winston Churchill wrote of the fall of Singapore as 'the worst disaster and largest capitulation in British history'.[33] Among those who had experienced its appalling consequences, Watt's fellow 18th Division prisoner Ronald

30. Peter Calvocoressi, Guy Wint, and John Pritchard, *The Penguin History of the Second World War* (London: Penguin, 1999), 909.
31. Rohan D. Rivett, *Behind Bamboo: An Inside Story of the Japanese Prison Camps* (Sydney: Angus & Robertson, 1946), unpaginated section title. Russell Braddon, *The Naked Island* (Edinburgh: Birlinn, 2005).
32. Ian Watt, 'Too Much Foresight', Stanford University Special Collections, SC401-ACCN 1994-106, Box 22, Folder 'POW Stuff'.
33. Winston Churchill, *The Second World War*, iv. *The Hinge of Fate* (New York: Mariner, 1986), 81.

Searle and Malay Volunteer Ian Denys Peek summarized the surrender of Singapore with a different kind of bluntness: 'a wickedly inept political sacrifice' (Searle) by 'our piss-begotten politicians and military muttonheads, who not only did nothing but prevented anyone else from doing anything' (Peek).[34] 'Seldom in the history of war can there have been such a skein of muddle, confusion and stupidity,' marvelled Scottish journalist Tom McGowran.[35] Searle, Peek, and McGowran were among the staggering 62,000 British, Indian, and Australian personnel who were taken prisoner at Singapore alone.

Capture

'My military career was on the comic side,' Watt wrote in a 1967 letter to Brigadier Philip Toosey, the legendary senior officer often misidentified as the original of Alec Guinness's monomaniacal Colonel Nicholson in *The Bridge on the River Kwai*:

> I was chosen to deny Singapore Zoo to the enemy and I think that the first shot fired in anger on the island was by me, with an anti-tank rifle, after I'd decided that certain buffalo, orang-outang and other large caged animals would be dangerous to leave at large once the balloon went up. My beloved Swedes of the 5th Suffolks made it clear that they would regard it as murder if I also disposed of the two zebras; and as a result they were let loose, and eventually followed us from Pongol [Punggol] Point to Bukit Timah crossroads, at a wary distance.[36]

The picture called up here of the young Lieutenant Watt and his gentle subordinates (the 'Swede-bashers' of agricultural Suffolk) withdrawing down Singapore alongside a pair of worried zebras is certainly 'on the comic side'. Watt and his correspondent obviously never needed to remind each other that what followed the hopeless battle for Singapore was even worse, and that their situation would continue to get worse still over the following three and a half years.

34. Ronald Searle, *To the Kwai—and Back: War Drawings 1939–1945* (London: Souvenir Press, 2006), 7. Ian Denys Peek, *One Fourteenth of an Elephant: A Memoir of Life and Death on the Burma–Thailand Railway* (London: Bantam, 2005), 140, 526.
35. Tom McGowran, *Beyond the Bamboo Screen: Scottish Prisoners of War under the Japanese* (Dunfermline: Cualann Press, 1999), 14.
36. Letter from Ian Watt to Brigadier Philip Toosey dated 9 August 1967, Stanford University Special Collections, SC401-ACCN 1994-106, Box 24, Folder 1.

Hospitalized by shrapnel wounds from a mortar shell during the futile resistance in the north-east of the island—he would still be undergoing surgery on those wounds decades later—Watt had another extremely marginal escape when he was helped out of hospital just before invading Japanese troops slaughtered the patients there.[37] In the chaos of the British collapse, Watt was believed to have been killed in action on 15 February 1942, the day Singapore was surrendered, and the casualty branch of the War Office sent a letter to that effect to his next of kin, his recently widowed mother. A post-war correspondence between Watt and the War Office indicates that personnel who had managed to reach British lines in India when Malaya and Singapore fell had given unofficial but ostensibly reliable reports of Watt's death.

It was not until 17 December, ten months after the fall of Singapore, that official information passed through the International Red Cross Committee at Geneva that Watt was alive and imprisoned. A telegram from the War Office was sent to Renée Watt two days later. Watt may have been among the fortunate prisoners who got to send a pre-printed Japanese postcard of the axiomatically fictitious 'I am in captivity and treated well' variety (nothing of that description appears to have survived); otherwise the news from the Red Cross would have been the last heard directly of Watt at home until the liberation of the camps in August 1945. In stark contrast to the situation of many Allied prisoners in Germany, where the Red Cross was able to facilitate remarkable feats of communication between prisoners and their homes, incarceration under the Japanese meant almost total isolation from the outside world. 'We cannot look out and nobody can look in,' a former prisoner remembered, describing life in the camps where he, too, spent three and a half years as 'a totally sealed and seamless void'.[38]

The difficulty of looking into or out of the Japanese camps can be gauged by the extreme paucity of contemporary information about them. Responding to the hunger for knowledge among prisoners' families, who could not know whether their men were even alive or dead, there emerged in February 1944 the indicatively flimsy first number of *Far East*, a special monthly edition of *The Prisoner of War*, the

37. Moser, 'Some Reminiscences', 37. The story most likely refers to the massacre at the Alexandra Barracks Hospital, where Japanese troops killed some two hundred patients and staff in supposed retaliation for shots fired from the hospital grounds by the retreating British.

38. Peek, *One Fourteenth*, 229.

free newsletter published by the Red Cross and the St John War Organisation for the next of kin of captured personnel. The inaugural editorial would have consoled few readers: 'Unfortunately, owing to the attitude of the Japanese in matters relating to prisoners of war, contact with the prison camps has been only partial, intermittent and uncertain, and we know nothing reliable about the camps holding most of our men.'[39] This newsletter is altogether a thin document: some miscellaneous snippets of information from camps in Korea, Taiwan, Hong Kong, and Japan; a feature on the civilian internment camp at Stanley on Hong Kong, and another on the work of the Far East section of the Red Cross and St John Prisoner of War Department in London. Most tellingly, the centrefold is a two-page map of the Far East prison camps on which the location of camps is recorded as 'unknown' for Thailand: by now, Watt and many thousands of other prisoners would already have passed as much as eighteen months there, slaving on the Burma–Thailand Railway. As if trying to account for the newsletter's comfortless insubstantiality, the second issue of *Far East* included a longish feature subtitled 'The Story of What Has Been Done', which recounted the failed efforts made by the Red Cross and the customary 'Protecting Power' of neutral Switzerland to secure access to the prison camps.[40]

In his statement to the House of Commons on 10 March 1942, Foreign Secretary Anthony Eden had already—presciently—put the darkest construction on the Japanese refusal to allow the customary neutral oversight of their camps: 'It is clear that their treatment of prisoners and civilians will not bear independent investigation.'[41] Over the following months the government suppressed what was known about conditions on the Burma–Thailand Railway for fear, Sybilla Jane Flower explains, of jeopardizing their covert channels of information and provoking reprisals against prisoners whom they had no way of helping.[42] Only as the tide turned in favour of the Allies did Eden give a statement to the Commons (on 28 January 1944) in which he

39. 'The Editor Writes', *Far East*, 1/1 (February 1944), 1.
40. 'Red Cross in the Far East: The Story of what Has Been Done', *Far East*, 1/2 (March 1944), 4–5, 8.
41. 'Hong Kong (Japanese Barbarities)', *Hansard*, 10 March 1942.
42. Sybilla Jane Flower, 'Memory and the Prisoner of War Experience: The United Kingdom', in Kevin Blackburn and Karl Hack (eds), *Forgotten Captives in Japanese-Occupied Asia: National Memories and Forgotten Captivities* (Abingdon: Routledge, 2008), 61.

reported on the abysmal conditions under which the prisoners were believed to be held in the railway camps, and on the atrocities (tortures, executions) committed in Shanghai, Manila, and at sea. These were 'revolting disclosures', in the words of the following morning's *The Times*.[43]

'Revolting' was not an exaggeration. From the point of view of mere survival, it is hard to imagine how Watt's prospects could have been worse, as a wounded officer taken prisoner by an army taught that it was irredeemably shameful for even the lowliest of troops to outlive their defeat in combat. The directive of 'death before dishonour' had recently been written into the Japanese soldier's own Field Army Service Code: 'You shall not undergo the shame of being taken alive. You shall not bequeath a sullied name.'[44] As a result of this prevailing ethos, if it can be called that, prisoners were disgraced not only by their military defeat but also by their efforts to survive it. Perhaps most consequentially, the asymmetry of interests that resulted from Japan's public indifference to the fate of its own captured personnel—an 'ostentatious lack of interest', *The Times* editorialized in 1944—deprived Allied governments of the usual leverage for securing the humane treatment of their own servicemen in what is normally (as the War Office reminded relatives of prisoners of the Germans and Italians) a mutual hostage situation.[45] Only in what proved to be the war's final year did the British have leverage of any description, in the form of threats of future punishment underwritten by Japan's foundering military fortunes. Thus the Secretary of State for War, Sir James Grigg, reported in the House of Commons on the account of the Burma–Thailand Railway delivered by sixty British survivors of their enslavement there; they had been rescued by an American crew after the sinking

43. 'Outrages by Japanese', *The Times*, 29 January 1944, 4.
44. Quoted in Clifford Kinvig, 'Allied POW's and the Burma–Thailand Railway', in Philip Towle, Margaret Kosuge, and Yoichi Kibata (eds), *Japanese Prisoners of War* (London: Hambledon and London, 2000), 48.
45. 'A Grave Indictment' (Leader), *The Times*, 18 November 1944. The mutual hostage scenario was invoked to reassure families: 'remember that the German and Italian Governments are for their part equally anxious to secure good treatment for their own service men and merchant seamen who are prisoners in our hands and they know that the surest way to obtain it is to treat the British prisoners whom they have captured fairly and decently' (War Office, *A Handbook for the Information of Relatives and Friends of Prisoners of War* (London: HMSO, 1943), 2). This foreword ends: 'The information in this pamphlet relates to the conditions and treatment of prisoners of war in Germany and Italy, and **not** in Japan' (2; emphasis in original).

of a Japanese prison ship in September 1944: 'it is necessary that the Japanese should know that we know how they have been behaving, and that we intend to hold them responsible.'[46]

Back in the impenetrable camps, conditions were seldom better than life-threatening, but prisoners became adept at distinguishing between bad camps and those that were even worse, or the spectrum that one military historian crisply describes as 'an existence that varied from the harsh to the intolerable'.[47] When Singapore fell, surrendered personnel had been taken first to a massive holding camp at Changi, a former British military base in the north-east of Singapore, where disease, hunger, and overcrowding soon became dangerous. Nonetheless, so far superior were conditions at this miserable first site, where the prisoners had established their own quasi-autonomous internal administration from the outset, to other camps where the Japanese made their supremacy more intrusively and brutally felt, that internment at Changi was, according to R. P. W. Havers's history of the camp, 'in many ways a unique experience'.[48] There were many among the thousands of prisoners taken away in forced work parties who came to think back nostalgically about even Changi. 'You know, I used to dream of Changi and how good it was compared to where we were,' recalled Fred Ransome-Smith, like Watt a young lieutenant in the 5th Suffolks.[49] Changi 'seemed a paradise in comparison with those we were to know later', another veteran remembered; it was 'like a P. O. W. heaven', 'a haven of rest', and 'like the Mecca of all prisoner of war camps', others wrote.[50]

46. 'British Prisoners of War, Siam (Conditions)', *Hansard*, 17 November 1944.
47. S. P. MacKenzie, 'The Treatment of Prisoners of War in World War II', *Journal of Modern History*, 66/3 (September 1994), 515. Flower importantly points out that even on the Burma–Thailand Railway conditions varied 'between nationalities, between ranks, between camps or even within the same camps over a period of time' (Sibylla Jane Flower, 'Captors and Captives on the Burma–Thailand Railway', in Bob Moore and Kent Fedorowich (eds), *Prisoners of War and their Captors in World War II* (Oxford: Berg, 1996), 247).
48. R. P. W. Havers, *Reassessing the Japanese Prisoner of War Experience: The Changi Camp, Singapore, 1942–5* (London: RoutledgeCurzon, 2003), vii.
49. Pattie Wright, *Men of the Line: Stories of the Thai–Burma Railway Survivors* (Carlton, Victoria: Miegunyah Press/Melbourne University Publishing, 2008), 38.
50. Ernest Gordon, *Miracle on the River Kwai* (London: Collins, 1963), 52. Rivett, *Behind Bamboo*, 158. Roy Whitecross, *Slaves of the Son of Heaven: A Personal Account of an Australian POW, 1942–1945* (East Roseville, New South Wales: Kangaroo Press, 2000), 11. Ray Parkin, *Into the Smother: A Journal of the Burma–Siam Railway* (London: Hogarth, 1963), 12.

On the Line

This longing for bleak Changi was never more understandable than among the men sent north from the summer of 1942 to be assimilated into the 64,000 or so Allied prisoners of war, and in total more than a third of a million largely coerced labourers, on the new railway that the Japanese were building from Thailand into neighbouring Burma. 'Being a POW of the Japanese was to become an involuntary subscriber to an extraordinary lottery', was how one former prisoner remembered their predicament: 'You could remain hungry and bored in Changi . . . or you could crack the bad-luck jackpot and end up on the Burma–Siam railway.'[51] Along with the other unlucky ones, Watt was packed in the autumn of 1942 into a closed goods wagon shared by forty prisoners—his close friend and fellow prisoner John Durnford remembered their transportation as 'a Black Hole of Calcutta on wheels'; Scottish veteran Alistair Urquhart likened it to 'being buried alive'—to commence a punishing five-day, 900-mile journey up to Ban Pong in Thailand.[52] From the staging camp there, prisoners were dispersed to sites on the prospective railway to Burma either by trucks or on what were sometimes, in outcome if not intention, death marches.

The building of the Burma–Thailand or Burma–Siam Railway (Thailand had taken its present name only in 1939) proved to be the most grimly significant feature of the war experience of prisoners like Watt; historian Meg Parkes estimates that two-thirds of all British prisoners in the Far East worked on its construction at some point.[53] The purpose of the railway was to complete an overland military supply route between Bangkok and Moulmein, or, in effect, between the South China Sea and the Indian Ocean. Burma was now among the furthest outposts of a new Japanese empire that stretched across five time zones, and there was always a chance that the British and Americans over the border in India, which Japan also planned to

51. Quoted in Van Waterford, *Prisoners of the Japanese in World War II* (Jefferson, NC: McFarland, 1994), 32.
52. John Durnford, *Branch Line to Burma* (London: Macdonald, 1958), 24. Alistair Urquhart, *The Forgotten Highlander: My Incredible Story of Survival during the War in the Far East* (Abacus: London, 2011), 122.
53. Meg Parkes, 'Tins, Tubes and Tenacity: Inventive Medicine in Camps in the Far East', in Gilly Carr and Harold Mytum (eds), *Cultural Heritage and Prisoners of War: Creativity behind Barbed Wire* (New York: Routledge, 2012), 52.

invade, would launch a counterattack. The projected railway would cut many hundreds of miles off what was otherwise a laborious and looping sea journey between the land-bordering countries of Burma and Thailand, and allow Japanese troops to bypass the Malacca Strait, a vulnerable shipping channel, shallow and narrow, between the southern tip of Singapore and the north coast of Sumatra.

Probably because an overland route connecting Burma and Thailand would have been so direct a way of linking imperial India with colonies in the Malay Archipelago, British engineers had surveyed a railway route back in the 1880s. But everyone contemplating this project had given it up as a prohibitively bad job, with literally hundreds of miles of rock, mountain, river, swamp, bamboo, and tropical jungle to be blasted or bridged in one of the least humanly hospitable and most endemically disease-ridden (malaria, typhus, cholera) environments in Asia. But Japanese forces were triumphant in the early months of 1942—they had taken Guam, Wake Island, Hong Kong, and Malaya in January, Singapore in February, the Dutch East Indies in March, as well as Burma and the Philippines in April—and, with the attendant windfall of expendable foreign labour, military and civilian, they embarked upon the railway regardless of its manifest difficulties. They compounded the difficulties incalculably by using sick and malnourished people bearing rudimentary native hoes, picks, and bamboo baskets rather than physically fit and properly equipped manpower, and so the enterprise proved predictably deadly. The Allied War Graves Registration established in 1946 that 12,399 Allied prisoners had died there, although, in his authoritative account of the railway project, military historian Clifford Kinvig explains that this official figure clearly underestimates the real death toll, given that the continuing effects of starvation, disease, and hard labour continued to kill men long afterwards.[54] This undertaking also killed perhaps 100,000 so-called native labourers, such as Burmese conscripts and Indian Tamils from the Malayan rubber plantations, brought by force and fraud from their homes across south-east Asia.

Probably because their compatriots suffered and died in captivity in numbers disproportionate to the size of the nation's fighting forces (around 22,000 Australian personnel fell into Japanese hands), Australian

54. Clifford Kinvig, *River Kwai Railway: The Story of the Burma–Siam Railroad* (London: Brassey's, 1992), 198.

memoirists recorded most extensively Allied prisoners' experiences on the Burma–Thailand Railway. At the other extreme, very little can be learned at source of the atrocious suffering of the illiterate forced labourers from Asia, although they died in even worse circumstances and far higher numbers than Allied prisoners. Theirs were 'the greatest losses but the hardest to measure', writes Kinvig, 'and only the most general indication can be given of the scale of the tragedy'.[55] Uncounted and unrecorded, their bodies were buried or incinerated en masse. The memoirs of Allied prisoners give appalled accounts of how the enslaved Asian workforce was destroyed by those who had posed as liberators from European colonialism in the name of the 'Greater East Asia Co-Prosperity Sphere', as the imperialist and racist Japanese project of conquest named itself, in one of those terminological hypocrisies so characteristic of the period.[56] 'We must never forget them', writes one English prisoner, 'nameless and suffering and dying in squalor, their kinfolk not even knowing what has happened to them'.[57]

If only from the stricken testimonies of Western prisoners, we know that the Asian workers died in huge numbers from lack of food, clean water, and any medical care. They 'were shovelled into graves ten at a time', according to a prisoner friend of Watt who had himself served in a burial party.[58] Another prisoner working in brutal conditions near the Burma border reported that the enslaved Tamils in the camp next to his own 'died like flies and were buried as, or just before, they died in huge communal graves'; another described how 'every few days a huge hole was dug, and into this were thrown the dead, and sometimes the not-quite dead'.[59] When starvation and disease left the Asian labourers too weak to work, the Japanese simply slaughtered them outright. In the highly documentary 1948 memoir that he wrote from his hidden camp diaries, C. F. Blackater, a Scottish officer in the Indian Army, describes deliberate mass poisonings of sick Tamils.[60] Half a century later, Lomax still remembered with cold disgust how the Japanese

55. Kinvig, *River Kwai Railway*, 166.
56. The classic account of the Pacific theatre as a race war is John W. Dower, *War without Mercy: Race and Power in the Pacific War* (London: Faber, 1986).
57. Peek, *One Fourteenth*, 244.
58. Stephen Alexander, *Sweet Kwai Run Softly* (Bristol: Merriots, 1996), 139.
59. Braddon, *The Naked Island*, 210. Ronald Hastain, *White Coolie* (London: Hodder & Stoughton, 1947), 146.
60. C. F. Blackater, *Gods without Reason* (London: Eyre & Spottiswoode, 1948), 108, 112.

discovered 'a novel way of containing' a cholera epidemic in another Tamil camp: 'they shot its victims.'[61] But even aside from the notorious brutality with which they were treated, the Asian workers had another insurmountable difficulty. Brought to the Burma–Thailand Railway individually (or, even worse, with dependent families) from far-flung sites of origin, they lacked even the Allied prisoners' slim vestigial resources: a shared language and cultural assumptions similar enough to make organization possible, and the understanding of collective discipline instilled by their training as soldiers. 'At least we had our military discipline,' one Australian veteran recalled: 'They had nothing.'[62]

That Watt had seen collective organization save thousands of lives when those without it died in such sickening circumstances speaks to some of his strongest intellectual commitments. For a start, it helps to explain the intensity of his sympathy with Conrad, the subject of much of his major critical work. We can guess how important Conrad had become to Watt in captivity because within ten days of his repatriation he had visited Conrad's grave.[63] Perhaps the location would always have evoked Conrad to a literary-minded prisoner; we find in the memoir of British Warrant Officer Ronald Hastain that the view of the tropical ocean from the Changi camp on Singapore brought to life the 'sun and colour saturated prose of Conrad'.[64] But Watt's thoughts on Conrad suggest something darker in all senses. Throughout his work Watt always described admiringly Conrad's conservative faith in the virtues of duty, renunciation, and solidarity, even while acknowledging that in the face of such atrocities as those Conrad had witnessed in the Belgian Congo the famous Conradian ideals of 'restraint' and 'fidelity' (Watt glosses these as renunciation and duty) constitute only a 'meagre moral armament' (*C.* 151). Watt describes the experience of Conrad's surrogate Marlow in *Heart of Darkness* as 'a nightmare in a common usage of the term: an experience in which the individual's thoughts and actions are dominated by a terrifying and inexplicable sense of personal helplessness' (*C.* 240). 'In the last stages of the breakdown of

61. Lomax, *The Railway Man*, 149.
62. Quoted in Tim Bowden, *Changi Photographer: George Aspinall's Record of Captivity* (Sydney: ABC Books, 1993), 119.
63. Ian Watt, 'Around Conrad's Grave in the Canterbury Cemetery: A Retrospect', in Watt, *Essays on Conrad*, 187.
64. Hastain, *White Coolie*, 99.

his own health in the Congo, Conrad had faced alone the fact of his own mortality,' Watt wrote, knowing better than most Conrad critics what that confrontation must have felt like: 'He later considered the physical and moral assault of his African experience the turning point of his life' (*C.* 146). Here, we might also recall that the dehumanized African labourers described in the famous grove of death scene in *Heart of Darkness* ('They were not enemies, they were not criminals, they were nothing earthly now—nothing but black shadows of disease and starvation') are being forced to build a railway through a jungle.[65] Watt notices that detail as if entirely neutrally, without any autobiographical comment (*C.* 220).

Yet, even with their 'meagre moral armament', or what military discipline survived a chaotic and unexpected defeat, the death rate among Allied prisoners on the railway was one in three. Thousands died from combinations of the gruesome illnesses caused by performing hard labour on starvation rations and without medical supplies, with primitive and infested bamboo huts as their only shelter from an impossibly hostile environment of tropical monsoon-belt jungle. Among the killers were beriberi, dengue fever, diphtheria, dysentery, malaria, pellagra, scurvy, and typhus. Compounding the prisoners' misery were the skin diseases scabies and ringworm, and, much worse, the hideous tropical phagedena, whereby even a mere scratch (unavoidable by anyone labouring almost naked like these prisoners, whose clothes the jungle had quickly rotted away) turned septic, and flesh putrefied down to the exposed bone. In the camps, tropical ulcers frequently meant gangrene, and gangrene meant primitive amputations and an agonizing death, because surgical tools and anaesthetics largely had to be improvised or done without. Periodic outbreaks of cholera, as happened at Chungkai and Konkuita, the camps in Thailand where Watt spent the worst periods of his incarceration, exacerbated—as, for that matter, they attest to—the squalor of the conditions prevailing. There were periods at some camps when open pyres were needed to burn the cholera dead. 'I've never seen anything so horrible in my life... the sight of mates melting and disintegrating,' recalled elderly veteran Reg Twigg,

65. Joseph Conrad, *Heart of Darkness and The Congo Diary* (London: Penguin, 2007), 20. Watt writes that *Heart of Darkness* 'must have seemed grotesquely pessimistic to its original readers. It surely seems a good deal less so eighty years later, except to those who have had a very blinkered view of the century's battlefields' (*C.* 252–3).

who had been involved in carrying out some of these mass cremations seventy years earlier.[66]

But not even the worst of these degrading and disfiguring diseases need be fatal, and they would not have been here had their captors thought the prisoners' lives worth saving. The Japanese refusal even to cooperate with the Red Cross must have cost hundreds if not thousands of lives. What little the Red Cross managed to send to prisoners appears to have been stolen as a matter of course by their captors: Durnford first saw a Red Cross package only in June 1944, while Stephen Alexander (who was also in Watt's circle of prison-camp acquaintances late in the war) recalls a Japanese handout of Red Cross packages marked April 1942 only on 17 August 1945, when the war was already over.[67] The memoir of prisoner Alan Carter, captured in Java and a forced labourer in Japan, describes an entirely staged inspection in the familiar Potemkin style, with guards subsequently boasting to the starved inmates about their enjoyment of the prisoners' Red Cross packages ('they must have had about four parcels each').[68] Although there were occasions on which individual prisoners were knowingly worked, starved, or beaten to death, or shot, bayoneted, or beheaded, there is substantial consensus among both veterans and historians that the main cause of death was not so much deliberate cruelty as an absolutely universal indifference among their captors as to whether these expendable bodies lived or died. 'The labourers on the railway are essentially the victims, not of calculated brutality, but of the blindness to their needs of an alien and more powerful order,' Watt wrote: 'they are being mercilessly destroyed by a system which is administered by [those] who make a point of not noticing what they are really doing' (*C.* 220). This claim echoes those of many other former prisoners—victims, it has often been said, of 'the indifference, unpredictability and incompetence of the Japanese'—except that here Watt was ostensibly discussing the enslaved railway workers in *Heart of Darkness* rather than reflecting on his own wartime experience.[69] In the same vein, it is in the surprising context of a talk on Dickens that we find Watt proclaiming

66. Reg Twigg, *Survivor on the River Kwai: The Incredible Story of Life on the Burma Railway* (London: Penguin, 2013), 224.
67. Durnford, *Branch Line to Burma*, 153. Alexander, *Sweet Kwai*, 215.
68. Alan Carter, *Survival of the Fittest: A Young Englishman's Struggle as a Prisoner of War in Java and Japan* (Great Britain: Paul T. Carter, 2013), 91–2, 99.
69. Christopher Dowling, 'Introduction', in Robert Hardie, *The Burma–Siam Railway: The Secret Diary of Dr Robert Hardie 1942–45* (London: Imperial War Museum, 1983), 9.

'that all power relations, whether between nations, or classes, or age groups, are most directly and yet most hypocritically expressed in the distribution of food and drink'.[70]

It tells its own story that the prisoners who got to stay hungry and ragged at the less remote base camps recorded with such emphasis their horror and disgust at the desperate state in which survivors of the railway trickled back. Braddon called these returned prisoners 'wreckages of humanity', and he, himself, had been among them:

> These did not look like men; on the other hand, they were not quite animals. They had feet torn by bamboo thorns and working for long months without boots. Their shins had no spare flesh at all on the calf and looked as if bullets had exploded inside them, bursting the meat outwards and blackening it. These were their ulcers of which they had dozens, from threepenny bit size upwards, on each leg. Their thigh bones and pelvis stood out sharply and on the point of each thigh bone was that red raw patch like a saddle sore or monkey's behind. All their ribs showed clearly, the chest sloping backwards to the hollows of throat and collar bone. Arms hung down, stick-like, with huge hands, and the skin wrinkled where muscle had vanished, like old men. Heads were shrunken on to skulls with large teeth and faintly glowing eyes set in black wells: hair was matted and lifeless. The whole body was draped with a loose-fitting envelope of thin purple-brown parchment which wrinkled horizontally over the stomach and chest and vertically on sagging fleshless buttocks.[71]

The Australian official war artist Murray Griffin, who had been imprisoned in Changi throughout, made it his task to record in secret sketches the medical conditions of railway survivors in the absence of other ways of documenting the experience. A similar medical-documentary compulsion shapes much of the work of the British cartoonist Searle, captured at Singapore aged 21. A pre-war Cambridge acquaintance of Watt, Searle had experienced some of the most terrible of the camps as part of the notorious 'H Force' (two-thirds of his party of 600 were dead within seven months); many of his drawings are almost unbearable documents of the physical deterioration of dying prisoners.[72]

70. Ian Watt, 'Oral Dickens', *Stanford Humanities Review*, 8/1 (2000), 210. This reprint of Watt's lecture is prefaced by a sensitive account by John O. Jordan of how, in an overlapping of criticism and personal memory, Watt identifies with the starving prisoner Magwitch. John O. Jordan, 'The Critic as Host: On Ian Watt's "Oral Dickens"', *Stanford Humanities Review*, 8/1 (2000), 197–205.

71. Braddon, *The Naked Island*, 203.

72. Searle, *To the Kwai—and Back*, 98.

Synthesizing the eyewitness accounts, Daws writes thus of the railway survivors as they returned to the base camps:

> Some were dead on arrival; others collapsed and died before they could get to the sick huts. The rest were walking skeletons, the whites of their eyes gray, pupils just a splotch in the middle, like broken eggs. They stank to high heaven. The men in the receiving camps could smell them hundreds of yards off. They came crawling in like frightened rats; if they were offered food and help they would burst into tears.[73]

These young men had been—literally—fighting fit as little as eighteen months earlier, and it is instructive to find the view that one military doctor put on record in the *British Medical Journal* in April 1946. Lieutenant-Colonel R. Kemball Price of the Royal Army Medical Corps had studied 1,000 recently liberated prisoners sent to a hospital in India, and his report on their condition details as clinically as one would expect the physical damage inflicted by years of disease and starvation. But, of the prisoners' emotional condition, he writes much less dispassionately that 'anyone who saw them could never forget the experience':

> There was great superficial gaiety, but beneath this was a deep-rooted fear which showed itself when their faces were at rest. The frequent blinking and the shaking hand were a legacy of what they had been through. Their condition was aptly compared to that of the whipped dog returning to his master.[74]

Recording the 'Kwai'

In the United Kingdom, the Burma–Thailand Railway is now among the merely half-remembered of the war's atrocities. This is not true in Australia, where it is 'accepted as a central part of the modern Australian experience' and part of 'the national mythology'.[75] We can see something of this in novels like Richard Flanagan's Man Booker prizewinner *The Narrow Road to the Deep North* (2013): its protagonist is an elderly surgeon with a post-war public career recalling that of the real-life

73. Daws, *Prisoners of the Japanese*, 219.
74. R. Kemball Price, 'R. A. P. W. I.: An Impression', *British Medical Journal*, 1/4451, 27 April 1946, 647.
75. Gavan McCormack and Hank Nelson (eds), *The Burma–Thailand Railway* (Chiang Mai: Silkworm Press, 1993), 5, 6.

Australian army doctor Colonel Sir Edward 'Weary' Dunlop, a celebrated national figure for his heroic leadership on the Burma–Thailand Railway. David Malouf's *The Great World* (1990), which opens in the late 1980s but reaches back as far as the Diggers of the First World War, also puts the lives and deaths of the prisoners on the railway at its centre, as if it were the core of modern Australian history.

Of course, there was also widely read mid-century fiction explicitly about the prisoners of the Japanese, and Nevil Shute's *A Town Like Alice* (1950) and Laurens van der Post's *The Seed and the Sower* (1963) both became well-known films, too, the latter as *Merry Christmas, Mr Lawrence* (1983). Perhaps more tellingly, though, we find that a surprising range of post-war British novels turns to these prisoners' experience almost as shorthand for wartime fear and horror. This is especially significant because of how far realist fiction tends to rely upon what it takes to be shared cultural knowledge and attitudes, although the more experimental Anthony Burgess must also have thought that imprisonment under the Japanese could serve in readers' minds as a byword for gratuitous violence when footage from the camps is deployed during the thug Alex's aversion therapy in *A Clockwork Orange* (1962). The heroine of middlebrow bestseller Angela Thirkell's *Miss Bunting* (1945) has heard nothing for four years of her prisoner-of-war husband. 'This Japanese business is as black as midnight,' reflects her father, a retired Royal Navy man.[76] A character in Alan Sillitoe's short story 'The Disgrace of Jim Scarfedale', from *The Loneliness of the Long Distance Runner* (1959), is so prematurely aged by shock that he looks 'as if he'd just been let out of a Jap prisoner-of-war camp'.[77] Finally, when Anthony Powell's Charles Stringham, the charming alcoholic socialite of *A Dance to the Music of Time* (1951–75), is taken prisoner at the fall of Singapore and dies in a Japanese camp, Powell clearly assumes that his reader will know what a terrible end Stringham's has been. A character who knew Stringham in the camp is asked after the war about their incarceration, and we are told that 'there shot, like forked lightning, across his serious unornamental features that awful look, common to those who speak of that experience'.[78] Noting the 'instantaneous,

76. Angela Thirkell, *Miss Bunting* (Wakefield, RI: Moyer Bell, 1996), 52.
77. Alan Sillitoe, 'The Disgrace of Jim Scarfedale', in Alan Sillitoe, *The Loneliness of the Long Distance Runner* (New York: Vintage, 1987), 147–8.
78. Anthony Powell, *Temporary Kings*, in Anthony Powell, *A Dance to the Music of Time, Fourth Movement* (Chicago: University of Chicago Press, 1995), 206.

petrifying exposure of hidden feeling', Powell's narrator elaborates no further—'I had seen it before,' he says, to readers who had also, perhaps, seen it before.[79]

At the same time, many former prisoners of the Japanese felt that their wartime situation was subject to a form of misremembering, and they singled out for special opprobrium the fictionalization of their experience in David Lean's multiple-Oscar-winning *The Bridge on the River Kwai*. The film adaptation of Pierre Boulle's novella of the same title, Lean's movie appeared in 1957, the same year as *The Rise of the Novel*. Boulle's 1952 novella describes how Colonel Nicholson, a senior British officer imprisoned on the Burma–Thailand Railway, comes to rescue a vital Japanese bridge project from (crudely stereotypical) Asiatic incompetence. All the while, the oblivious traitor Nicholson's progress on the bridge is ironically doubled by a commando unit preparing, with the same technological expertise and single-mindedness of purpose, to blow the bridge up. A rubber planter in Malaya, the Free-French-supporting Boulle had spent the war in French Indochina, a prisoner of its collaborationist regime; he could have learned only at second hand of the historical events at the camp, Tamarkan, where prisoners bridged the Mae Klong River (the railway followed the course of its tributary, the Kwae Noi), and where Lieutenant-Colonel, later Brigadier, Toosey successfully took much of the internal organization of the camp out of Japanese hands. The situation at Tamarkan was close enough to Boulle's setting as to reveal the origin of his absurdist fable about the moral indifference of the military–industrial enterprise, where it is all the same whether you build bridges or blow them up.

Watt had no fundamental problem with Boulle's novella, believing that its schematic and quasi-allegorical form made it impossible to read as a work purporting to describe the actual experience of building the Burma–Thailand Railway. The story was 'intended to be self-evidently absurd', Watt wrote, and Boulle's epigraph from Conrad's *Victory* on 'the Great joke' underscored his ironic intent.[80] If Boulle's novella was historical at all, it was only in so far as the parallel narratives of obsessed bridge-builders and bridge-destroyers gave the novel 'its own kind of truth': 'the conflict between the technical skill of the West and the

79. Powell, *Temporary Kings*, 206.
80. Ian Watt, 'The Humanities on the River Kwai', in Watt, *The Literal Imagination*, 241.

blindly destructive way it is used'.[81] He had much harsher words for Lean's film adaptation, which, unlike Boulle's self-conscious fable, used an uncomplicatedly digestible realist style in its substitution of masculine adventure for the brute fact of the prisoners' total disempowerment.

Importantly for my purposes, the film's worldwide success seems to have done more than anything else to irritate Watt into publishing on his wartime experiences. He otherwise said little about it in print, although the fact that his personal papers include numerous stories, poems, essays, and fragments of memoir about his imprisonment, written in the 1940s and sometimes surviving in fairly polished drafts, indicate that he must have considered publishing more about this period in his life than he eventually did. (His papers include, for example, the table of contents for a projected autobiographical war book, of which around half the named contents survive.) The only material about the war Watt published prior to the release of *The Bridge on the River Kwai* is 'The Liberty of the Prison', which appeared in the *Yale Review* in 1956, shortly before the publication of *The Rise of the Novel*. In that essay, recognizably a product of its existentialist time, Watt addressed the psychological difficulties of becoming a prisoner, and then of ceasing to be one. His former Stanford colleague W. B. Carnochan writes in another context that, although notions of struggle are typically central to the literature of imprisonment, 'the very absence of struggle, the radical acceptance of confinement—the desire not to escape or even the love of being imprisoned—is sometimes the real story'.[82] 'The Liberty of the Prison' comes close to this uncomfortable conclusion that psychologically it may have been even harder to come home and have to make choices again than it was to be imprisoned and choiceless. This was the feeling of being 'conditioned by captivity, and sickly secure in it', of which former prisoner David Piper wrote, as he recalled the terrible freedom of being helpless in the face of his likely death, when 'there were no decisions to take'.[83]

'The Liberty of the Prison' is much more explicit than Watt's other writings about the toll taken by (in his words) 'one of the least-known

81. Ian Watt, 'Bridges over the Kwai', *Listener*, 6 August 1959, 216, 217.
82. W. B. Carnochan, 'The Literature of Confinement', in Norval Morris and David J. Rothman (eds), *The Oxford History of the Prison: The Practice of Punishment in Western Society* (Oxford: Oxford University Press, 1995), 428.
83. David Piper, *I Am Well, Who Are You? Writings of a Japanese Prisoner of War* (Exeter: Anne Piper, 1998), 15.

tragedies of the Second World War'.[84] Unusually, Watt touches on painful matters such as the 'numb and bewildered fear' of the initial phase of captivity, the months where he lay sick with malaria ('a state of dull insensibility and exhaustion'), and his survivor guilt (a 'case of conscience about his survival', he dryly calls it).[85] In perhaps the most overtly confessional passage he ever published, Watt recalls watching a production of *Uncle Vanya* not long after demobilization and trying not to cry 'so violently that I got a cramp in my throat': 'I might have shrugged it off: feeling only that the people in Tchehov could express their self-pity, but that one shouldn't in ordinary life, except for something else that happened a few days later.'[86] That 'something' was the experience of sitting in an auditorium with other former prisoners watching a film compilation made by a Civilian Resettlement Unit to update them on the major war events that they had missed in captivity:

> I didn't enjoy the battle scenes much, but when they came to the pictures of the relief of Stalingrad, and one saw two endless lines of muffled people slowly advancing to greet each other across the waste of snow, I found that that awful crying had started again; and here was I in uniform, and with men who'd been prisoners with me.[87]

But rather than allow this anecdote to generate more pathos than it inevitably does—a psychologically defenceless former prisoner overcome by his unforeseen identification with the survivors of Stalingrad—Watt almost immediately explains that he and the other prisoners had been forced in the camps not 'to realize how sorry for ourselves we were'.[88] This is a punishingly dismissive way of talking about his own pain, but it is in keeping with the derisive reference to 'self-pity' a few sentences earlier. There is a marked habit in all Watt's published writings about his war experience of neutralizing moral outrage with ironic self-deprecation. (As he wrote of Conrad, it is 'the standard modern prescription—when fearful of self-exposure, take cover in irony' (*C.* 346).) Still, this essay comes closer than any other to saying how terrible his experience had been. His other purportedly autobiographical essays about his imprisonment, the essays about what he came to call the 'myth' of the Kwai, understate almost to the point

84. Watt, 'The Liberty of the Prison', 514.
85. Watt, 'The Liberty of the Prison', 516, 522, 522.
86. Watt, 'The Liberty of the Prison', 530.
87. Watt, 'The Liberty of the Prison', 530.
88. Watt, 'The Liberty of the Prison', 531.

of misrepresenting the depth of personal suffering that had taught him how falsely David Lean had represented the Burma–Thailand Railway.

Perhaps it is not surprising that Watt's war experience is largely unspoken in his published work: he was a critic rather than a creative writer, after all. But this special kind of reticence seems to me attributable in part to his membership of a generation of mid-century British literary critics who were never attracted to contemporary dogmas about the irrelevance of the writer's intentions and the critic's ability to interpret them, but, on the contrary, expected from serious readers a high level of what we would now call emotional intelligence. Watt's friend William (in correspondence 'Billy') Empson, for instance, argued to the end of his life that the reader 'ought to be trying all the time to empathize with the author (and of course the assumptions and conventions by which the author felt himself bound); to tell him that he cannot even partially succeed is about the most harmful thing you could do'.[89] In another attack on what he considered the inhuman nullity of New Critical orthodoxy, Empson deplored the ('petulant') critical position that says 'that you won't be bothered with anything but the words on the page . . . If you cared enough you would.'[90] 'There is always an appeal to a background of human experience which is all the more present when it cannot be named,' Empson wrote in 1947, in his preface to the post-war edition of *Seven Types of Ambiguity*.[91] It is difficult not to sense an unnamed meaning in the strange apology that opens Watt's *Conrad in the Nineteenth Century*, where Watt announces that any critic embarking on a discussion of Conrad's troubled life 'must wonder how far the triviality of his own deprivations may have disabled him for the task' (*C.* 1). Watt obviously did not specify what constituted this particular critic's knowledge of 'deprivation'; it was self-evidently not 'trivial', but this was not the place to discuss it. Indeed, even when he appeared to be writing directly about his imprisonment, he tended strongly towards self-effacement, as Frank Kermode noticed

89. William Empson, *Using Biography* (London: Chatto & Windus and the Hogarth Press, 1984), viii.
90. William Empson, 'Still the Strange Necessity', in William Empson, *Argufying: Essays on Literature and Culture*, ed. John Haffenden (London: Hogarth, 1988), 125.
91. William Empson, *Seven Types of Ambiguity* (2nd edn; London: Chatto & Windus, 1947), xv.

when he wrote that in his late lecture '*The Bridge over the River Kwai* as Myth' Watt 'nowhere dwells on his own work and suffering'.[92]

In any case, the received wisdom on dealing with returned prisoners in 1945 was to encourage them to avoid speaking about their experiences. That this was characteristic of the time is suggested by Ruth Leys's influential *Trauma: A Genealogy* (2000), which notes the surprising failure of the phenomenon of trauma to command much interest at mid-century, even in the aftermath of the Holocaust and the Second World War.[93] It is not remotely surprising to find that prisoners' memoirs often attest to the clinically traumatic effects of their experience: life-threatening levels of depression and anxiety; unmanageable anger, restlessness, and hyper-vigilance; insomnia, flashbacks, and nightmares. Having worked closely with these men for decades, the Liverpool School of Tropical Medicine found that over a third of Far East prisoners suffered from 'classical PTSD' long before the syndrome had been named, let alone understood.[94] A full sixty-five years after his liberation, Urquhart mentioned nightmares that were still 'so bad that I fight sleep for fear of the dreams that come with it'.[95] Judith Herman explains that chronic post-traumatic symptoms such as these are longest lasting when they emerge from a period of terrorizing and entrapping circumstances, as distinct from Freud's single instance of 'fright'.[96]

Former prisoners of the Japanese had almost certainly needed more help than they received. The War Office established twenty Civilian Resettlement Units (CRUs) across the country to help reintegrate former prisoners of war through a residential stay of five or six weeks. In his history of British demobilization, Alan Allport rightly notes that, 'considering how blasé the Forces could be about the difficulties of readjustment, it stands out as a humane and imaginative initiative that must have done much good'.[97] Writing specifically about former

92. Frank Kermode, Foreword, in Watt, *Essays on Conrad*, x.
93. Ruth Leys, *Trauma: A Genealogy* (Chicago: University of Chicago Press, 2000), 5.
94. D. Robson, E. Welch, N. J. Beeching, and G.V. Gill, 'Consequences of Captivity: Health Effects of Far East Imprisonment in World War II', *QJM: An International Journal of Medicine*, 102/2 (2009), 94.
95. Urquhart, *The Forgotten Highlander*, 302.
96. Judith Lewis Herman, *Trauma and Recovery: From Domestic Abuse to Political Terror* (London: Pandora, 1992), 74–95.
97. Alan Allport, *Demobbed: Coming Home after the Second World War* (New Haven: Yale University Press, 2009), 203.

prisoners of the Japanese in his history of modern military psychiatry, Ben Shephard likewise notes the valuable work of these units; the problem was that they were voluntary, and relatively few Far East prisoners attended them.[98] Indeed, that only approximately 4,500 out of the 37,583 returned prisoners of the Japanese attended raises the possibility that many of these men were psychologically far too unwell to know how ill they really were. Shephard identifies another problem, though: 'a general, officially orchestrated repression of the "unpleasantness" in the Far East, born of a very British combination of concern for relatives' feelings and obtuse official secretiveness': prisoners were urged not to speak about their experiences, and families were urged not to ask about them.[99]

Watt alludes to this prescription when he describes returning to the family home after the war, where he encountered his mother's puzzling (and implicitly hurtful—although this is not the sort of thing he would say outright) incuriosity, an apparent indifference maintained only until 'awkwardly' she told him that she had been urged by the repatriation authorities not to mention the prison camps.[100] In *The End of a Hate* (1958), the second volume of his prisoner-of-war memoirs, Braddon also describes his mother dutifully following all the advice conveyed by a psychiatrist on the treatment of former prisoners of war. This was 'a long list of *Dos* and *Don'ts*... wrong, without fail, in every one of them': 'We, whose only experience over the past four years was captivity, were never to be questioned about either those years or our captors.'[101] Another Australian veteran reports: 'We were told not to discuss our experiences with relatives and friends; and they in turn were advised not to ask us about our experiences. (This was the current medical thinking—which these days is completely reversed.)'[102]

Many other former prisoners refer to the same presumably well-meaning but damaging conspiracy of silence when they recount their homecoming in their memoirs, and no doubt with self-conscious irony, given that these memoirs are by their mere existence contravening the injunction of forgetful reticence, and their authors' felt need to write them so plain a testament to its failure. Durnford opens his memoir with a verse in which 'friends avoid, with genuine regret, | Mentioning

98. Ben Shephard, *A War of Nerves* (London: Jonathan Cape, 2000), 320.
99. Shephard, *A War of Nerves*, 320.
100. Watt, 'Dover, November 1945'.
101. Russell Braddon, *End of a Hate* (London: Cassell, 1958), 56.
102. Whitecross, *Slaves of the Son of Heaven*, vi.

days they like us to forget'.[103] He ends with his homecoming, in a conclusion that offers no closure:

There was news of friends, familiar things, of public and private matters all in the cheerful, unemotional manner of English family conversation. But there was no time then over the knives and forks—and somehow there has never been an opportunity since—to explain that things were not the same, and could not be.[104]

Piper recalled a different kind of reticence, when people 'politely ... asked us what it had been like, and we could not tell them; when we tried to tell them, they changed the subject soon enough, and soon too we learned not to try'.[105]

In any case, the stiff upper lip was already highly developed among prisoners. In a memoir published, instructively, only half a century after the end of the imprisonment it records, Lomax wrote that 'we survivors almost competed with each other in laconic understatement'; during their imprisonment they had 'all tried to be patterns of courage to each other, and the price we paid would not be exacted in full until much later'.[106] Durnford gives an imperishable instance of this verbal stoicism in captivity when he writes of two artillery subalterns 'whose stock-in-trade expression for starvation, murder and sudden death was "Never a dull moment"'.[107]

Christopher Hitchens attributed to Watt a similar combination of reticence and gallows humour, when he recounted in his autobiography a 1987 visit to the 'dry, wry, and donnish' Watt on the Stanford campus:

He [Watt] admitted later that, detecting other people's reserve after returning home from these wartime nightmares, he had developed a manner of discussing them apotropaically, as it were, so as to defuse them a bit. And he told me the following tale, which I set down with the hope that it captures his memorably laconic tone of voice:

Well, we were in a cell that was probably built for six but was holding about sixteen of us. There wasn't much food and we hadn't been given any water for quite a while. The heat was absolutely ferocious. Dysentery had begun to take its toll, which was distinctly disagreeable at such close quarters...

103. Durnford, *Branch Line to Burma*, v.
104. Durnford, *Branch Line to Burma*, 207.
105. Piper, *I Am Well, Who Are You?* 16.
106. Lomax, *The Railway Man*, 200, 196.
107. Durnford, *Branch Line to Burma*, 71.

Added to this unpleasantness, we could hear one of our number being rather badly beaten by the Japanese guards, with rifle-butts it seemed, in their guardroom down the corridor. At this rather trying moment one of my young subalterns, who'd managed to fall asleep, started screaming and flailing and yelling. He was shouting 'No, no—please don't... Not any more, not again, Oh God please.' Hideous noises like that. I had to take a snap decision to prevent panic, so I ordered the sergeant to slap him and wake him up. When he came to, he apologized for being a bore but brokenly confessed that he'd dreamed he was back at Tonbridge.[108]

Hitchens uses this blackly comic anecdote to introduce his discussion of his own schooldays, but it also speaks to his admiration for the culture of sardonic reticence that this kind of education had instilled in British men of Watt's generation.

And reticence is itself among Watt's own critical preoccupations. Late in life, he wrote approvingly of Cervantes as 'the least confessional of writers, much too proud to give us any notion of his own personal experiences of humiliation and defeat'—Cervantes in fact had also been a war-wounded soldier, a prisoner, and a slave labourer (a captive for five and a half years, according to his prologue to the *Exemplary Stories*).[109] This correspondence was hardly lost on Watt, although, perhaps needless to say, it elicited no autobiographical disclosures; his comment appears in *Myths of Modern Individualism*, where he comments merely as if in passing that all the book's subjects had experienced imprisonment at some stage in their lives (*MMI* 137). Watt used similar terms in *Conrad in the Nineteenth Century*, where it is even clearer that they were meant as praise: Conrad 'scorned the confessional genre', and was 'the last man either to provide raw biographical data for public consumption, or to disclose anything which might prove in the slightest embarrassing to himself or to others' (*C.* 25). Watt speculated that Conrad's reluctance to 'explain... to the uninitiated' the culture from which he had been painfully severed must have been a form of psychic defence against 'traversing endless tracts of national, family, and personal history, all of them too painful to contemplate and too complicated to share. It was better to keep quiet' (*C.* 9). We learn that Conrad had

108. Christopher Hitchens, *Hitch-22* (London: Atlantic Books, 2010), 47, 48; ellipses in original.

109. Ian Watt, *Myths of Modern Individualism: Faust, Don Quixote, Don Juan, Robinson Crusoe* (Cambridge: Cambridge University Press, 1996), 88. Subsequent references are to this edition and are cited parenthetically as *MMI*, followed by page number. Miguel de Cervantes, *Exemplary Stories*, trans. Lesley Lipson (Oxford: Oxford University Press, 2008), 3.

concealed a psychological breakdown to avoid 'deeply humiliating explanations of the sufferings of a distant past which nobody else would ever really understand anyway' (*C.* 13). Conrad himself had Marlow declare that 'the wisdom of life . . . consists in putting out of sight all the reminders of our folly, of our weakness, of our mortality; all that makes against our efficiency—the memory of our failures, the hints of our undying fears, the bodies of our dead friends', in a novel with ventriloquistic qualities that, appropriately enough, interested Watt deeply.[110] Watt quotes these lines from *Lord Jim*—lines about good form and repression—shortly before he turns to Conrad's representation of the stiff upper lip. The 'stiff upper-lip' is 'the special reticence of the anglo-saxon masculine code', Watt writes, and its observance is either 'social decorum' or 'a strenuous and unnatural psychological posture' (*C.* 317). Among all readers of Conrad, he was placed to see both sides.

The fifty years after the war's end saw the publication of many memoirs by former prisoners; and indeed more than fifty years, allowing for books such as Peek's acclaimed *One Fourteenth of an Elephant* (2003), Urquhart's *The Forgotten Highlander* (2010), and Twigg's posthumously published *Survivor on the River Kwai* (2013). Reflecting on the fact that he wrote directly of his wartime internment under the Japanese only forty years later, the English novelist J. G. Ballard told an interviewer that 'those experiences took a long time to forget, and a long time to remember'.[111] But some had documented their years of imprisonment as they unfolded, and all these prison-camp diarists and artists had consciously risked their own lives to do so, in the full knowledge that the Japanese had prohibited such record-keeping among their prisoners. (And once defeat looked imminent, the Japanese would also destroy many of their own records of the camps: 'documents that would be unbearable in the hands of the enemy,' as their directive put it in August 1945.[112]) The inordinately brave George Aspinall managed to take secret photographs from his capture at Singapore (at the age of only 18) all the way up to the Burma–Thailand Railway; his commanding officer saved the contraband negatives by hiding them in a latrine

110. Joseph Conrad, *Lord Jim* (Oxford: Oxford University Press, 2002), 125–6.
111. J. G. Ballard, '1986: Solveig Nordlund. Future Now', in *Extreme Metaphors: Interviews with J. G. Ballard 1967–2008*, ed. Simon Sellars and Dan O'Hara (London: Fourth Estate, 2012), 226.
112. Quoted in Waterford, *Prisoners of the Japanese*, 41.

borehole. Medical officer Dr Robert Hardie kept a diary on army message forms stashed inside a flask; the Scottish artist John Mennie hid his drawings in the hollow of a bamboo walking stick; with the help of dying prisoners, Searle hid his work in the cholera huts that the guards were too afraid to enter; Blackater wrote notes on flimsy India paper ('the broad margin from pages of "The Oxford Book of English Verse"') and hid them inside the back of a hairbrush; Rivett kept his papers under the coverings on his ulcerated legs.[113] Another memoirist, Roy Whitecross, fearfully had a friend bury his diary in two tin cans 'thirty-seven paces due south of the well we had dug in the camp'; he saw another prisoner beaten to death by Japanese guards for being discovered with a pencil.[114] John Coast, a close friend of Watt's, published one of the earliest of the memoirs in 1946, but *Railroad of Death* was written on the ship home, because Coast had never been able to find the manuscript that he had hurriedly buried at Chungkai in anticipation of one of the potentially deadly Japanese searches.[115] The camp's commanding officer buried his own diary two feet down in the grave of another English prisoner.[116]

Decades later, Watt recalled visiting a liberated camp two days after the war's end, where he watched 'scores of ex-prisoners circling aimlessly about with their eyes on the ground, like mushroom pickers', looking for the buried diaries for which they had risked their lives.[117] 'I did not realise how many had taken that risk until long after the end of the war,' Watt explained in 1981, in a public lecture defending the humanities as a reflection of a universal 'need to record and testify' and 'an assertion of the individual's sense that his memory of his past, his historical experience, is an essential part of his sense of self'.[118] In *The Rise of the Novel* he praised Defoe's memoir style of narrative for creating 'a sense of personal identity subsisting through duration and yet being changed by the flow of experience' (*RN* 24); in *Conrad in the Nineteenth Century*, he praised *Lord Jim* for showing how 'the internal sense of the duration of the self and of others is given a context, shaped, and made real, through memory' (*C.* 302). The real-world witnesses to the Japanese

113. Blackater, *Gods without Reason*, 185.
114. Whitecross, *Slaves of the Son of Heaven*, vii.
115. John Coast, *Railroad of Death* (Newcastle: Myrmidon, 2014), xvi.
116. Cary Owtram, *1000 Days on the River Kwai* (Barnsley: Pen & Sword, 2017), 92.
117. Watt, 'The Humanities on the River Kwai', 232.
118. Watt, 'The Humanities on the River Kwai', 232.

prison camps must also have been on Watt's mind when, in an essay on George Orwell's *Nineteen Eighty-Four* written around the same time as he contemplated the relevance of humanistic enquiry even in catastrophic conditions, he emphasized the power of the inner motives driving Orwell's hero to keep a diary that he knows could get him killed. Winston Smith is not the last man in Europe, nor is he the last human being of his torturer O'Brien's taunts, but, rather, he is 'the last humanist', because his diary 'is a literary *acte gratuit* of a heroic kind, since endangering his life merely to give an objective testimony to his view of the truth about himself and his time surely bespeaks Winston's deep need for self-expression'.[119]

There is an oblique and rather moving manifestation of the same compulsion 'to record and testify' in Watt's habit of diagnosing fictional characters with diseases whose lethal progress he had witnessed in the prison camps. Robinson Crusoe's life-endangering but soul-saving fever is 'presumably malaria', Watt supposes in a parenthetical afterthought (*MMI* 159), while Conrad's skeletal Kurtz, turning into symbolic ivory at the point of death, is based on someone who is probably 'in the last stages of dysentery—a disease peculiarly repulsive in its physical manifestations, and usually marked by an unimaginable degree of emaciation' (*C.* 142). Here, Watt also feels compelled to note that the real-world source for Kurtz was absolutely not buried 'in a muddy hole', as Marlow describes Kurtz, 'but in a proper grave in the cemetery at the Baptist mission' (*C.* 141–2). This would seem an almost pedantic correction were it not that Watt had once seen so many friends buried with the same lack of ceremony as the hastily dispatched Kurtz.

Disease, starvation, and exhaustion had left Watt gravely ill by the end of the war. If his mere survival showed that he was 'one of the lucky ones... back', as a character tells the returned prisoner-of-war protagonist of Henry Green's *Back*, Watt felt that he had been one of the lucky ones all along, if only in a somewhat relative sense, as an officer. He believed that 'those who were not officers had a much harder time in nearly all respects'.[120] That other prisoners had it worse is a common theme of prisoners' memoirs, and at times the reader senses something like survivor guilt (or, in Watt's laconic phrase, a 'case of conscience about his survival') in their insistence on this point. Of course, the

119. Ian Watt, 'Winston Smith: The Last Humanist', in Watt, *The Literal Imagination*, 220.
120. Watt, 'The Liberty of the Prison', 532.

contrasts that they drew have some factual basis: prisoner-memoirists often resort to the all-surpassingly terrible predicament of the Asian labourers by way of contrast; and, as an officer, Watt would usually have had enough money to pay for black-market duck eggs or bananas, where they could be found, to supplement the lethally inadequate prison-camp ration of dirty, weevil-riddled rice.[121] Even so, he had suffered in the course of his captivity with malaria, beriberi, diphtheria, and permanently scarring tropical ulcers, not to mention the psychological and other after-effects of having been beaten up and seen others beaten up by the unpredictably violent Korean guards.[122] (Japan had annexed Korea in 1910, and even their victims supposed that the racially subordinated Korean conscripts were mostly taking out their own bad treatment on the prisoners in their power.) Watt's repatriation was delayed by what was now extremely fragile health, which meant hospitalization in Burma, and he was finally demobilized only in March 1946. The year in which he published *The Rise of the Novel* opened with his receipt on 3 January of the only monetary compensation he seems to have received: a cheque for $85.40 supplied via the Red Cross for his share as a former prisoner in a liquidation of Japanese assets.[123]

The Rise of the Novel Revisited

'We were superficially quite normal enough for the idea that nothing had left its mark to survive for quite a time; but the idea, of course, was not altogether true,' Watt wrote in 'The Liberty of the Prison'.[124] In the

121. In theory, though barely in practice since the Japanese held most of it back, prisoners forced to work on the railway were paid. Around half of what little remained to an officer then went to the camp collection for the sick, whom the Japanese considered useless mouths and refused to feed. Blackater, *Gods without Reason*, 48.
122. 'I suppose every prisoner of war has seen or heard his companions being murdered by the Korean guards, the Japanese camp officers, or the Kempitai, the hated security police; and he has certainly been beaten himself many times' (Watt, 'The Liberty of the Prison', 523). In an unpublished essay, he describes collapsing (he was sick with diphtheria) after being beaten up in March 1943 by a Korean guard who had once given him some fruit; he attributes the beating to 'the fact that even after I had received the gifts I had not shown complete and uncritical approval of this particular Korean's actions with other prisoners' (Ian Watt, 'The Japanese', Stanford University Special Collections, SC401-ACCN 1990-131, Box 56, Folder, 'The Gahanese Character').
123. The British—not Japanese—government made payments of £10,000 to surviving prisoners in 2001. Watt died in 1999.
124. Watt, 'The Liberty of the Prison', 529.

decade since demobilization, Watt had commenced and abandoned a book about orality and literacy with the social anthropologist Jack Goody, with whom he had been an English student at Cambridge, and who was, not incidentally, a former prisoner of war in Italy and Germany. (Goody believed that it was their shared wartime experience of having 'for the first time in our lives been deprived of books and newspapers' that led them to contemplate 'the role of writing in human societies'.[125]) Eventually Watt returned to his pre-war research on the emergence of the novel in relation to eighteenth-century print culture. This project went through many drafts and titles: 'Public Taste and the Development of the Novel, 1719–1754', 'The Novel and its Society, 1719–1754', 'The Novel and its Reader, 1719–1754', and 'The Reading Public and the Rise of the Novel, 1719–1754'. But, in the more resonantly titled book to which this research ultimately led, the growth of the reading public, once so important, is allotted merely an avowedly 'brief and tentative' chapter with only a heavily qualified claim about the extent of eighteenth-century literacy (*RN* 35). The emphasis of *The Rise of the Novel* falls elsewhere. The rise of the novel as the rise of the reading public gets replaced by what became Watt's canonical argument about the rise of the novel as the rise of realism: 'realism of presentation', an implicitly individualistic new empiricism, and 'realism of assessment', or the effort to judge subjective experience by shared social and moral values. As all students of the eighteenth-century novel learn, Watt uses Defoe and Richardson to represent 'realism of presentation', while Fielding exemplifies more briefly 'realism of assessment'.

Watt's preface to *The Rise of the Novel* mentions his dissatisfaction with his earlier focus on literacy: reading eighteenth-century novelists doubtless requires us to take into account the impact of changing audiences for prose fiction, 'but their works are surely more profoundly conditioned by the new climate of social and moral experience which they and their eighteenth-century readers shared' (*RN* 7). I show in the coming chapters how Watt's book, too, was 'profoundly conditioned' by a 'new climate of social and moral experience'. It is no accident that one of Watt's own keywords is 'environment' ('fateful' and 'lacerating'

125. Jack Goody, 'Watt, War, and Writing', *Stanford Humanities Review*, 8/1 (2000), 224. What survived is published as Jack Goody and Ian Watt, 'The Consequences of Literacy', *Comparative Studies in Society and History*, 5/3 (April 1963), 304–45.

are other expressive tics), although it is overshadowed in *The Rise of the Novel* by Watt's no less instructive recourse, on well over two hundred occasions, to 'reality' and its cognates.

The Rise of the Novel starts from the assumption that the works of Defoe, Richardson, and Fielding are axiomatically important, and Watt's aim is to illuminate the historical, social, and moral conditions that made them possible. This book, in turn, assumes that critics such as Watt matter, and pursues a similarly reconstructive wish to explore the extraordinary conditions that shaped early post-war thinking about literature in ways that only historical distance makes legible. We see there the circuit connecting literature and non-literary life: the lived experiences through which we read literature, and which shape the ways in which we read it, produces readings that in turn make sense of the experiences that drove the readings. So I assume that there is a fundamental sincerity in literary criticism that survives the occasionally anaesthetizing circumstances under which it is produced, and even that sincerity in humanistic enquiry is a good thing; and that academic writing—for once, the urbane Watt uses words more sentimental than mine—'should above all contain nothing which the writer doesn't believe in his heart of hearts'.[126] 'Should Criticism be Humanist?' Watt asked in a talk on the BBC's Third Programme in 1952. For Watt, the humanist approach was exemplified by the work of Richards, Empson, Leavis, Lionel Trilling, and implicitly himself, against the formalisms of the New Criticism: 'the humanists giving pride of place to the extrinsic interest and values of the literary work, to its value for the reader, and for society as a whole'.[127] Literary criticism was about both the individual and the common good.

As Watt wrote, literary criticism is 'subject to the processes of history', and, if the orientations underlying this book are close enough to those that formed Watt's work to explain why anyone would write a book about another critic in the first place, distance as much as affiliation defines our relationship to mid-century literary critics. Other mid-century humanists have attracted renewed interest in recent years: on the British side, pre-eminently Empson, although intermittently Leavis; and, on the American side, Trilling and perhaps F. O. Matthiessen.[128]

126. Watt, 'Realism and Modern Criticism of the Novel', 84.
127. Ian Watt, 'Should Criticism be Humanist?', *Listener*, 4 September 1952, 378.
128. See, e.g., John Rodden, *Lionel Trilling and the Critics* (Lincoln, NE: University of Nebraska Press, 1999), Randall Fuller, *Emerson's Ghosts: Literature, Politics, and the*

Like Watt, they wrote too long ago to be actually imitable, but also long enough ago to benefit from the powerful charisma of a time when literary study felt secure about its own purposes. That said, something more than nostalgia should encourage us to read mid-century classics with fresh eyes. In the closing paragraph of his survey of the 'rise of the novel' debates, Seager insists that his readers should 'test against the original *all* claims about what Ian Watt argues'; his blunt rationale is only momentarily surprising: 'In the course of my reading for this study I have found a considerable extent of misprision and, what is worse, misrepresentation of *The Rise of the Novel*. It has unfortunately become a book more often caricatured than consulted.'[129]

The obvious precedent for my reading of the life in Watt's work is one of the books to which he explicitly declared his indebtedness, Erich Auerbach's 'brilliant panorama' *Mimesis: The Representation of Reality in Western Literature* (*RN* 79). The origins of *Mimesis* (1946) in its author's wartime exile in Istanbul as a Jewish German scholar separated from his library and his country by Nazi race laws have been known for so long that Auerbach's wartime experience is almost inseparable from the story he tells in the book. To name another work to which Watt avows his indebtedness (*RN* 84), Georg Lukács' *Theory of the Novel* (1920) declares its own historical provocations at the outset, when Lukács writes in his preface that this book was his response to the First World War. The pain of being a hostage to geopolitical upheaval finds expression in its famous theory of 'transcendental homelessness': although Lukács's *Obdachlosigkeit* is the 'homelessness' of ordinary English usage, the standard English translation also renders as 'homelessness' what Lukács calls *Heimatlosigkeit*—which is not (just) about losing the roof over your head but about a spiritual, even existential, sense in which you have been uprooted from your own homeland, your habitat. *The Rise of the Novel* confirms no less the truism about what is hidden in plain sight. Watt's former colleague Carnochan wrote

Making of Americanists (New York: Oxford University Press, 2007), Matthew Bevis (ed.), *Some Versions of Empson* (Oxford: Clarendon Press, 2007), Adam Kirsch, *Why Trilling Matters* (New Haven: Yale University Press, 2011), and Michael Wood, *On Empson* (Princeton: Princeton University Press, 2017). Leavis makes several appearances in Stefan Collini, *Absent Minds: Intellectuals in Britain* (Oxford: Oxford University Press, 2006), and naturally receives extended treatment in Christopher Hilliard, *English as a Vocation: The* Scrutiny *Movement* (Oxford: Oxford University Press, 2012).

129. Seager, *The Rise of the Novel*, 189.

of Watt's past as 'an experience that some of Defoe's characters could have survived—but...not many others', when he mentioned Watt's war in an essay published shortly after his former colleague's death, in the only discussion of *The Rise of the Novel* that comes close to implying that Watt's intellectual life may have been affected by his military experience.[130] Carnochan is not concerned with Watt's imprisonment as such, but he conveys powerfully the sense that there is a 'protective' quality to Watt's urbane style that only partly conceals 'the existential dread that underlies the rise of the novel'.[131] A few years later, Roger Bourke discussed Watt's Kwai essays in his valuable survey of fiction about the Far East prisoners, although he supposed that 'it would be wrong to claim that the shadow of his imprisonment hangs over *The Rise of the Novel*'.[132] But Bourke quotes the passage where the 'shadow of his imprisonment' is most obvious. Here is Watt closing his discussion of Defoe:

> The Second World War, especially, brought us closer to the prophetic nature of Defoe's picture of individualism. Camus used Defoe's allegorical claim for *Robinson Crusoe* as epigraph to his own allegory, *La Peste* (1948): 'It is as reasonable to represent one kind of imprisonment by another, as it is to represent anything that really exists by that which exists not.' At the same time André Malraux wrote that only three books, *Robinson Crusoe, Don Quixote* and *The Idiot*, retained their truth for those who had seen prisons and concentration camps. (*RN* 133)

Or prisoner-of-war camps, Watt could have added, but did not. We will see these incomplete and private references frequently in what follows.

This passage Watt quotes is explicitly about obliquity—Defoe and then Camus using one kind of imprisonment to represent another—but is itself deploying indirection in occluding Watt's own biographical situation. For many among this generation of critics, an interest in indirection followed their easy acceptance of psychoanalysis, as when Watt wrote of the difference between Conrad's early and late fiction: 'it was in the early works that Conrad had drawn most directly upon his own experiences of disillusionment, isolation, and suffering; and

130. W. B. Carnochan, 'The Persistence of *The Rise of the Novel*', *Stanford Humanities Review*, 8/1 (2000), 92.
131. Carnochan, 'The Persistence of *The Rise of the Novel*', 92.
132. Roger Bourke, *Prisoners of the Japanese: Literary Imagination and the Prisoner-of-War Experience* (St Lucia, Queensland: University of Queensland Press, 2006), 24.

after he had once painfully discovered his own ways of coming to imaginative terms with these experiences, there was no longer the need, and there could hardly be the wish, to do it again' (*C.* 358). Another British prisoner of the Japanese who became a literary critic, Graham Hough argued that Freud had 'altered the moral and emotional landscape of the West more fundamentally than anyone since Rousseau'.[133]

What Freud can do for us ... is to show that what might appear to be a rather perverse literary device, a meaningless obliquity, is in fact deeply rooted in our psychological habit. The elaboration of a raw personal situation into a form in which it can be more readily accepted is not a matter of evasiveness or decorum, but a profound psychological necessity.[134]

This book is centrally concerned with Watt's 'elaboration of a raw personal situation into a form in which it can be more readily accepted'. The 'raw personal situation' from which we write is unlikely to be as terrifying as those Watt and Hough had known, but perhaps it is true that literature—or literary criticism—allows us to say what we would never say on our own behalf, some of which we never even knew we wanted to say before the encounter with the text that licensed its saying. Watt would have recognized this phenomenon too, for, as he wrote in yet another loaded passage in *Conrad in the Nineteenth Century*, the need 'to be articulate about matters which have hitherto been more or less private or unconscious, is perhaps the commonest way in which we clarify our own perceptions and convictions' (*C.* 257).

Essentially this book suggests that Watt's criticism thinks through painfully distinctive modern experiences: problems of subjectivity, individuality, and the demands of communal existence; the lived effects of violence, dispossession, and fear; tensions between the impulse towards testimonial expression and the sense of emotional and verbal decorum. An American colleague greeted the publication of the Conrad book as 'More Watt on Life', and Watt professed not to mind 'the ironic aspersion' implied in the suggestion that his criticism drifted far beyond the ostensible subject of analysis.[135] It is hard to guess how conscious Watt was that he was often writing about more than the

133. Graham Hough, *Image and Experience: Studies in a Literary Revolution* (London: Duckworth, 1960), 130.
134. Hough, *Image and Experience*, 126.
135. Quoted by Watt in Todorov, *Literature and its Theorists*, 118.

literary works in front of him, but his own comments on how far Richardson knew what he was doing as a novelist seem apt: 'it seems reasonable to say that, in general, although a writer does not always know what he has written, he cannot write what he does not know.'[136] What any critic ends up actually writing about is dizzyingly overdetermined, and accidents of many kinds stand behind scholarly interests that appear to be freely chosen. But there is surely some accounting for taste. Perhaps what Watt wanted to say in the autobiographical work he never published he could say most expressively when he was not writing about himself. Here, one recalls the most influential insight of trauma theory, that symptomatic project of historicism meeting poststructuralism as the Second World War generation reached the end of their lives: traumatic experience is not directly available to consciousness but can be reconstructed from its rehearsal.

My debt to that transformative body of work must be obvious even in the basic premise of this book, but Watt's story is more than a confirmation of what are now psychoanalytic truisms, whereby untimeliness and indirection are of the essence, and the return in criticism to his harming evinces merely what Freud's foundational model of traumatic recurrence had called 'the impulse to work over in the mind some overpowering experience so as to make oneself master of it'.[137] Naturally, we could elaborate ingeniously the parallel between Cathy Caruth's emphasis on the image of 'falling' in traumatic discourse with the utterly blindsiding fall of Singapore. An experience of traumatizing fright on the grand scale, this previously unthinkable event opens many prisoners' memoirs. Borrowing Caruth's terms, it is 'the traumatic accident' that 'takes place too soon, too suddenly, too unexpectedly, to be fully grasped by consciousness'.[138] 'When Singapore capitulated, late in the afternoon of Sunday 15 February, our lives were split into two with the brutal finality of a guillotine blade,' one veteran recalled with extraordinary psychological acuity: 'It could not have been more

136. Ian Watt, 'Samuel Richardson', in Ian Watt et al., *The Novelist as Innovator* (London: British Broadcasting Corporation, 1965), 10.
137. Sigmund Freud, *Beyond the Pleasure Principle*, trans. James Strachey (New York: Norton, 1961), 16.
138. Cathy Caruth, *Unclaimed Experience: Trauma, Narrative, and History* (Baltimore: Johns Hopkins University Press, 1996), 101.

abrupt, more complete, or more destructive to our personalities.'[139] But to show how the war finds expression in Watt's writing is to make a more affirmative argument than to cast criticism as a symptom of unresolved trauma. While this is the story of someone surviving experiences that might have killed him several times over, so to speak, it is also about potentially annihilating experiences being turned into something creative, durable, and analytically powerful.

But—finally—to say so is merely to reprise Watt's views once more. These transformations of personal loss and fear into sanely measured perspectives on the external world were the basis of his deepest critical affinities, Conrad and Samuel Johnson: 'Neither Johnson nor Conrad wrote directly about their inner lives, and in each case it is only our subliminal sense of great energies at play to keep turbulent and destructive personal feelings under conscious control which makes us feel that we are in touch with one of the great heroes of the wars of the mind' (*C.* 25). The traditional stiff upper lip again, perhaps, except that Watt is suggesting that the codes of stoicism are finally transparent to the 'subliminal sense' of a sympathetic reader who is attuned to the ways in which private pain can be turned into shareable insights about the world. This presumption of profound but tacit understanding cannot have been unusual among those who experienced the Second World War, a war in which, as Tony Judt so memorably wrote, 'everyone lost something and many lost everything'.[140]

'Sympathy is a form of knowledge', R. H. Tawney wrote just after the war, in a line from his classic essay on the relationship between literature and history that Watt was given to quoting: 'It cannot be taught. It can only be absorbed by association with those the depths of whose natures has enabled them most profoundly to feel and most adequately to express it.'[141] For Watt this kind of encounter is a reflection of 'how people become human', a move towards 'the prime condition of civilized life: awareness of the reality of the other'.[142] Reading, he continued, 'involves a deep and unconditional awareness of the real and

139. Peek, *One Fourteenth*, 663.
140. Tony Judt, *Postwar: A History of Europe since 1945* (New York: Penguin, 2005), 41.
141. R. H. Tawney, *Social History and Literature* (London: Cambridge University Press for the National Book League, 1950), 14. See Watt, 'The Humanities on the River Kwai', 235, and Watt, 'Realism and Modern Criticism of the Novel', 77.
142. Ian Watt, 'Writing about Literature', *Glosses*, 1/1 (1970), 3.

independent existence of all the multiplicity of things and experiences outside the individual's subjective world'.[143] What Tawney called sympathy Watt said was no more or less than the imagination, 'the literal imagination': our means of 'entering as fully as possible in all the concrete particularities of a literary work or the lives of others or the lessons of history'.[144]

143. Watt, 'Writing about Literature', 3.
144. Watt, 'The Humanities on the River Kwai', 235.

2

Defoe's Individualism and the Camp Entrepreneurs

'So certainly does Interest banish all manner of Affection, and so naturally do Men give up Honour and Justice, Humanity, and even Christianity, to secure themselves.'

Daniel Defoe, *Moll Flanders* (1722)[1]

'Camp life, which surpasses in savagery all that we know about the lives of cannibals or rats, had almost broken him.'

Aleksandr Solzhenitsyn, *In the First Circle* (1968)[2]

The story told in *The Rise of the Novel* begins in 1719 with the publication of *Robinson Crusoe*, but Watt's opening paragraph acknowledges that extended fictional prose narratives predate 'the novel' by millennia. Margaret Anne Doody developed the challenge that this longer history of prose fiction presents to Watt's argument in her erudite and iconoclastic *The True Story of the Novel* (1996), where the origins of the novel are found instead in the cosmopolitan and polyglot worlds of classical antiquity. Doody identifies in that era's productions many of the characteristics that we have come to take as decisively constitutive of the modern 'Western' novel. In Watt's influential view, however, what distinguishes the eighteenth-century novel, the first *novel*, from such prior works is 'the amount of attention it habitually accords both to the individualisation of its characters and to the detailed presentation of their environment' (*RN* 18).

1. Defoe, *Moll Flanders*, 58.
2. Aleksandr Solzhenitsyn, *In the First Circle*, trans. Harry Willets (New York: Harper Collins, 2009), 261.

Many critics have complicated or amplified Watt's argument that the rise of the novel reflects and implicitly advances the rise of individualism and 'a growing tendency for individual experience to replace collective tradition as the ultimate arbiter of reality' (*RN* 14). This has proved to be among the most influential, and thus the most frequently contested, of all the claims made in *The Rise of the Novel*. Indeed, given that Doody rejects all Watt's other main premises, it is striking that even she believes that there is a connection between the rise of the novel and the rise of individualism, even if she finds it in an altogether different place and time: the novel, she argues, 'comes into being and flourishes during a period—an extended period—of self-consciousness and of value for the individual'.[3] Much closer to Watt's eighteenth-century story, Michael McKeon's essential *Origins of the English Novel* describes how and why it matters that aristocratic anti-individualism, with its view of worth as birth and its romance sensibility, is still demonstrably present in the early eighteenth century, although his book ends up in a similar place to *The Rise of the Novel*, with individualism and the realist novel triumphant by the end of the century.[4] Differently concerned with the novel's making of the individual, D. A. Miller attributes the dominance of the novel from the eighteenth century onward to its 'superior efficacy in producing and providing for privatized subjects', whereas Deidre Shauna Lynch has shown compellingly how this novel-as-individualism equation evades the economic history of character-reading from which emerged only belatedly our familiar conceptions of novelistic subjectivity as deep interiority and particularized personhood—conceptions that Watt and those who followed him present as if they were somehow timeless and self-evident.[5] Finally, perhaps Nancy Armstrong takes Watt's thesis about the rise of the novel as the rise of liberal individualism as far as it will go when she proposes that 'the history of the novel and the history of the modern subject are, quite literally, one and the same'.[6] In *How Novels Think*, she argues that the realist novel largely invented

3. Doody, *The True Story of the Novel*, 24. See also her reading of Roman art, with its 'interest in the inward and the personal'; these are figures who 'look reflective, self-involved or self-questioning'; 'we cannot help feeling that here are people capable of internal reflection, of introspection—like the characters in the novels, in fact' (25).
4. McKeon, *Origins of the English Novel*, see esp. 21, 419.
5. D.A. Miller, *The Novel and the Police* (Berkeley and Los Angeles: University of California Press, 1988), 82. Deidre Shauna Lynch, *The Economy of Character: Novels, Market Culture, and the Business of Inner Meaning* (Chicago: University of Chicago Press, 1998), 1–20.
6. Armstrong, *How Novels Think*, 3.

the liberal individual, meanwhile edging out of the picture those competing and less easily assimilated notions of selfhood circulating in non-realist forms of fiction.

But what is noticeable and surprising when *The Rise of the Novel* is read in the contexts of Watt's historical situation and his other writings is that its understanding of 'individualism' is neither innocently descriptive nor, as it is often taken to be, particularly celebratory. Watt is often thought of as the literary-historical spokesman for a Whiggish, *Bildungsroman*-like narrative of the progressive enfranchisement of the modern individual; in fact, he seems to have understood individualism not so much as a heroic emancipation of the autonomous self from the shackles of pre-Enlightenment caste determinism and benighted religious orthodoxy but as something much more frightening in its capacity to uproot and isolate people, setting them against one another as competitors and rivals. In fact, it is really no exaggeration to say that for Watt the rise of social and economic individualism entails a potentially chilling cultural transformation, because 'it posits a whole society mainly governed by the idea of every individual's intrinsic independence... from other individuals' (*RN* 60). As a result of 'the hypostasis of the economic motive [and] a devaluation of other modes of thought, feeling and action', 'the various forms of traditional group relationship, the family, the guild, the village, the sense of nationality—all are weakened' (*RN* 64). The aftermath of a total war, and of all war's constitutive involuntary collectivities, from the armed forces and prison camps to the nation itself, perhaps helps to explain why Watt places such emphasis on the fragility of community; and the national community, specifically, is one to which he keeps returning in his account of Defoe: 'Crusoe, one feels, is not bound to his country by sentimental ties, any more than to his family; he is satisfied by people, whatever their nationality, who are good to do business with; and he feels, like Moll Flanders, that "with money in the pocket one is at home anywhere"' (*RN* 66).

The literature of individualism turns its protagonists into 'solitary nomads', Watt wrote in *Myths of Modern Individualism*, turning at the end of his career to what he saw as the debilitating extent to which individualism precludes personal loyalty and all other forms of human solidarity. 'Somehow', J. Paul Hunter muses, in an account of individualism and the novel more sympathetic to Watt than most, 'the novel has always communicated a terrible sense of isolation and articulated dramatically the breakdown of the relationships between individuals'.[7] To understand why that sense of breakdown made Defoe a 'portentous and timely figure', as Watt put it in a passage that I quoted early in Chapter 1, we need to look at the mid-twentieth rather than the mid-eighteenth century as the decisive moment for thoughts on individualism and the novel.

King Rat

Recounting the critical history of the famous 'destructive element' passage in Conrad's *Lord Jim*, Watt remarked that every decade 'has discovered in the passage an image of its own characteristic preoccupations' (*C.* 325). As he knew, acts of interpretation have a situational element, and we see this plainly in the modern reception of Defoe's characters. Between the wars, Virginia Woolf found in Moll Flanders a 'robust understanding', 'noble tolerance', and 'good-will', while her friend and contemporary E. M. Forster presented an even more affirmative Moll, with her 'decent and affectionate heart', 'innate goodness', 'humour and good sense'.[8] Now scholars, rejecting Watt's much harsher reading, find different ways of accommodating Moll Flanders by, for example, focusing on the redemptive durability of her bonds with other women characters, or recuperating her individualism as Defoe's critique of corrupted communities.[9] But, writing shortly after the war, the best Watt could say for Moll's 'most positive qualities' was that she shows 'a restless, amoral and strenuous individualism', and the most he could say of her psychological make-up was that she shares the reflexes of 'Pavlov's dog', quick to react to the stimulus of 'profit or danger' (*RN* 114, 108). His robustly instinctive, not to say downright feral, Moll Flanders is no more nor less than a survivor:

> Her wisdom is not impressive; it is at best of a low atavistic kind wholly directed to the problems of survival; but nothing could be more impressive

7. Hunter, *Before Novels*, 40.
8. Virginia Woolf, *The Common Reader, First Series* (Orlando, FL: Harcourt, 1984), 89, 90, 90. E. M. Forster, *Aspects of the Novel* (San Diego: Harcourt, 1955), 56, 57, 58.
9. Srividhya Swaminathan, 'Defoe's Alternative Conduct Manual: Survival Strategies and Female Networks in *Moll Flanders*', *Eighteenth-Century Fiction*, 15/2 (January 2003), 185–206. Melissa Mowry, 'Women, Work, Rearguard Politics, and Defoe's Moll Flanders', *Eighteenth Century*, 49/2 (Summer 2008), 97–116.

than her energy, and it too has a moral premise, a kind of inarticulate and yet fortifying stoicism. Everything happens to Moll Flanders and nothing leaves scars. (*RN* 132)

Temperamental and political differences surely contribute to Watt's divergence from canonical prior readings—of course the humanist Forster and the feminist Woolf would be predisposed to offer more redemptive readings of Moll—but there is a key historical difference too.

That is, perhaps Watt's invulnerable Moll Flanders might be seen as a product of the Second World War, the outbreak of which had helped to create Bertolt Brecht's profiteering Mother Courage. Watt's version of Moll shares her ruthless economic priorities, her unreflective fortitude, and what at times feels like a barely human resilience. Mother Courage earns her name because she risks her life by driving through the bombardment of Riga, fearing that the bread in her wagon will go mouldy before she can sell it: 'what else could I do?', she asks, and it is not a stupid question when she believes that the alternative is starvation.[10] We might compare Watt's early post-war summary of *Moll Flanders* as 'a comprehensive image of the ambiguous and dehumanizing conflicts into which modern civilization plunges its unhappy natives'.[11]

Of course, there is plenty in *Moll Flanders* to support Watt's dark and disenchanted reading of its principal. Witness the unmixed delight with which she learns of the judicial execution of an accomplice, now incapable of incriminating Moll in their shared crimes: 'the joyful News that he was hang'd, which was the best News to me that I had heard a great while'.[12] This is among the starkest confirmations in the novel of Moll's declared view that people 'naturally . . . give up Honour and Justice, Humanity, and even Christianity, to secure themselves'. But this is only one facet of Moll Flanders, and for Watt to make her begin and end there is surely to betray the impact of wartime forms of unfeeling. More specifically still, I would argue that Watt's influential version of Moll Flanders is the product not simply of the war but of the war's prison camps, and that her closest counterparts are to be found among the camp entrepreneurs of whom former prisoners wrote, envious and appalled, in their memoirs and autobiographical fiction. These were the

10. Bertolt Brecht, *Mother Courage and her Children: A Chronicle of the Thirty Years' War*, trans. Eric Bentley (New York: Grove, 1991), 25.
11. Watt, 'The Recent Critical Fortunes of Moll Flanders', 126.
12. Defoe, *Moll Flanders*, 219–20.

'mighty men' of Watt's friend John Durnford's war memoir: 'mighty men, nabobs of the black-market in tobacco, clothing and even, it was suggested, quinine, grew fat and sleek like merchants.'[13] (In desperately short supply, quinine was the only reliable remedy for the malaria that was killing hundreds in the camps.) Durnford was not always derogatory about prisoners' business activities; he himself briefly sold rawhide sandals for a talented entrepreneur. Some camps had 'a brisk economic life on strictly free-enterprise lines', according to another former prisoner acquaintance of Watt's; he had sold ersatz 'marmalade' at Chungkai.[14]

These rawhide sandals and fake marmalade make possible a more affirmative reading of the relationship between Defoe and the prison camp than the one Watt's analysis of Defoe's characters suggests. Surveying fiction produced by or about former Far East prisoners, Roger Bourke notes the *Robinson Crusoe* quality of these works, recounting the compellingly Crusoe-like feats of ingenuity performed in the camps: medical equipment was made from bamboo thorns and old bicycle wheels; prosthetic limbs from rubber-tree wood and filing cabinets; toothbrushes from coconut fibre; soap from palm oil.[15] Russell Braddon writes of prisoners making 'soap, brooms, brushes, false teeth, paper, radios, book bindings, artificial limbs, pressure cookers'.[16] Rohan Rivett and Ernest Gordon describe how surgical supplies were made from butchers' saws, curettes from sharpened spoons, bedpans from bamboos, anaesthetics from narcotic plants, surgical sutures from dried cow entrails; at a pinch—so to speak—a pair of scissors amputated ulcerated toes.[17] As Robinson Crusoe satisfyingly proclaims, 'by making the most rational judgment of things, every man may be in time master of every mechanick art'.[18] Indeed, Watt wonders if part of the reading pleasure of *Robinson Crusoe* in its own time was that Defoe reminded readers of an era before economic specialization. On Crusoe's island 'there is an absolute equivalence between individual effort and individual reward' (*RN* 72).

What is less comforting, and I think more directly relevant to Watt's bigger claims about Defoe, is how far the prison-camp 'triumph of

13. Durnford, *Branch Line to Burma*, 126.
14. Graham Hough, 'Prisoners', *London Review of Books*, 8 May 1986, 8.
15. Bourke, *Prisoners of the Japanese*, 28–9.
16. Braddon, *End of a Hate*, 17.
17. Rivett, *Behind Bamboo*, 279–91; Gordon, *Miracle on the River Kwai*, 165–6. Meg Parkes and Geoff Gill from the Liverpool School of Tropical Medicine, where many former prisoners were treated after the war, review medical conditions in the camps and the improvisations that helped to relieve them in *Captive Memories: Starvation, Disease, Survival* (Lancaster: Palatine Books, 2015), 94–144.
18. Daniel Defoe, *Robinson Crusoe* (London: Penguin, 2003), 55.

improvisation', as Braddon called it, was directed towards individually self-serving commercial ends.[19] Among the best known of the prison-camp entrepreneurs is the title character of James Clavell's *King Rat* (1962), a bestselling novel also known from the English director Brian Forbes's film adaptation of 1965. *King Rat* was the work of a British-turned-American writer otherwise known for authoring the screenplays of, somewhat ironically on both counts, *The Great Escape* and *Shogun*. Even aside from its wide dissemination in the 1960s, Clavell's account of entrepreneurship is worth pausing on because he and Watt were captured around the same time and spent time in at least one of the same camps, Changi on Singapore, where *King Rat* is set. The title character is Corporal King, a charismatic but intimidating American prisoner who establishes a successful black-market enterprise within the camp, and who is ultimately ruined by the outbreak of peace because his instinct for commercial opportunity flourishes best in conditions of near-total privation. This is why, when all the other camp inmates are mere skin and bone (the liberating officer is aghast at these 'zombies in rags, zombies in loincloths, zombies in sarongs—boned and meatless'), King, in contrast, 'ate like a man, smoked like a man, slept like a man, dreamed like a man and looked like a man'.[20]

Doing whatever is necessary to survive is all that matters in *King Rat*, and the prison-camp principle of every man for himself proves more durable by far than the conventional ideas of honour that Clavell associates with the life-denying and hypocritical class system embodied in the novel's English characters. And, notwithstanding the novel's sometimes fatiguingly macho tenor, the camp-instilled rethinking of values that puts self-interest first is embraced by Clavell's women as well as his men; among the characters forced to reconsider their pre-war assumptions is the Roxana-like wife of a Scottish prisoner, a young mother whose experience of defencelessness and deprivation as an interned enemy alien means that she quickly adapts to her new situation as courtesan to a Japanese colonel. This anti-ethic of opportunistic adaptation proves pervasive: the mercantile-criminal credo of the racketeering Corporal King is explicitly linked to his American nationality, but its utility in these harsh conditions means that it potentially contaminates everyone in the novel. King sums up that 'American' credo: 'Number

19. Braddon, *The Naked Island*, 228.
20. James Clavell, *King Rat* (New York: Delta, 1999), 469, 8.

one, poverty's a sickness. Number two, money's everything. Number three, it doesn't matter how you get it as long as you get it.'[21]

Clavell's title refers most explicitly to the rat farm Corporal King establishes in the camp. King raises rats for meat and sells the product as black-market mouse deer to unwitting officers, in a gratifying marriage of war-aggravated class hatred and the irresistible profit motive, and in a darkly ironic, if presumably unintended, echo of Robinson Crusoe's discovery that his island's wild goats can be domesticated and bred for food and skins. William H. McDougall, an American journalist imprisoned in a Japanese camp on Sumatra, writes in his war memoir of 'that barometer of desperation, rodent prices': the camp price of 'cooking-rats', as he refers to them with disarming casualness, could range between one guilder and five depending on how bad conditions were.[22] But Clavell's title also suggests the gruesome folkloric phenomenon of the 'rat king'. A rat king is said to be formed when rats have been living in such close proximity as a pack that their tails become entangled, fused by blood and excrement, with the result that they gradually become a single animal because their constituent individuals are no longer functionally individual in any meaningful sense. The Ukrainian Holocaust survivor Piotr Rawicz used the crypto-zoological rat king as a grotesque figure for involuntary solidarity in another retrospective novel of the Second World War, *Blood from the Sky* (1961), in which the narrator tells a story likening his endangered fellow Jews to this 'monster, created out of sickness and starvation':

It sometimes happens that one hears squeakings and pipings and yelpings coming from a rafter in some old loft—different and louder than those usually made by rats. It gets on your nerves and you pick up an ax and split the rotten beam. Whereupon it releases a monster, created out of sickness and starvation in the cramped and filthy nest: a score or so skeleton-thin rats have become so conjoined, their legs and their long tails have grown so fused and knotted, that it is no longer possible for them to disunite; the blood system of this collective organism is now one, the same blood flowing through the entanglement of tails and legs. None of them will ever again be capable of leading an independent existence. They will have to live communally, enjoying the incomparable bliss that comes from self-surrender.[23]

21. Clavell, *King Rat*, 275.
22. William H. McDougall Jr, *By Eastern Windows: The Story of a Battle of Souls and Minds in the Prison Camps of Sumatra* (London: Arthur Barker, 1951), 192.
23. Piotr Rawicz, *Blood from the Sky*, trans. Peter Wiles (New Haven: Yale University Press, 2003), 89.

Thus, when Clavell evokes the simultaneously abject and threatening figure of the rat king, reversing its terms in order to bring out the parasitism always implied in the original, he suggests that the most attractive alternative to such deadly collectivity is exploiting your no-less-brutalized fellows in order to become the king of the rats. Looking back in 1972 on his time on the Burma–Thailand Railway, artist Leo Rawlings evoked similarly figurative rats when he recalled that 'even the rats among us, and rats there were, can be forgiven their petty crimes. We had now reached the state where every man had to put himself first just to survive.'[24] Clavell also presents the temptation as virtually insurmountable, but it means disgrace at the end of *King Rat* when, able once more to judge by the professed standards of the outside world, the liberated prisoners shun the racketeer whose favour they sought so sycophantically in captivity.

'Nothing more awful than to watch a man who has been found out, not in a crime but in a more than criminal weakness,' Conrad wrote in *Lord Jim*: 'weakness unknown, but perhaps suspected, as in some parts of the world you suspect a deadly snake in every bush,—from weakness that may lie hidden, watched or unwatched, prayed against or manfully scorned . . . not one of us is safe.'[25] The future Conradian Watt had long since been thinking about such questions of weakness and temptation by the time Clavell addressed them in *King Rat*. He had already written in the late 1940s a short story titled 'A Chap in Dark Glasses' in which the narrator, an urbane, cultured, and (not to put too fine a point on it) thoroughly Watt-like junior officer, saves his own life by becoming a small-scale entrepreneur, one of the camp's 'racketeers as we were called'.[26]

The dark glasses of the story's title suggest the autobiographical investments of what is substantially a work of fiction; in straightforwardly non-fictional essays, the short-sighted Watt mentions wearing dark glasses throughout his captivity because his ordinary glasses were smashed during the battle for Singapore, and he was still wearing dark lenses (which were all he had) on repatriation, leading an old friend at the railway station in Dover to suppose that he had been blinded in

24. Leo Rawlings, *And the Dawn Came up like Thunder* (Newcastle upon Tyne: Myrmidon, 2015), 126.
25. Conrad, *Lord Jim*, 32; ellipsis added.
26. Watt, 'A Chap in Dark Glasses'.

the war.[27] These glasses also feature in Watt's tellingly-titled 'A Man Must Live', another unpublished story from the late 1940s, which focuses on rivalries among racketeers in a Thai camp. The entrepreneurial central character, a cynical middleman known as 'the Professor', appears to be an unsparing self-portrait of the author as 'a fat, sallow young man in dark glasses'—'fat' being altogether relative here, needless to say, and most likely a symbolic reflection of his racketeering successes. Since it is vanishingly unlikely that Watt was involved in much camp trading—all his friends discuss their own and others' mercantile efforts, whereas Watt only ever appears in relation to the intellectual activities of the camps—it seems all the more interesting that he identified with the entrepreneur enough to be able to inhabit his world view imaginatively in his fiction a decade before he did so in his writings on Defoe. McDougall, that keen observer of fluctuating rodent prices, found in captivity 'two classes' of 'entrepreneur': 'he who works solely for the purpose of keeping himself alive and he who works for profits he can bank . . . a loan shark or racketeer trading on the cupidity or hunger of his fellows.'[28] The pseudo-autobiographical entrepreneurs of Watt's stories are in the first category, while Clavell's protagonist is more like the second.

As far as Clavell's treatment of racketeering is concerned, Watt's private impression of *King Rat* was that it was a bit overblown in its handling of Changi, which they had both known at first hand (Watt, though, had experienced much worse camps than Changi). A scribbled note about *King Rat* records that there was 'minor endless crookery; less dramatic conflict'.[29] His more considered verdict was that 'no one crook got quite as much on top as that. But one recognises the picture all right, though one doesn't want to. Every kind of thieving and brutality.'[30]

Like the king rat of the prison camp, Watt's Moll Flanders has no sense of sorority with other members of her oppressed and forlorn group. 'Who is the convict's worst enemy?' asks the gulag veteran Solzhenitsyn:

27. In 'Reunion on the Kwai', for instance, Thai civilians whom Watt met as he awaited repatriation remember him decades later for wearing dark glasses day and night. Ian Watt, 'Reunion on the Kwai', *Southern Review*, 5 (1969), 714–15.
28. McDougall, *By Eastern Windows*, 186.
29. This is on a piece of scrap paper headed 'King Rat'. Stanford University Special Collections, SC401-ACCN 1994-106, Box 22, Folder 'Siam Notes'.
30. Ian Watt, 'Kings, Rats, and Opticians', Stanford University Special Collections, SC401-ACCN 1994-106, Box 23, Folder 9.

'Another convict.'[31] Watt makes much of such passages as that in which Moll Flanders, her death sentence commuted, buys for herself and her husband better treatment than all the other convicts being transported to Virginia as forced labourers, although few among them could be as infamous as this notorious thief and her highwayman husband. These other transported criminals are 'a dreadful Gang' and 'as harden'd vile Creatures as ever *Newgate* produc'd in my time', Moll informs us, as if she had been leading a life of benign respectability all these years, rather than the life we have been reading about up to this late point in the novel.[32] The boatswain of the ship is not to be fooled by superficially criminal appearances, Moll urges, but should know that she and Jemy are 'Persons of a differing Character from the wretched Crew that we came with'.[33] So much, we might say, for the proverbial thickness of thieves. Commenting on Watt's dark reading of Defoe, Robert Alter wrote in his 1965 study of the picaresque that the 'moral universe of *Moll Flanders*, we find, is bare and depressingly cold', with its subordination of human relationships to the pursuit of gain.[34] Interestingly, Watt is much less judgemental than this implies. A 'healthy amorality' is how he sums up Moll's easy ability to shake off the usual claims of conscience (*RN* 128). In conditions of shared suffering, sympathetic identification with the other prisoners might entail that blissful 'self-surrender' of which Rawicz sardonically writes: the death-in-life of the rat king. Watt's Moll, in contrast, is as healthy and self-sufficient as King Rat. Still, Watt wonders if Defoe is using her to purvey some questionable fictions about the social and psychological impunity of the total individualist: 'no vicissitude can ever impair her comfortable vitality; our grossest crimes and our most contemptible moral weaknesses, apparently, will never deprive us of the love of others or even of our own self-respect' (*RN* 132).

Cannibals

'He wasn't evil,' one of Clavell's characters protests in *King Rat*, when challenged to account for his growing admiration for the camp

31. Alexsandr Solzhenitsyn, *One Day in the Life of Ivan Denisovich*, trans. H. T. Willetts (New York: Farrar, Straus & Giroux, 2005), 131.
32. Defoe, *Moll Flanders*, 294, 295.
33. Defoe, *Moll Flanders*, 313.
34. Robert Alter, *Rogue's Progress: Studies in the Picaresque Novel* (Cambridge, MA: Harvard University Press, 1965), 49.

entrepreneur: 'All he did was adapt to circumstances.'[35] Among the most searching literary treatments of the moral costs of adaptation is J. G. Ballard's *Empire of the Sun* (1984), a fictionalized treatment of Ballard's wartime incarceration by the Japanese as a child in the Lunghua civilian internment camp near Shanghai. Ballard's *oeuvre* offers multiple versions of his war experience, all a little different in emphasis. His harrowing short story 'The Dead Time' (1977) is a surrealistic rendering of his feeling that he was tied forever to those who did not survive imprisonment. The young protagonist drives around the paddy fields outside Shanghai with a truckload of corpses to whom he now feels closer than his own family (which he is ostensibly trying to find) and whom he cannot bring himself to dispose of: an unusually literal example of what Cathy Caruth calls 'the survivor whose life is inextricably linked to the death he witnesses'.[36] Ballard then describes his internment at greater length in a realist idiom in *Empire of the Sun* and *The Kindness of Women* (1991), and finally in his autobiography *Miracles of Life* (2008). *Empire of the Sun* is particularly significant because it separates the autobiographical child protagonist Jamie, or 'Jim' as he grows up, from his family, although Ballard had actually spent the whole period of captivity with his parents and younger sister: he explained in his autobiography that he 'felt that it was closer to the psychological and emotional truth of events to make "Jim" effectively a war orphan'.[37] As he told an interviewer in 1986, the separation of the child protagonist from his parents means that he 'is forced to live like a sort of young Robinson Crusoe, almost'.[38] Like Watt's, Ballard's preoccupation with Defoe would last a lifetime.

But Jim is not the most ruthless individualist in *Empire of the Sun*. Here, the prison-camp entrepreneur is Basie, the American sailor—of course American again, since, as a number of historians have remarked, 'Americans were the great individualists of the camps, the capitalists, the cowboys, the gangsters'; they were 'the most entrepreneurial, but some of their rackets were worthy of the Mafia'.[39] (Gavan Daws further

35. Clavell, *King Rat*, 487. 36. Caruth, *Unclaimed Experience*, 102.
37. J. G. Ballard, *Miracles of Life: Shanghai to Shepperton: An Autobiography* (London: Harper Perennial, 2008), 82.
38. Ballard, '1986: Solveig Nordlund', 225. On Ballard's different versions of his imprisonment, see Roger Luckhurst, 'Petition, Repetition, and "Autobiography"', *Contemporary Literature*, 35/4 (Winter 1994), 688–708.
39. Daws, *Prisoners of the Japanese*, 23. Brian MacArthur, *Surviving the Sword: Prisoners of the Japanese in the Far East, 1942–45* (New York: Random House, 2005), xxvii.

notes that Americans were the only national group whose members are known to have murdered compatriots in captivity.[40]) Like Moll Flanders, to whom, as Watt wrote, 'everything happens . . . and nothing leaves scars', Ballard's sinister, opportunistic Basie has 'a bland, unmarked face from which all the copious experiences of his life had been cleverly erased'.[41] At various points in the novel Basie tries to sell Jim or uses him as a decoy to draw Japanese fire away from himself; Jim even comes to suspect that Basie and the other American prisoners are sending him to the edge of the camp in order to gamble—literally take bets—on how far away Jim can get before being shot by the guards.

This savage pastime echoes one of the most cold-hearted exploitations of others in the Far East camps, when some prisoners literally starved because they had gambled away their rice rations to tougher comrades. Daws describes 'life and death' stakes when he tells of two veteran American cardsharps who profited from the willingness of desperate prisoners to gamble for food or cigarettes: 'the end product of classic American free-enterprise capitalism'.[42] (Smoking proved an even deadlier habit than usual because some would risk even more severe malnutrition by trading or gambling their food ration for cigarettes.) According to Australian Roy Whitecross, 'some practically lived on the hunger and stupidity of others'; his memoir describes how American prisoners from the Philippines introduced into the camps capitalist practices such as trading rice on usurious terms—practices previously unknown and initially unthinkable to the more communally oriented prisoners of other nationalities.[43] David Piper, imprisoned on Formosa (Taiwan), remembered a fellow prisoner found on the verge of starvation because he had lost six days' rice playing at Blackjack. 'In the camps it could seem as if, when it came to the crunch, the ultimate, the only essential quality of man was animal hunger,' Piper surmises, and 'all other qualities were but fatty accretions, inessential and permissible only in certain artificially contrived conditions of civilisation'.[44]

40. Daws, *Prisoners of the Japanese*, 23.
41. J. G. Ballard, *Empire of the Sun* (New York: Simon & Schuster, 2005), 69.
42. Daws, *Prisoners of the Japanese*, 147, 311.
43. Whitecross, *Slaves of the Son of Heaven*, 199. Daws confirms Whitecross's claim that British and Australian prisoners were disgusted by this 'American' practice (*Prisoners of the Japanese*, 309).
44. Piper, *I Am Well, Who Are You?*, 23.

Solzhenitsyn's view that life in the prison camp 'surpasses in savagery all that we know about the lives of cannibals or rats' is thus confirmed in the Far East as in the gulags. Watt's sense of the timeliness of Defoe now becomes most explicable, since the world of the Second World War camps can read so much like the cannibalistic psychological universe of *Robinson Crusoe*.[45] Defoe's hero is a former slave who enslaves others; a man whose greatest fear is of being devoured and yet who can readily envision circumstances in which one might literally consume other people to survive, as when he contemplates the purely hypothetical survivors of the novel's second shipwreck who, floating on their no-less-hypothetical raft, 'might by this time think of starving, and of being in a condition to eat one other'.[46] Watt acknowledged that it might seem a little perverse of him to treat *Robinson Crusoe* as the first 'novel' given its conspicuous lack of interest in personal relationships (*RN* 92); for all his pained yearning for companionship, thoughts of other people only terrorize Crusoe the moment they threaten to materialize:

> Then terrible thoughts rack'd my imagination about their having found my boat, and that there were people here; and that if so, I should certainly have them come again in greater numbers, and devour me; that if it should happen so that they should not find me, yet they would find my enclosure, destroy all my corn, carry away all my flock of tame goats, and I should perish at last for meer want.[47]

Other people are always a threat to Crusoe's stomach, for instinctively Crusoe senses that, even if incomers will not literally eat him, they will assuredly starve him to death.

John Richetti describes 'Crusoe's inner turmoil' as 'the psychological effects of a longing for human contact and a terror of unknown others against whom the building of fortified shelter and mastering of the environment are defensive reactions': this is 'a productively fearful competitive separation from others', Richetti writes, putting his finger on the paradoxical way in which civilization (culture, productivity) is

45. Although I use the term only figuratively, cannibalism featured in the Pacific War, as when Japanese troops invaded (and were left to die on) islands that could not support them. Lizzie Collingham treats the issue with restraint in her impressive food history of the war, *The Taste of War: World War II and the Battle for Food* (London: Penguin, 2011), 297–300.

46. Defoe, *Robinson Crusoe*, 148.

47. Defoe, *Robinson Crusoe*, 123.

dependent upon the individual's fear of others in *Robinson Crusoe.*[48] Thanks to thinkers ranging from Hobbes to Freud, we think of civilization as founded on our fear of other people in a different sense, as the logic of the social contract or the protective 'civilization' that stops people from killing or enslaving each other: '*Homo homini lupus*', Freud writes of the alternative in *Civilization and its Discontents.*[49] What incomers are emphatically not in Defoe's novel is an opportunity for some kind of community, and, when an island community begins to materialize after the mutiny, Crusoe is on the first boat out. On surviving the shipwreck Crusoe finds it 'particularly afflicting... that I had no weapon either to hunt and kill any creature for my sustenance, or to defend my self against any other creature that might desire to kill me for theirs'; when he flees the sight of the footprint in the sand, he tells us that 'never frighted hare fled to cover, or fox to earth, with more terror of mind'.[50] His first night on the island is spent in the treetops for fear of being eaten by wild animals, but it takes him little time to learn to think of himself as predator rather than prey.

This transformation in Crusoe's self-understanding prefigures the ugly lesson described in prison-camp writings when the naive protagonist's first arrival at the camp supplies predatory older hands with new opportunities for gain. The war memoir of American literary critic and infantry veteran William V. Spanos recounts his arrival at a German camp following his capture during the Allies' last major setback of the war, the Ardennes counteroffensive at the end of 1944. (Worse was to come for Spanos, for in the spring of 1945 he not only watched the destruction of Dresden, like fellow Ardennes prisoner Kurt Vonnegut, but was forced to participate in the excavation of corpses from the rubble.) Upon entering the prison camp Spanos is met by two surprisingly well-dressed and self-assured British prisoners, in a rare reversal of the 'convention' that prison-camp profiteers are rackety American servicemen whose wartime exploitations are continuous with their lives as peacetime crooks. These sleek men proceed to rifle through his pockets: 'To these British prisoners I wasn't a comrade, an unfortunate ally who, like them, had been captured and was suffering the hell of dislocation and the hostility of the enemy. I was, it

48. John Richetti, *The English Novel in History, 1700–1780* (London: Routledge, 1999), 67.
49. Sigmund Freud, *Civilization and its Discontents*, trans. James Strachey (New York: Norton, 1961), 69.
50. Defoe, *Robinson Crusoe*, 39, 122.

seemed from their crude manner and actions, simply an object to be exploited.'[51] This ugly introduction to camp life outlines the shape of things to come. Spanos tells of an American prisoner in his cohort who steals from others, and of the brutal retribution enacted by these 'comrades' from whom he steals; in fact, the Americans' only experience of camaraderie during their entire captivity is in this horrible episode when they are united by their lust for revenge against the fellow-American whom they savagely beat up (it is unclear if he even survives).[52] Best equipped for the world of the prison camp are those who 'take a severely functional view of their fellows' (*RN* 112). The phrase could serve as the verdict of Clavell, Ballard, or Spanos on the camp entrepreneurs and exploiters, but it is actually Watt's summing-up of Defoe's protagonists. The ultimate drive of Defoe's fiction is '*ego contra mundum*' (*RN* 132).

'He's a survivor, though survivors can be dangerous,' one of Ballard's characters observes: 'Wars exist for people like Basie.'[53] When equal shares mean that everyone might die, opportunism, pragmatism, and the morally insensible spirit of capitalist enterprise are potential life-savers. 'What is the calorie count on friendship, on personal loyalty, on moral agreements, on altruism?' asks Daws.[54] A version of that question was asked by all the early post-war novelists who revisited Defoe, although, perhaps because of contemporary environmental fears, *A Journal of the Plague Year* rather than *Robinson Crusoe* seems the twenty-first-century preference, rewritten in a range of contemporary novels from Geraldine Brooks's *Year of Wonders* (2001) to Cormac McCarthy's *The Road* (2006) and Jim Crace's *The Pesthouse* (2007). But, no less symptomatically, what Albert Camus's war allegory *The Plague* (1947) had found in that text back in the 1940s was that 'there is no denying that the plague had gradually killed off in all of us the faculty not of love only but even of friendship'.[55]

51. William V. Spanos, *In the Neighborhood of Zero: A World War II Memoir* (Lincoln, NE: University of Nebraska Press, 2010), 67.
52. Spanos, *In the Neighborhood of Zero*, 87–9. Terrence Des Pres recounts similar stories from camps and gulags where a bread-thief is beaten up, murdered, or in some unspecified other way 'punished...so severely that he lost his taste for stealing' (Terrence des Pres, *The Survivor: An Anatomy of Life in the Death Camps* (Oxford: Oxford University Press, 1980), 140–2).
53. Ballard, *Empire of the Sun*, 166.
54. Daws, *Prisoners of the Japanese*, 19.
55. Albert Camus, *The Plague*, trans. Stuart Gilbert (New York: Vintage, 1991), 182.

Alone and forced to survive by his own wits, Ballard's hitherto protected upper-middle-class Jamie learns immediately that 'kindness, which his parents and teachers had always urged upon him, counted for nothing'.[56] The idea returns in Ballard's autobiography when he recalls a minor theft that he had committed at Lunghua. 'Moral principles, along with kindness and generosity, are worth less than they might seem.'[57] In *Empire of the Sun* this epiphany means that Jamie must scavenge from the ruins of his old life, and the ruined lives of others, just as in *Robinson Crusoe*. It is unnerving how clearly the reader remembers Crusoe's enterprising salvage from the first shipwreck, of which Crusoe was the solitary survivor, and yet forgets the profit he gleans from the novel's second foundering, as if by that point the novel has acculturated even its reader into its uncompromising survivalist world: 'I had indeed gotten two pairs of shoes now,' Crusoe tells us, 'which I took off of the feet of the two drown'd men, who I saw in the wreck'.[58] The shoes are of no use to Defoe's drowned sailors, of course, but survival in Ballard entails stealing from the old and the dying as well as the dead; and it means strategic alliances with the strong and desertion of the weak so that they cannot drag you down with them.

Like Ballard a British civilian prisoner of the Japanese, Daphne Jackson wondered at

> the speed with which some degenerated into little more than animals... Thieving, lying, telling tales to curry favour with guards or staff went on all the time. As far as I could see, the old saying that 'trouble brought out the best in one' was very much a half-truth. The good people in camp got better, but the bad ones got far, far worse.[59]

In *Empire of the Sun*, collaboration with the Japanese is a universally accepted way of getting by: a crime for which no one is blamed, let alone punished, since anyone else would do the same if the opportunity arose. Defoe himself repeatedly stated versions of the old adage that necessity knows no laws, and it is the central insight of prisoners' memoirs, which I think helps to explain Watt's fascination with his resiliently entrepreneurial cast of mind, or Defoe's conviction that 'he that gave me Brains will give me Bread'.[60]

56. Ballard, *Empire of the Sun*, 62.
57. Ballard, *Miracles of Life*, 94.
58. Defoe, *Robinson Crusoe*, 153.
59. Daphne Jackson, *Java Nightmare* (Padstow: Tabb House, 1979), 77.
60. Quoted in Novak, *Daniel Defoe*, 232.

Ballard shared Watt's lifelong interest in Defoe, and specifically the Defoe who considered self-preservation the main engine of human activity. In the overlapping sequel to *Empire of the Sun*, Ballard's hybrid novel-memoir *The Kindness of Women*, Jamie's father tries to distract the boy Ballard from the attractions of Shanghai's wartime streets by promising him that if he stays home he will be allowed to finish, of all things, *Robinson Crusoe*.[61] Ballard recalled in his autobiography that he 'loved' *Robinson Crusoe* as a child, and he rewrote *Robinson Crusoe* over and over across his career.[62] In his atmospheric early work of science fiction *The Drowned World* (1962), set amid the (tellingly malarial) cityscape of a flooded London that is (no less tellingly) populated only by looters, the main character undertakes what the novel calls 'inverted Crusoeism—the deliberate marooning of himself'.[63] Ballard's *Concrete Island* (1974) offers a postmodern version of Defoe's novel: a selfish loner is marooned after a car crash on an 'island' of waste ground between two highways, falling victim to a dystopian extreme of the familiar social atomization attendant on modern individualism.

With the unrivalled insight of the prison-camp survivor, an unconvinced Watt dryly noted that Defoe's heroes and heroines must be uniquely fortunate in the unhesitating willingness of other people to serve the protagonist's interests over their own. Robinson Crusoe 'is conspicuously lucky to find other people who want to devote themselves to his personal advantage . . . to exist only to be the perfectly reliable and wholly devoted servants of Crusoe's interests' (*MMI* 170), while Moll Flanders apparently elicits only 'the most unqualified and selfless devotion' from the characters around her: 'Everyone seems to exist only for her, and no one seems to resent it' (*RN* 112). (Again, this could not be further from Forster's pre-war reading: 'She and most of the characters in Defoe's underworld are kind to one another, they save each other's feelings and run risks through personal loyalty.'[64]) Ballard implies similar scepticism in his rewritings of Defoe: the anti-social modernity of *Concrete Island* means the obliteration of any expectation of aid. This was a 'completely false' assumption, the marooned

61. J. G. Ballard, *The Kindness of Women* (New York: Picador, 1991), 8.
62. Ballard, *Miracles of Life*, 20.
63. J. G. Ballard, *The Drowned World* (London: Fourth Estate, 2014), 48.
64. Forster, *Aspects of the Novel*, 56–7.

main character recognizes, and merely 'part of that whole system of comfortable expectations he had carried with him'.[65]

But 'you were on an island long before you crashed here', another character tells this proto-yuppie protagonist; Ballard is making the same point about the moral effects of economic individualism as Watt had drawn from Defoe's characters when he wrote that they are so 'essentially solitary' that they 'all belong on Crusoe's island' (*RN* 112).[66] For Watt, Crusoe's 'inordinate egocentricity condemns him to isolation wherever he is' (*RN* 86). Crusoe, he later remarked, 'is in general devoid of any pretense of "loving thy neighbor as thyself," or indeed of any civic spirit whatever'—a significant phrasing on Watt's part, given how close it comes to implying that 'loving thy neighbor as thyself' is more a performance ('any pretense') than a plausible psychological reality (*MMI* 162). Their shared background of wartime imprisonment explains why both Ballard's and Watt's readings of Defoe should have emphasized so strenuously the inherent likeness between the capitalist and the criminal as literally antisocial forces. In an autobiographical reflection Ballard restated explicitly in *Miracles of Life*, versatile Jamie in *Empire of the Sun* is 'resented... for revealing an obvious truth about the war, that people were only too able to adapt to it'.[67] 'It was not that war changed everything', Ballard writes, 'but that it left things the same in odd and unsettling ways'.[68] Or, as Watt wrote in 1959 in even more deflationary terms: 'The commonest lesson of the prison camp, I think, is one that everybody really knows but does not like to admit: that survival, always a selfish business, gets more so when it is difficult.'[69]

'Perceptions of not really being alive'

This is a 'lesson of the prison camp' that resonates for decades in Watt's criticism, as we find in his much later thoughts on Conrad and the purported moral benefits of suffering. Describing the end of Conrad's *'Narcissus'*, in which the narrator recasts as a human triumph what the

65. J. G. Ballard, *Concrete Island* (New York: Picador, 2001), 43.
66. Ballard, *Concrete Island*, 141.
67. Ballard, *Empire of the Sun*, 163. Ballard wrote in *Miracles of Life*: 'In many ways I was the opposite of a misfit, and adapted too well to the camp' (81).
68. Ballard, *Empire of the Sun*, 46.
69. Watt, 'Bridges over the Kwai', 218.

reader has already witnessed as a disastrous voyage marked by shipboard sickness, death, and social disintegration, Watt attributed to critics the 'superstition' that 'in literature, at least, all suffering and error are automatically digested into maturity of understanding' (*C.* 118); Hannah Arendt had used similar terms when she objected in *The Origins of Totalitarianism* (1951) to 'the superstition that something good might result from evil'.[70] Watt was writing specifically against humanist strategies of interpretation that ignored the peculiarly unearned optimism of Conrad's ending, with its laudatory closing address to fellow seamen: 'You were a good crowd,' declares the captain of the *Narcissus*: 'As good a crowd as ever fisted with wild cries the beating canvas of a heavy foresail; or tossing aloft, invisible in the night, gave back yell for yell to a westerly gale.'[71] But this is almost a mutiny novel. The captain's peroration is so far removed from the novel's substance as to sound hollow if not delusional, and only the most uncomprehendingly optimistic could accept it at face value. Watt's Conrad book is scathing about the consolatory tropes of this kind of criticism, as when he asks of the talismanic phrase 'in the destructive element immerse': 'What can be more universally acceptable than a saying which announces that its user has survived his ritual immersion in life's destructive traumas and has now emerged into the maturity of tragic acceptance?' (*C.* 328). It is all part of what he calls a 'hunger for a magical transformation of reality' in much mid-century novel criticism as it strains to find evidence of protagonists' final atonement or redemption (*C.* 339); or, for that matter, of their awakened self-knowledge, and, for Watt, the fetish of 'self-knowledge' is just 'another of the modern secularised versions of the consolations which religion offers in the face of suffering, waste, and evil' (*C.* 349).

When Watt derided what he and Arendt called 'superstition' about suffering and virtue, he participated in a much wider mid-century debunking of old truisms about the ennobling effects of pain. This was among the redemptive fictions exploded by those contemporaries of Watt who survived even worse forms of wartime imprisonment. 'It

70. Hannah Arendt, *The Origins of Totalitarianism* (Orlando, FL: Harcourt, 1979), 442. Watt and Arendt knew each other in the 1970s because they both served on the taskforce that led to the creation of the National Humanities Center. See Watt, 'The Humanities on the River Kwai', 12.

71. Joseph Conrad, *The Nigger of the 'Narcissus' and Other Stories* (London: Penguin, 2007), 136.

goes without saying', wrote Jean Améry, Austrian–Jewish member of the Belgian Resistance, 'that in Auschwitz we did not become better, more human, more humane, and more mature ethically. You do not observe dehumanized man committing his deeds and misdeeds without having all of your notions of inherent human dignity placed in doubt.'[72]

Among all the literature of mid-century imprisonments, Holocaust writing offers the most extended critique and, at the same time, defence of individualism. To evoke this body of work is emphatically not to suggest that the experience of prisoners in the Far East could ever be considered equivalent to what was done to Jewish contemporaries by Japan's most powerful European ally. For a start, and completely unlike that of Jewish prisoners in Germany and the countries it occupied, the predicament that Watt shared with other Allied personnel had a comprehensible history and context, since the prisoner of war had for so long been a recognized feature of armed conflict. The *OED* dates the term's first English usage to 1608 and its Middle French equivalent to 1475, although the prisoner of war as a historical fact may be about as old as warfare itself. The Japanese treated their prisoners of war as disposable labour, believing their very lives, to say nothing of human dignity and rights, to have no inherent value, but that manifestly is not the same situation as that of people actively intended to die. 'There are no parallels to the life in the concentration camps,' Arendt wrote: 'Forced labor in prisons and penal colonies, banishment, slavery, all seem for a moment to offer helpful comparisons, but on closer examination lead nowhere.'[73] But Arendt, who had been imprisoned at the squalid concentration camp at Gurs, also shows that one can make descriptive comparisons that imply no false evaluative equivalences. She offers a taxonomy of camps in accordance with traditional notions of the afterlife: if the refugee or displaced person's camp is Hades, then the gulag is Purgatory, and the Nazi camps were Hell, where cruelty was not an incidental feature of incarceration but a deliberately refined one. 'All three types have one thing in common: the human masses sealed off in them are treated as if they no longer existed, as if what happened to them were no longer of any interest to anybody.'[74] Primo

72. Jean Améry, *At the Mind's Limits: Contemplations by a Survivor on Auschwitz and its Realities*, trans. Sidney Rosenfeld and Stella P. Rosenfeld (Bloomington: Indiana University Press, 1980), 20.

73. Arendt, *Origins of Totalitarianism*, 444.

74. Arendt, *Origins of Totalitarianism*, 445.

Levi likened his first hours in the camp to 'being already dead'.[75] A prisoner of the Japanese wrote that the total severance 'from our old world...creates perceptions of not being really alive'.[76]

Margot Norris notes in her study of modern war writing that there are similarities between Holocaust experiences and other mid-century imprisonments—she names the civilian internees of the Japanese among them—but rightly proposes that any similarities inevitably stop with 'the *final phase*' of bureaucratized mass killings, which 'bear no analogues'.[77] Strictly speaking, the closest parallel is probably to be found between the beginning of the Far East prisoners' captivity, when many prisoners experienced the albeit highly relative normalcy of Changi, and the end of the Jewish prisoners' incarceration, as documented in books like Levi's *The Truce/The Reawakening* (1963), a world of material scarcity and antic theatrical productions in Red Army camps. (In a well-known interview with Levi, Germaine Greer likened the book to a 'more sceptical, more pessimistic' *Robinson Crusoe*.[78])

Yet some similar *effects* obtained across the multiple forms of mid-century imprisonment. I shall return to the social and moral effects, but the most obviously comparable of the physical and psychological effects are evidenced in descriptions of prisoners terminally shattered by the building of the Burma–Thailand Railway. Those in Ernest Gordon's memoir of Chungkai, where he and Watt were incarcerated, are redolent of nothing so much as the concentration camp '*Muselmann*': 'a staggering corpse, a bundle of physical functions in its last convulsions,' Améry recalled; Levi remembered them as 'non-men who march and labour in silence, the divine spark dead within them, already too empty to really suffer'.[79] 'One hesitates to call them living,' Levi chillingly wrote: 'one hesitates to call their death death.'[80] Gordon's memoir likewise describes defunct human shells of slave labourers, whom starvation, exhaustion, and disease had rendered wholly oblivious to sensation

75. Primo Levi, *Survival in Auschwitz: The Nazi Assault on Humanity*, trans. Stuart Woolf (New York: Simon & Schuster, 1996), 22.
76. Peek, *One Fourteenth*, 478.
77. Margot Norris, *Writing War in the Twentieth Century* (Charlottesville, VA: University Press of Virginia, 2000), 117; emphasis in original.
78. Primo Levi, 'Germaine Greer Talks to Primo Levi', in Primo Levi, *The Voice of Memory: Interviews 1961–87*, ed. Marco Belpoliti and Robert Gordon, trans. Robert Gordon (Cambridge: Polity, 2001), 6.
79. Améry, *At the Mind's Limits*, 9. Levi, *Survival in Auschwitz*, 90.
80. Levi, *Survival in Auschwitz*, 90.

and incapable of speech. 'They seemed to have no centre left with which to hear and respond,' Gordon remembered, and no one could 'reach them' as 'they shuffled along in a grey, twilight existence, waiting for death'.[81] 'They had been killed in a way more fiendish than physical torture,' he concluded: 'They were dead before they stopped breathing.'[82] Or, as the imprisoned medic Robert Hardie put it in his illicit diary, 'they are so far gone that there is nothing to work on in attempting to save them'.[83] Reg Twigg remembered them with painful vividness: 'I don't think they felt anything. You knew by their eyes, they'd got nothing left. They were walking skeletons, blistered and ulcerated, their skin glistening with lesions and lacerations, their tongues thick in their mouth, their stares vacant.'[84] Prisoners called this last feature the 'atap stare', referring to the atap (nipa palm) leaves providing the prisoners with their rudimentary shelters, and it was a virtually catatonic form of withdrawal from which no one was expected to come back. The memoirs are haunted by the image of absolute self-loss these victims embodied.

Writing of a journey down-country with a group of these men, Durnford described them dying at his feet:

> So imperceptible was the change, that there was little difference between those who passed as living and those who had died. Their faces drew into a piece of grey gristle, from which the eyes stood like those of wounded cattle. The hair was matted, and arms and legs so thin that they scarcely seemed to own the flesh. Only their bellies, swollen and distended with rice, showed grossly from the cage of bare ribs in which, somehow, beat a human heart... Without the muscular strength to sit upright they lolled against each other, their mouths hanging open without support. And no one in the boat spoke a single word.[85]

Durnford contended that this monstrous spectacle must give the lie to the then-current identification of the reduction of people to things with purely European totalitarian ideologies. This was notoriously an era in which the human being was being 'alienated and eradicated, altered and undone', as Mark Greif put it in his study of mid-century thought, although this was happening not only across Europe.[86] Durnford

81. Gordon, *Miracle on the River Kwai*, 183.
82. Gordon, *Miracle on the River Kwai*, 183–4.
83. Robert Hardie, *The Burma–Siam Railway* (London: Imperial War Museum, 1983), 91.
84. Twigg, *Survivor on the River Kwai*, 160.
85. Durnford, *Branch Line to Burma*, 116–17.
86. Greif, *The Age of the Crisis of Man*, 3.

described what he took to be the unthinking cruelty of a rehabilitation agency showing the newly liberated prisoners newsreels from Belsen and Buchenwald. 'Somewhat unnecessarily', Durnford thought, as if former prisoners of the Japanese did not know what (to borrow Levi's famous phrase) 'the demolition of a man' actually looked like.[87]

Durnford is an outlier here, however, because survivors of the Japanese camps were usually very careful to point out that their experience could not meaningfully be likened to the Holocaust—the incomparable horror of which they probably grasped better than most people in the years immediately after the war precisely because they had also experienced starvation, slave labour, and the fear of extermination. Among the saddest treatments of the problems of uneven comparison and sympathetic identification is the memoir of Loet Velmans, who, after a brief stay in London as a Jewish refugee from the occupied Netherlands, had ended up in the Dutch East Indies because it falsely looked to be the safest refuge, after the German invasion of his homeland early in 1940 and before the Japanese conquests of its colonies. Writing about his liberation from the Japanese camps in which he spent years, Velmans recalled hearing for the first time of the Nazi camps from a British officer, himself also Jewish: 'We, who had considered ourselves hardened veterans and who thought that we had seen and lived through the worst, had great difficulty controlling our emotions. Most could not hold back their tears.'[88]

Japanese 'brutality did not approach the systematic Nazi torture and extermination of the Jews and others', Watt stressed, even when 'the fear of it was always there'.[89] The fear of extermination reached its height as the war drew to a close and the prisoners believed that they were going to be liquidated en masse in order to obliterate these most material of witnesses to Japanese war crimes; Korean camp guards had told them so, and Japanese orders to that effect were subsequently discovered on Formosa and Borneo.[90] Historian Clifford Kinvig writes that prisoners had 'a very close call'.[91] Writing in the mid-1990s, Watt's

87. Durnford, *Branch Line to Burma*, 196. Levi, *Survival in Auschwitz*, 26.
88. Loet Velmans, *Long Way back to the River Kwai: Memories of World War II* (New York: Arcade, 2003), 186.
89. Watt, 'The Liberty of the Prison', 523.
90. MacArthur, *Surviving the Sword*, 383. See also Jack Chalker, *Burma Railway: Images of War: The Original War Drawings of Japanese POW Jack Chalker* (Shepton Mallet: Mercer Books, 2007), 119–20.
91. Kinvig, *River Kwai Railway*, 191.

friend Stephen Alexander was still referring to the last camp to which he was taken as 'an extermination camp', from which prisoners were 'rescued by the atom bomb'; he recalled having been told by Korean guards that this was 'the officer bumping-off camp'.[92] Sir David Piper, after the war the director of the National Portrait Gallery, the Fitzwilliam in Cambridge, and the Ashmolean in Oxford—so another highly educated man—also wrote of 'our inevitable liquidation': the atomic bomb, he unequivocally declared, 'had saved my life'.[93] Ballard told an interviewer the same in 1985 (and, so 'far from being an instrument of death, the atomic bomb has become for me an instrument of protection'), and the fear of extermination is something he revisits constantly in his fiction.[94] Watt always believed that the Japanese command were intent on 'liquidating all prisoners in fighting zones', and thus 'the atomic bomb had, incidentally, saved the lives of many thousands of Allied prisoners'.[95] But, even as they believed that they had survived a planned massacre, former prisoners of the Japanese were typically careful to avoid crude comparisons with even worse war-era imprisonments.

Graham Hough is an instructive case. A slightly older Cambridge acquaintance of Watt, Hough was captured as an 'other rank' rather than an officer; he, too, became a literary critic after the war, crediting the origins of his *The Last Romantics* (1949)—a survey of late Romantic thought running from John Ruskin to W. B. Yeats—to the fact that he had managed to hold on to his copy of Yeats all the way through captivity. The irony in this would not have been lost on Hough. Yeats's notorious exclusion of First World War poetry from the 1936 *Oxford Book of Modern Verse* on the grounds that 'passive suffering is not a theme for poetry' must have been at the back of Watt's mind when he proposed that 'the actual life of a prisoner of war is probably the last subject in the world for fiction'.[96] Other than mentioning in his preface

92. Alexander, *Sweet Kwai*, 2, 2, 208.
93. Piper, *I Am Well, Who Are You?*, 13, 21.
94. J. G. Ballard, '1985: Tony Cartano and Maxim Jakubowski. The Past Tense of J. G. Ballard', in Ballard, *Extreme Metaphors*, 222. *Empire of the Sun* includes a death march that never happened; 'The Dead Time' alludes to 'rumours we had heard that before they surrendered the Japanese planned to slaughter their civilian prisoners' (J. G. Ballard, 'The Dead Time', in *The Complete Stories of J. G. Ballard* (New York: Norton, 2009), 927). The Ballard character in *The Kindness of Women* recalls learning from war crimes trials that the Japanese planned to move their prisoners up-country where 'they would have been free to dispose of us' (60–1).
95. Watt, 'The Liberty of the Prison', 514.
96. W. B. Yeats (ed.), *The Oxford Book of Modern Verse, 1892–1935* (Oxford: Oxford University Press, 1936), xxxiv. Watt, 'Bridges over the Kwai', 218.

the origins of *The Last Romantics*, Hough typically avoided self-revelation in his critical writing as rigorously as Watt, but in a 1986 review of Ronald Searle's drawings from the Japanese prison camps he recalled how, shortly after his release, he had found himself scrutinizing the newspaper photographs of the liberation of the Nazi camps:

> Not all of it was unfamiliar. We looked on the pictures of individual survivors with a practised eye: this one might pull through; that one, no, he's finished. But in respect of the sheer scale of the catastrophe, and its hideous deliberation, it was plain at once that we had known nothing like it. Those piles of shoes, those heaps of bodies, the ordered systematic massacre, were perhaps more horrifying to us who had seen other but lesser horrors than to those who had been spared them altogether. No one would talk of it. *Wovon man nicht sprechen kann, darüber muss man schweigen.*[97]

Hough's assignment was to review Searle's drawings alongside the Polish underground fighter Gustav Herling's memoir of the Soviet gulags, *A World Apart*. 'Comparative ratings of suffering are always an impertinence,' Hough declared, but nonetheless he was struck by the varieties of incarceration experience.[98] To the extent that any 'comparative ratings' are implied, his review suggests that Hough considered the gulag experience worse than what he had experienced in the Far East, but viewed the Holocaust as of a different order altogether. 'Even the Japs didn't do that sort of thing!' is how Ian Denys Peek summed up one collective response to watching with his fellow ex-prisoners a film of the liberation of the Nazi camps: 'We are shaken, disgusted, frightened—all this was happening while we were dying slowly on that accursed railway, and thinking we were having a hard time! Well, we were, but look what was going on in other places.'[99]

Obviously, then, former prisoners of the Japanese were generally careful not to diminish the horror of the Holocaust with false identification ('it was plain at once that we had known nothing like it'), perhaps because their interest in that experience as the terminally extreme version of their own was so deeply felt. This interest is not surprising, given how many similar concerns circulate across the different literatures of wartime imprisonment. In the context of individualism, what emerges most pressingly is their shared sense that customary moral distinctions have to be suspended. 'It is difficult for those who consider the morality

97. Hough, 'Prisoners', 8. 98. Hough, 'Prisoners', 8.
99. Peek, *One Fourteenth*, 648.

of this activity from the contented perspective of a full stomach and an unthreatened future to make a satisfactory judgment', writes Kinvig, discussing the common prison-camp practice of stealing from the dead.[100] Writing by former prisoners in the Far East, like that of former inmates of the concentration camps, typically describes some type of adjustment—Levi wondered at what he called 'an invaluable activity of adaptation'; Watt wrote of 'silent and forgotten miracles of adaptation'—as they ask readers to understand why acts that are antisocial or shameful by pre-war or post-war standards cannot be understood outside of their context.[101]

Levi found the memorable phrase when he wrote of a 'grey zone', where customary moral judgements may no longer apply.[102] But few people experienced or elaborated more brutally the gap between the intellectual acceptance of this fact and the emotional impossibility of living in accordance with its furthest implications than the young Polish political prisoner Tadeusz Borowski. In his horrifically self-lacerating story 'This Way for the Gas, Ladies and Gentleman', the narrator, who shares his author's name, has the 'privilege' of unloading transports of Jewish prisoners for the gas chambers, and survives by stealing from them: his great fear is that the Nazis will 'run out of people'.[103] (It is impossible not to wonder if his war experience had something to do with Borowski committing suicide by gas a few years later, at the age of only 28.) Levi explains that, because there was no way to live on what was given, the mere fact of a prisoner's survival was already evidence that he or she had attained a 'privilege' that others lacked: 'large or small, granted or conquered, astute or violent, licit or illicit—whatever it took to lift oneself above the norm'.[104] He regards the individualist scramble for advantage as simply a standard feature of all prison camps and not simply their most extreme iteration, the Nazi death camps; the 'prominent' prisoner is built into the brutally

100. Kinvig, *River Kwai Railway*, 97.

101. Levi, *Survival in Auschwitz*, 56. Ian Watt, 'The Ways of Guilt', Stanford University Special Collections, SC401-ACCN 1990-131, Box 56, Folder 'Revenge of Mercy'.

102. Primo Levi, *The Drowned and the Saved*, trans. Raymond Rosenthal (New York: Vintage, 1989), 36–69.

103. Tadeusz Borowski, *This Way for the Gas, Ladies and Gentlemen*, trans. Barbara Vedder (London: Penguin, 1976), 31.

104. Levi, *The Drowned and the Saved*, 41. Levi describes the camps' black-market economy in the chapter titled 'This Side of Good and Evil' in *Survival in Auschwitz*, 77–86.

hierarchical structure of prison camps more generally, as 'an indispensable component of camp sociology'.[105]

Levi is equally explicit on what happens to human relationships when prisoners are confronted with a struggle to survive that divides them precisely because they share it. 'One entered [the Lager] hoping at least for the solidarity of one's companions in misfortune, but the hoped for allies, except in special cases, were not there; there were instead a thousand sealed off monads, and between them a desperate covert and continuous struggle,' Levi wrote in *The Drowned and the Saved*: this was 'a Hobbesian life, a continuous war of everyone against everyone'.[106] 'The principal rule of the place', Levi writes, 'made it mandatory that you take care of yourself first of all': 'almost everybody feels guilty of having omitted to offer help. The presence at your side of a weaker—or less cunning, or older, or too young—companion, hounding you with his demands for help or with his simple presence, in itself an entreaty, is a constant in the life of the Lager.'[107] That same atmosphere of struggle and competition persists in Levi's story of his return home, in which the most memorable characters are ruthlessly self-serving and entrepreneurial, distinguished from each other not according to their particular actions or relative degrees of moral culpability but with reference to Levi's liking for each of them. Mordo Nahum is 'a lone wolf, in an eternal war against all, old before his time, closed in the circle of his own joyless pride', whereas the young Italian Cesare, 'child of the sun', receives comprehensive amnesty from Levi for all his thefts and swindles.[108]

The moral atmosphere of the prison camp spills over into the fiction of the early post-war era. 'I was interned near Tripoli in a camp where we suffered from thirst and destitution more than from brutality,' recounts the 'judge-penitent' of Camus's novel *The Fall* (1956): 'I'll not describe it to you. We children of the mid-century don't need a diagram to imagine such places.'[109] *The Fall* is a novel about the guilt of witnessing someone else's death: the guilt not of perpetrating an active killing but of a passive letting-die, it seems, when the narrator describes how

105. Levi, *The Drowned and the Saved*, 99.
106. Levi, *The Drowned and the Saved*, 38, 34.
107. Levi, *The Drowned and the Saved*, 79, 78.
108. Primo Levi, *The Reawakening*, trans. Stuart Woolf (New York: Simon & Schuster, 1995), 80.
109. Albert Camus, *The Fall*, trans. Justin O'Brien (New York: Vintage, 1991), 123.

he saw a woman fall from a bridge and made no attempt to save her from drowning. But at the end of the novel the narrator discloses how he stole the water of a dying comrade in a Libyan prison camp where the prevailing logic was 'my life or yours', to borrow a phrase from one of Watt's early post-war stories about the Japanese camps.[110] That merely ensuring one's own survival means risking the lives of others is said outright in *The Plague*, when the narrator, Dr Rieux, learns that unstinting 'vigilance' is required never to be the cause of someone else's death.[111] In a stunning reading of culpability in eighteenth-century fiction, Sandra Macpherson finds a form of tragedy there when she considers the emergent novel in relation to a contemporary legal logic based not on liberal concepts of contract, consent, and agency but on the principle of strict liability. According to strict liability, your intention is no longer relevant to a legal judgement; having hurt someone without ever consciously having wished him or her harm, you can be 'responsible without being at fault', both 'innocent and to blame'.[112] If there is one question that mid-century incarceration writing also asks, it is how far we are responsible for the lives of others.

'What care they to Die, that can't tell how to Live?'

'Everyone he had ever helped was still clinging to him,' Ballard's Jim resentfully notices, in a sentence that recalls Levi's comments on the oppressive needs of weaker prisoners; Jim's insight comes on the death march out of the Lunghua camp, when every prisoner is assessing the physical condition of everyone else, critically evaluating each exploitable other to find a potential instrument of personal survival.[113] Imprisonment has turned everyone into a version of Robinson Crusoe, who, Watt wrote, sees other people only 'in terms of their commodity value' (*RN* 69), and tends 'to judge his friends and acquaintances not as persons in themselves, but as objects he may be able to use for his own personal advantage' (*MMI* 167).

These moral claims made by the weaker on anyone perceived to be likelier to survive are also the subject of one of the most developed

110. Watt, 'The Ways of Guilt'. 111. Camus, *The Plague*, 253.

112. Sandra Macpherson, *Harm's Way: Tragic Responsibility and the Novel Form* (Baltimore: Johns Hopkins University Press, 2010), 9, 12.

113. Ballard, *Empire of the Sun*, 194.

of Watt's stories about the camps. Titled in different papers either 'The Ways of Guilt' or 'The Revenge of Mercy', this story appears to have been written within a year or so of demobilization; the surviving manuscript is dated 9 February 1948, but references in correspondence indicate that it was already drafted at least as early as the previous summer.[114] This is the text with which I bring this chapter to a close because it speaks so directly to the interests in individualism that Watt would address a decade later in *The Rise of the Novel*. As in his other stories, the biographical detail of Watt's narrator follows Watt's own even when the names are changed or (as here) simply not provided. The link between the two resembles that between Conrad and his second-self Marlow (Conrad's 'in part self-portrait', Watt designated him (*C.* 19)), to name the literary model the stories follow most closely.

The narrator of 'The Ways of Guilt' is recalling, shortly after the war, his time as a junior officer at Chungkai. It is the summer of 1943, a year into the building of the railway, and parties of desperately sick men are being returned to the base camps in lower Thailand from the even worse camps up country. Other Chungkai memoirists also described this sickening spectacle. Jack Chalker remembered unloading barges full of the 'dead, dying and desperately ill... few were recognizable and I cannot remember one conscious occupant who was able to speak'.[115] For Chungkai's commanding officer Cary Owtram, 'only those of us who witnessed it as I did, not once but scores of times, could possibly visualize to what point the human body can suffer and still survive'.[116]

In this 'scrap heap for everything the railway had smashed', as Watt's story calls Chungkai, 'the struggle for existence fill[ed] the foreground'. The narrator cherishes his own illness for fear that, if he is thought anything less than deathly unwell, and therefore worthless to the Japanese, he will 'be forced up the line again on one of those up-country drafts that terrorized the camp like the opening words of a death sentence'. The narrator is hailed by a foully dirty and emaciated body being carried on another soldier's back; this is the 'other rank' Robinson, whom he has previously met in the makeshift Roberts Barracks hospital when Singapore fell. Robinson's recognizing him leaves the narrator feeling obliged to look out for Robinson: not only because he is an officer, but

114. The story is described in a 10 June 1947 letter from a 'Mark S' at the University of California, Berkeley—almost certainly Mark Schorer—whose advice Watt appears to have sought.

115. Chalker, *Burma Railway*, 74.

116. Owtram, *1000 Days on the River Kwai*, 67.

also because, in a climate of every man for himself, he knows that if he does not help him then no one else will. The 'guilt' of the story's title is overdetermined: the guilt of superior military rank, the guilt of being less deathly ill than some and yet cherishing his illness as his paradoxical best hope of staying alive, and, finally, the guilt at resenting the demands that Robinson's need for acknowledgement places upon him.

For, increasingly, Robinson's very existence imposes upon the narrator an unnamable burden—economic in the first instance, but plainly more than economic—that he does not wish to carry, rather like Levi as the liberation approaches and the camps are full of the sick and dying. 'I felt like crying,' Levi writes of the dying inmates who learned and called out his name: 'I could have cursed them.'[117] Nonetheless (and like Levi in the episode from which these lines come), Watt's narrator feels that he must carry the burden of Robinson's expectations anyhow, even as he knows that the natural outcome of prolonged exposure to one's own and other people's suffering is, as Watt crisply puts it, an 'economy of feeling'. (It is a version of the phenomenon Defoe described in *Journal of the Plague Year*: 'Mens Hearts were hardned, and Death was so always before their Eyes, that they did not so much concern themselves for the Loss of their Friends, expecting, that themselves should be summoned the next Hour.'[118]) Weak and dependent, Robinson wants help with everything, and, just as the Japanese have, once more, almost killed him at the start of the story by shoving him roughly off the cattle truck because he cannot climb down unaided, his own compatriots guarantee his death at the end when they ignore his cries for help. This is partly because they believe that Robinson could help himself, and partly because it feels dangerous in these circumstances to engage in any way with other people's suffering. Many veterans of the camps attested to this sense that 'the most valuable—and difficult—lesson you learn is not to get too close to anybody'.[119] 'Once you got started with sentimentality and grief you were a goner' is how Alistair Urquhart recalled reproaching himself for helping a fellow prisoner on his deathbed.[120]

Unlike his ironic namesake, Watt's miserable Robinson cannot get over his need for the pity and acknowledgement of others ('*Poor* Robin

117. Levi, *Survival in Auschwitz*, 166.
118. Daniel Defoe, *A Journal of the Plague Year* (London: Penguin, 2003), 18.
119. Twigg, *Survivor on the River Kwai*, 254.
120. Urquhart, *The Forgotten Highlander*, 168.

Crusoe', indeed), and, to borrow from Watt's account of the sailor dying on Conrad's *Narcissus*, 'he feels morally entitled to any power or privilege he can extort from his suffering' (*C.* 107).[121] In this respect Robinson is not unusual, since, as the narrator explains, 'we were all sick, or recovering from sickness: everyone felt he was entitled to special consideration'. But, if every prisoner is by definition a victim of his terrible circumstances, Robinson's primary sense of himself as one cruelly guarantees his continued victimization at the hands of the other prisoners, who instinctively resent the claims he makes on their own slender emotional resources. Robinson believes the other prisoners have taken an incomprehensible dislike to him, but the narrator understands it perfectly. 'Of course they had a down on him,' he thinks: 'No one could stand the strain of dealing with someone who made such large demands on the little pity we could spare from ourselves.' The narrator tries to explain to Robinson that he will need to take the initiative in order to save his own life—'Everything's up to you'—but he knows that Robinson is not listening. And so Robinson dies, and his death does not matter at the time, even if it comes to haunt the narrator after the war because of what it has shown him about himself, and about others.

In what is apparently meant to be a rhetorical question, Moll Flanders asks, 'what care they to Die, that can't tell how to Live?'[122] She dismisses as humanly irrelevant the deaths of the abject poor, who have proved incapable of looking out for themselves as she looks out for herself. Robinson is one of the incapable. Watt's narrator describes how camp inmates would stay in their huts rather than have to make the effort to stand to attention while others carried to the burial ground 'those who had failed to survive'—a brutal phrasing, characterizing these prisoners' deaths as no more than the final confirmation of their personal unfitness for life. However broken after their terrible and unforeseen reversals, most of the Chungkai prisoners have picked themselves up and adopted (in Conrad's phrase) 'the great mental occupation of wishing to live'.[123] The fitter prisoners who can still be bothered

121. Defoe, *Robinson Crusoe*, 113; emphasis in original. Watt's reading of James Wait is relevant here: 'pity . . . may seem to be based on a wholly altruistic concern for the welfare of others, but in reality it is intimately connected with the individual's unconscious fear of his own sickness and death' (*C.* 109).

122. Defoe, *Moll Flanders*, 255.

123. Conrad, *The Nigger of the 'Narcissus'*, 65. Another contemporary manuscript (dated September 1946) offers a more fable-like treatment of resilience. Japanese guards

looking out for more debilitated others can bring themselves to care only for those who are willing to help themselves; these albeit reluctant caretakers are at least 'rewarded', Watt writes, 'with the unreasoning vigor of their [patients'] urge to live'. For capturing Watt's unsparing view of Robinson Crusoe and Moll Flanders there could hardly be a better phrase than 'unreasoning vigour of their urge to live': Defoe's victims of an indifferent and unpredictable modern fate command our sympathetic attention not because they suffer but because they survive.

have locked up a working-class soldier to die in a Tamil cholera hut. Watt's undaunted Bob Dawkes escapes and makes his way back to his camp: he has had no food or water, and was surrounded by dying labourers, and yet he tells his comrades in the story's final line that at least he had 'me fag-paper and me lighter—I could 'ave a roll when I felt like it'. Watt's epigraph is from *The Bhagavad Gita*: 'The strangest thing is that a man, seeing others die, does not think that he will die' (Ian Watt, 'The Strangest Thing', Stanford University Special Collections, SC401-ACCN 1990-131, Box 56, Folder 'The Strangest Thing').

3

Richardson, Identification, and Commercial Fantasy

'Vulgar, gross, sentimental, impoverished in style—our popular sub-art presents a dream of human possibilities to starved imaginations everywhere.'

Leslie Fiedler, 'Looking Backward: America from Europe' (1952)[1]

'Most mass-entertainments are in the end what D. H. Lawrence described as "anti-life". They are full of a corrupt brightness, of improper appeals and moral evasions. To recall instances: they tend towards a view of the world in which progress is conceived as a seeking of material possessions, equality as a moral levelling, and freedom as the ground for endless irresponsible pleasure. These productions belong to a vicarious spectators' world; they . . . pander to the wish to have things both ways, to do as we want and accept no consequences.'

Richard Hoggart, *The Uses of Literacy* (1957)[2]

'A prisoner-of-war camp has at least one thing in common with our modern world in general: both offer a very limited range of practical choices,' Watt proposed in an essay that elaborated a point he had made in passing decades earlier when he described the prisoner of war as 'not so much a person as an extreme case of a more general modern condition—the powerlessness of the individual caught in the grip of vast collective purposes; in the end what he does makes little difference, and he knows it'.[3] Both claims are taken from his essays

1. Leslie Fiedler, 'Looking Backward: America from Europe', in *The Collected Essays of Leslie Fiedler*, i (New York: Stein & Day, 1971), 125.
2. Richard Hoggart, *The Uses of Literacy* (London: Penguin, 1990), 340.
3. Ian Watt, '*The Bridge over the River Kwai* as Myth', in Watt, *Essays on Conrad*, 205–6. Watt, 'Bridges over the Kwai', 218.

about the film version of *The Bridge on the River Kwai*, which he criticized for its pretence that people are freer to act on their own individual desires than they can ever be even in ordinary life, let alone in a prisoner-of-war camp. For Watt, the prison camp is an exemplary site for understanding the limits of human freedom.[4]

Watt wrote of *Don Quixote* that 'the confusion of romantic wishes with historical truth is a universal tendency', but he believed that nothing had done so much to reinforce and sanction the confusion of what is desired and what is possible as modern entertainment industries from popular fiction to Hollywood cinema (*MMI* 65). Looking first at his handling of *The Bridge on the River Kwai*, I suggest in this chapter that Watt found the modern culture industry's historical and symbolic origin in the commercial successes of Richardson and took *Pamela* and *Clarissa* as paradigmatic fictions about inflated fantasies of individualist agency and, in the end, its virtual impossibility.

Constructing the Kwai Myth

Carl Foreman and Michael Wilson, the cold-war-blacklisted screenwriters of *The Bridge on the River Kwai*, recapitulated the dual-narrative structure of their source text, Pierre Boulle's *Le Pont de la Rivière Kwai*, in which plans almost simultaneously unfold for building and destroying

4. Like Giorgio Agamben, Watt casts the limit situation of the camps as a way to understand the norm, although he approached the question of the administered life as a Weberian whereas Agamben famously follows Carl Schmitt. See 'The Camp as the "Nomos" of the Modern', in Giorgio Agamben, *Homo Sacer: Sovereign Power and Bare Life*, trans. Daniel Heller-Roazen (Stanford: Stanford University Press, 1998), 166–80. The comparison only goes so far: it is impossible to imagine Watt making claims like Agamben's 'Auschwitz . . . is, by now, everywhere' (*Remnants of Auschwitz: The Witness and the Archive*, trans. Daniel Heller-Roazen (New York: Zone, 2002), 20). A useful account of the limits of Agamben's position—important limits given its intellectual appeal early in the war on terror—is in John Brenkman's *The Cultural Contradictions of Democracy: Political Thought since September 11* (Princeton: Princeton University Press, 2007), esp. 55–64. As Brenkman writes, Agamben's 'camp' sometimes covers everything from Auschwitz to the affluent gated communities of the United States, and 'Agamben thus furnishes his own argument with its reductio ad absurdum' (58). On Agamben's tendentious reading of Primo Levi to characterize incommensurate forms of guilt, see Debarati Sanyal, 'A Soccer Match in Auschwitz: Passing Culpability in Holocaust Criticism', *Representations*, 79/1 (Summer 2002), 1–27.

the railway bridge.[5] While the prisoners in the camp construct the bridge under the leadership of the deluded Colonel Nicholson, a crack force is making its way through the jungle to blow it up. Boulle told Watt in a 1976 letter that the story itself was purely fictional, and (even less plausibly) that the Kwai, the minor river along which the Burma–Thailand Railway mostly ran, was merely a name picked from an atlas as a suitable setting for a story that he had already imagined.[6] More recently, it has been proposed—maybe Watt even suspected as much when he wrote to Boulle—that the details that Boulle deploys about the Tamarkan camp, from the transformation of Khwae Noi into 'Kwai' to the name of the Japanese commanding officer, Saito, were lifted from *Railroad of Death* (1946), the almost instantaneously written prisoner-of-war memoir of Watt's close friend John Coast; Watt and Coast had been imprisoned only a couple of miles from Tamarkan.[7] But, as I mentioned in Chapter 1, Watt may have had misgivings about the transformation of an extremely painful episode into fiction, but he did not believe that Boulle's stylized fable would pass with any reader for historical truth. This was not at all his view of the film.

Although the screenwriters largely followed Boulle's plot, they made a crucial addition to its cast of characters when they invented Shears, a maverick American prisoner who escapes from the camp and joins the British special forces making their way through the jungle to destroy Nicholson's handiwork, and who unites the two parallel but antithetical groups of disempowered prisoner builders and dashing saboteurs. From Watt's point of view, this change would misrepresent the building of the Burma–Thailand Railway in a fundamental and historically symptomatic way. For Watt, the addition of the rugged American escapee effectively declares that prisoners who hated their enslavement could simply walk out of the camp to become bona fide war heroes rather than remain among the camp's nameless multitude of implicitly emasculated victims. As if to underscore the filmmakers' incomprehension of the specifically demoralizing realities of the Far East camps,

5. On the dispute about how far Foreman's initial work survived or was supplanted by that of Lean and Wilson, see Kevin Brownlow, 'The Making of David Lean's Film of *The Bridge on the River Kwai*', *Cineaste*, 22/2 (1996), 10–16.
6. Letter from Pierre Boulle to Ian Watt dated 11 August 1976, Stanford University Special Collections, SC 401-ACCN 1994-106, Box 24, Folder 1.
7. See Laura Noszlopy, 'Railroad of Death: An Introduction', in John Coast, *Railroad of Death* (Newcastle: Myrmidon, 2014), xxxiv.

Shears was played by William Holden, four years earlier the escapee Sefton in Billy Wilder's *Stalag 17*, a casting choice that falsely (although presumably accidentally) implied the interchangeability of two completely different kinds of wartime imprisonment.

'A golf course is for golf. A tennis court is for tennis. A prison camp is for escaping'—or so says the aristocratic officer De Boeldieu in Jean Renoir's classic *Grand Illusion* (1937). Released not long before the Second World War, this retrospective First World War film established the premise and plot arc of all such movies to come: that a prisoner-of-war narrative is the suspenseful story of a bid for freedom. Film historian Kevin Brownlow notes that *Grand Illusion* was among the films Lean 'most admired', and Lean's effort is a narrative of escape in every sense: most people watching *The Bridge on the River Kwai* would not have contemplated how far it was dealing in impossibilities when prisoners break out successfully from the jungle camps in accordance with the generic conventions of the war adventure.[8] Samuel Hynes attributes the popularity of Second World War escape bestsellers such as *The Great Escape* and *The Colditz Story* ('romances', he actually calls them) to the fact that 'they told the public the story it wanted to hear': 'They are all adventure stories that inject the old personal military virtues—courage, daring, ingenuity, endurance—into the anonymous mass narrative, with all its suffering and death, that modern war is.'[9] There are no equivalents from Thailand, where only the fictional Shears could escape and find willing helpers in a country that had declared war on his own, as Thailand had in January 1942, and encounter whole communities ready to risk their own and others' lives for a stranger whose very skin usually marked him out as an enemy escapee. Back in the stubbornly unsympathetic real world, the prisoners had prices on their heads: by way of carrot, villagers tempted to facilitate prisoners' escapes could seek a bounty for surrendering them to the Japanese; by way of stick, the likelihood of mass reprisals discouraged Thai villagers from harbouring or assisting escapees. The infrequent escape attempts typically concluded with men being recaptured and summarily executed in front of their officers.

'Have you any other matter of any kind which you wish to bring to notice?' asked the final question on Form M.I. 9/JAP, the War Office

8. Brownlow, 'The Making of David Lean's Film', 10.
9. Hynes, *The Soldiers' Tale*, 236.

questionnaire supplied to the liberated prisoners. Almost absurdly in these circumstances, the form seeks information primarily about escape attempts and recaptures. Watt's is among those that survive in The National Archives. To this final question he replied tersely: 'That owing to the distances involved, the colour difficulty, the language difficulty, & low conditions of help, the advice of my own Lt Colonel Baker 5 Suffolks, that escape except in very special circumstances was impossible. This was confirmed by the fate of the few attempts made.'[10] One of Watt's unpublished stories from the 1940s, 'A Chap in Dark Glasses', is narrated by an English officer on the Burma–Thailand Railway who fantasizes about escape to the point that he and another prisoner get as far as making contact with a group of local bandits with a view to buying their help. Watt's liberation questionnaire indicates that the story had some autobiographical basis. He and two other (named) officers had made contact with a group of Thai and Chinese men (Watt could not tell whether they were bandits or guerrilla fighters) late in the summer of 1943 with a view to escaping on the full moon in September, but before the attempt could take place Watt was sent up country to the Konkuita camp, near the Burmese border. According to Stephen Alexander, imprisoned there at the same time, Konkuita was 'an evil camp': perpetually filthy with human excrement, and thus disease-ridden even by the standards of its kind; supply problems made the diet even deadlier than usual; and, to add to the threats to their lives, theft among prisoners was endemic.[11] Yet Watt's story ends with the narrator's ambivalent relief when his being sent there thwarts the escape plan before a single step has been taken, as if he has always known that his dream of escape would have been suicidal in reality. Indeed, in his essay 'The Liberty of the Prison', Watt supposed that there may even have been some immunity from feelings of guilt in the knowledge that escape was out of the question, when a thousand miles of hostile mountain and jungle separated the prisoners from the closest Allied lines.[12]

'There are no escapes in these pages,' his friend John Durnford warned in the preface to his memoir, a book completed in the year in which both *The Rise of the Novel* and *The Bridge on the River Kwai* appeared.[13] That Durnford felt this needed to be said at the start indicates

10. The National Archives: WO 344/407/2.
11. Alexander, *Sweet Kwai*, 153.
12. Watt, 'The Liberty of the Prison', 524.
13. Durnford, *Branch Line to Burma*, xi.

his assumptions about what readers would expect of a prisoner-of-war story. 'On the Kwai, hundreds tried to escape; most of them were killed; not one succeeded; but for Bill Holden it was a breeze,' Watt writes in his staccato corrective to Lean's cinematic fantasy: 'Obviously, if our circumstances on the Kwai had been as pliable as those of the movie, there would have been no reason whatever for [Camp Commanding Officer] Toosey or anybody else to make all the compromises which their actual circumstances forced on them.'[14] The unreal heroics of the American escapee-saboteur made a mockery of the real prisoners' necessarily passive courage, and Watt was dismayed that the film could render the courageous Toosey a deluded madman. As a former prisoner-officer from Toosey's regiment put it, 'a colonel as bone-headed as "Colonel Nicholson" would soon have been pounding peanuts in the cookhouse while someone more pragmatic took over'.[15] Watt insisted flatly that the question was not whether or not the prisoners would build the Burma–Thailand Railway—dilemmas like this had been resolved at gunpoint back in 1942 when Singapore was surrendered—'it was merely how many prisoners would die, be beaten up, or break down, in the process', and how far it might be possible to minimize those losses, as Toosey tried to do.[16]

And there was never any question about the Japanese ability to build their own railways, bridges, and all, a point Watt stressed because he believed that the film's racist depiction of a technologically masterful West triumphing over primitive Asian ineptitude gratified the same white Western supremacy fantasies that the war in Vietnam should now have put to rest forever.[17] For 'nothing is more dangerous than man's delusions of autonomy and omnipotence', he wrote in the different racial context of *Heart of Darkness*, suggesting that the danger of the inflated Western self-image is the cautionary lesson embodied in the career of the megalomaniac Kurtz, whose lofty status as the supposed emissary of European enlightenment makes possible his subsequent career as a brutal Congo warlord (*C.* 168).

Both the novel and the film of *The Bridge on the River Kwai* are predicated on Western technological supremacy—Colonel Nicholson may be a prisoner, but he has the expertise to get the bridge built

14. Watt, 'The Humanities on the River Kwai', 243.
15. Alexander, *Sweet Kwai*, 251.
16. Watt, 'The Humanities on the River Kwai', 244.
17. Watt, '*The Bridge over the River Kwai* as Myth', 200.

when his Japanese counterpart, the erratic alcoholic Colonel Saito, does not—but the film finally departs from Boulle's novel in a directly contradictory way by playing up the triumph of technology when its beautiful bridge is blown up spectacularly in the climactic ending. Boulle's novel, in contrast, ends in pointless death and moral confusion when one commando kills the others as he tries to stop Nicholson protecting the bridge they have been sent to dynamite. That 'the West is the master of its means'—technology—'but not of its ends' is how Watt glossed the meaning of this original ending: 'Boulle used fantasy to convey a real and salutary truth; while the movie used realistic means to convey a false and—I think dangerous—collective contemporary fantasy.'[18] And then, as Watt noted, there was an all-too-historical moral problem that both the novel and the film avoided completely: the problem of forced collaboration with the enemy on a military project, in contravention of international law. Article 31 of the 1929 Geneva Convention mandated that any work to which prisoners were put should have no direct connection with the war; although Japan had not formally ratified the Geneva Convention, it was nonetheless bound, as Tokyo Trials legal advisor Lord Russell of Liverpool pointed out, by the same provision (to which they had agreed) in the Hague Convention of 1907.[19] To Watt's mind, the movie resolved all the problems around collaboration only with the cheapest of evasions. The troublesome bridge is blown to bits, eliminating with perfect finality the chief testament to the Allied prisoners' collaboration under duress, however far the grand dynamite explosion violates Boulle's further-reaching point about the West's unthinking faith in its military might, and irrespective of how much at odds this formally complete style of cinematic closure is with historical actuality: after all, a bridge that is built with forced labour can be rebuilt by forced labour too.

18. Watt, 'The Humanities on the River Kwai', 248.
19. Lord Russell of Liverpool, *The Knights of Bushido* (Bath: Chivers Press, 1985), 54. Although Japan had not ratified the Geneva Convention, which its delegates had signed, the Japanese Foreign Minister declared on 29 January 1942 that treatment of British and Dominions POWs would be in accordance with the convention '*mutatis mutandis*' (Kinvig, 'Allied POW's', 42). Some British politicians hopefully recalled Japan's exemplary modern reputation; for example, the Earl of Onslow reminded his fellow peers of the 'very good reports' from the Russo-Japanese War ('Japanese Atrocities at Hong Kong', *Hansard*, 10 March 1942). In contrast, the Foreign Secretary used that same record to point out that 'the Japanese know well what are the obligations of a civilised Power to safeguard the life and health of prisoners who have fallen into their hands' ('Japanese Treatment', *Hansard*, 28 January 1944).

All this, for Watt, compounded with a transparent form of wishful thinking the film's ignorance, and its 'stupefying indifference to the facts of geography or politics': he was darkly amused by the scene in which a strategist meant to be a Cambridge scholar of East Asian languages 'pointed impressively to Burma on the map, and called it Thailand'.[20] It was mere wishful thinking to believe that dynamite could solve all the problems the movie had raised, which the movie implied when it structured its plot according to a countdown to the destruction of the bridge, as if Foreman were reprising his success with *High Noon.* Indeed, this earlier movie may have been on Watt's mind when he described *The Bridge on the River Kwai* ending 'pure Western style, [as] the train tooted and chugged round the same old corner'.[21] Film critic Georges Joyaux quotes Boulle expressing his wish that the screenplay had given more attention to the suffering involved in the historical building of the railway: Joyaux calculates that in screen time the race to blow the bridge up takes much longer than the bridge has taken to build in the first place.[22] But passive suffering is evidently not the stuff of commercial fantasy, Watt believed: not when you can have maverick American heroes and a countdown to the big explosion.

Watt's essays on *The Bridge on the River Kwai*, then, are primarily concerned with the film as a negatively exemplary production in its promulgation of the commercial untruths associated with what Frankfurt School theorists had famously designated the Culture Industry. The vapidly unhistorical Anglo-American culture that could both generate and swallow a fiction like Lean's about a war that had ended only twelve years earlier becomes characteristic of modern individualism at large, forever nourishing what Watt mocked as 'the *hypertrophie du moi*' (*MMI* 177), an excessive sense of individual entitlement, or 'what Freud called the childish delusion of the omnipotence of thought'.[23] It would be bad enough were this merely the preserve of the most overtly commercial cinematic outputs, Watt suggested, but the same individualist fantasy now permeates culture at every level: 'Hollywood, the advertising industry, Existentialism, even the current counter-culture are alike in their acceptance or their exploitation of the delusion of the omnipotence of thought. From this come many of their

20. Watt, 'Bridges over the Kwai', 218.
21. Watt, 'Bridges over the Kwai', 218.
22. Georges Joyaux, '*The Bridge over the River Kwai*: From the Novel to the Movie', *Literature/Film Quarterly*, 2 (1974), 175, 180–1.
23. Watt, '*The Bridge over the River Kwai* as Myth', 204.

other similarities: that they are ego-centered, romantic, anti-historical; that they all show a belief in rapid and absolute solutions of human problems.'[24] Kwai veteran Graham Hough, whose tough-mindedness in this regard might have shared its source with Watt's, held a similar mid-century view of inferior creativity: 'There is neurotic fantasy, and the idle day-dreaming of normal persons, and, we must admit, a good deal of bad art, which are all, as Freud would say, an evasion of the demands of reality, a refusal, permanent or temporary, harmful or more or less innocent, to come to terms with the world.'[25]

Formal Realism and Pseudo-Realism

As importantly, however, Watt's mistrust of conventional Hollywood cinema has a markedly formal as well as thematic aspect. Popular film is dangerous when it gets near historical events precisely because its representational 'pseudo-realism', as he calls it, means that heartening frauds are liable to be taken for descriptive truth: 'the pseudo-realism of Hollywood has the accidental effect of making millions of people think they are seeing what something is really like when actually they are not.'[26]

> The movie's air of pseudo-reality was also inevitably enforced by its medium... the camera can't help giving an air of total visual authenticity; and the effect of this technical authenticity tends to spread beyond the visual image to the substance of what is portrayed. Every moviegoer knows in some way that—whenever he can check against his own experience—life isn't really like that; but he forgets it most of the time, especially when the substance of what he sees conforms to his own psychological or political point of view.[27]

Given how central the concept of realism was to Watt's thinking, it is easy to imagine how troubling the idea of 'pseudo-realism' must have been for him. After all, his canonical if much-disputed definition of the novel relied on what he termed its 'formal realism':

> the premise, or primary convention, that the novel is a full and authentic report of human experience, and is therefore under an obligation to satisfy its

24. Watt, '*The Bridge over the River Kwai* as Myth', 204–5.
25. Hough, *Image and Experience*, 110.
26. Watt, '*The Bridge over the River Kwai* as Myth', 201.
27. Watt, '*The Bridge over the River Kwai* as Myth', 200.

reader with such details of the story as the individuality of the actors concerned, the particulars of the times and places of their actions, details which are presented through a more largely referential use of language than is common in other literary forms. (*RN* 32)

But it is difficult to see what could distinguish realism from 'pseudo-realism', given that both rely on exactly the same 'primary conventions', the same illusionistic technologies of a straightforwardly referential medium and a verisimilar accumulation of circumstantial details in order to embed the characters and their actions in their specific and instantly recognizable environment.

Instructively, though, this phrase 'pseudo-realism' appears not only in Watt's denunciations of the ego-and-market-gratifying fictions of *The Bridge on the River Kwai* and the modern mass culture of which he considered the film depressingly representative. In fact, he first coined the phrase in *The Rise of the Novel*. But it appears in a slightly unexpected context there: not in the discussion of Defoe, despite that, among all his authors, 'pseudo-realism' would be most intuitively relevant to Defoe's assertions that the wholly fictional is also literally true. We find similar claims in his famous equivocating prefaces to *Moll Flanders* ('The World is so taken up of late with Novels and Romances, that it will be hard for a private History to be taken for Genuine where the Names and other Circumstances of the Person are concealed'), *Roxana* ('this Story differs from most of the Modern Performances of this Kind... Namely... the Work is not a Story, but a History'), and *Robinson Crusoe* ('a just history of fact; neither is there any appearance of fiction in it').[28] Instead, less predictably, the term 'pseudo-realism' is invented for Richardson, when Watt turns to the question of 'private experience and the novel' in his chapter of that title.

In that chapter, Watt reviews the familiar terrain of Richardson's prurient eroticism but then adopts a different line of attack. In the end, the 'major objection' to '*Pamela* and to the novelette tradition it inaugurates' can hardly be that it is 'salacious'—this aspect of Richardson's fiction, Watt seems to feel, can be taken as given—but rather that, with the air of authentic report that Richardson creates through Pamela's exhaustively documented psychological and social circumstances, apparently realist novels like *Pamela* lend 'a new power to age-old

28. Defoe, *Moll Flanders*, 1. Daniel Defoe, *Roxana* (Oxford: Oxford University Press, 1998), 1. Defoe, *Robinson Crusoe*, 3.

deceptions of romance' (*RN* 204). Pamela Andrews is an updated Cinderella, and the fairy-tale resolutions of both girls' stories 'are essentially compensations for the monotonous drudgery and limited perspectives of ordinary domestic life' (*RN* 204). The Cinderella comparison is amusingly apt: Pamela is no ordinary teenage skivvy, after all, but a natural aristocrat singled out by everyone who encounters her, for her beauty ('I never saw such a Face and Shape in my Life; why she must be better descended than you have told me!') and intelligence ('Said she, thou art as witty as any Lady in the Land. I wonder where thou gottest it'): 'For Beauty, Virtue, Prudence, and Generosity too, I will tell you, she has more than any Lady I ever saw.'[29] There is much of this in *Pamela*, and if it helps to rationalize what happens—how could Mr B not fall in love with this prodigy?—it also compounds the improbabilities to an almost absurd degree.

Yet what makes *Pamela* apparently 'realist', but in fact merely 'pseudo-realist', is not actually its Cinderella content but the formal mode through which it transforms 'the prince and the pumpkin' into 'a substantial squire and a real coach-and-six':

> This is no doubt the reason why Richardson, who so rarely gave his approval to any fiction except his own, was able to forget how close he was to providing exactly the same satisfactions as the romances he derided. His attention was so largely focussed on developing a more elaborate representational technique than fiction had ever seen before that it was easy to overlook the content to which it was being applied—to forget that his narrative skill was actually being used to re-create the *pseudo-realism* of the daydream, to give an air of authenticity to a triumph against all obstacles and contrary to every expectation, a triumph which was in the last analysis as improbable as any in romance.
>
> (*RN* 204–5; emphasis added)

This, then, is 'pseudo-realism'. The modern realist novel proves to be the kind of commodity in which 'what is fundamentally an unreal flattery of the reader's dreams appears to be the literal truth' (*RN* 205). Defoe, presumably, deploys a similar technology in prototype but not to the same indulgently escapist ends, even though Watt also considered Defoe's resilient individuals too heroically autonomous to be true ('a consolatory unreality has been made to appear real', he wrote of *Robinson Crusoe* in 1951[30]). So we find that realism is not only the formal

29. Samuel Richardson, *Pamela* (Oxford: Oxford University Press, 2001), 53, 46, 423.
30. Ian Watt, '*Robinson Crusoe* as a Myth', *Essays in Criticism*, 1/2 (April 1951), 107.

or technical category it promised to be in the opening chapters of Watt's book—'ethically neutral', he calls it (*RN* 117)—but a moral one, because of what pseudo-realism accomplishes. 'We are the creatures of our light literature much more than is generally suspected,' Conrad wrote in *Chance*, and Watt makes the same Conradian point in *The Rise of the Novel* when he proposes, with reference to Richardson, that 'the novel's power over private experience has made it a major formative influence on the expectations and aspirations of the modern consciousness' (*RN* 205).[31] The great paradox of the novel as a form is that 'the most apparently realistic of literary genres' should have proved 'capable of a more thorough subversion of psychological and social reality than any previous one' (*RN* 206).

This unease about a form that uses its realistic resources to animate unrealistic or downright anti-realistic fantasies has an unmistakably eighteenth-century quality. Watt's fears about entertainment media that mask their fantastical content with unprecedentedly authentic-seeming representational techniques recall many of the concerns expressed about the British novel in its earliest decades. The eighteenth-century novelist Clara Reeve had put a similar objection into the mouth of a disapproving male critic in her pioneering history and defence of the early novel, *The Progress of Romance* (1785), when she had him argue that novels mislead readers about what the world is like. The novel's verisimilitude encourages the reader to believe that he or she (probably 'she', in keeping with the association of women with the early novel) knows from reading novels what the world is like when she manifestly does not.[32] Samuel Johnson's famous 1750 essay is perhaps the best-known articulation of the fears about realistic fiction accompanying the phenomenon that came to be known as 'the rise of the novel': no one would take for truth the fantastical old-fashioned romance, Johnson supposed, so the reader is never really vulnerable to its seductions. In contrast, the real-worldly 'new novels' are accordingly more risky when they serve as 'the entertainment of minds unfurnished with ideas, and therefore easily susceptible of impressions; not fixed by principles, and therefore easily following the current of fancy; not informed by experience, and consequently open to every false suggestion

31. Joseph Conrad, *Chance* (Oxford: Oxford University Press, 2008), 215.
32. Clara Reeve, *The Progress of Romance*, ii (New York: Facsimile Text Society, 1930), 78–9.

and partial account'.[33] The innocent novel reader becomes a Lydia Languish discontented by the refusal of ordinary life to supply the excitements of fictional narratives. Watt's pessimistic view is that, two centuries later, the world has now come essentially to be rewritten for a culture-consumer whose sense of personal entitlement is shored up on every side by profitable promises that people should expect to get whatever they want. Watt admired Johnson unreservedly ('one of our great heroes of the mind', no less), and, like Johnson, he feared the propensity of fiction to 'undermine our experience of the stubbornness of facts', in the phrase he used when he wrote of 'the deep blindness of our culture and its media, both to the obdurate stubbornness of reality and to the stubborn continuities of history'.[34]

Yet—and also like Johnson—Watt nonetheless admired Richardson too. At times he seems to have admired Richardson's novels almost against his own will, presupposing as these novels do all kinds of bourgeois luxuries that Watt knew what it meant to live without: the luxury of privacy; the luxury of identification; the luxury of romantic love. He could only have become more attuned to the differences between people's rawest needs and their mere wants during his harsh life as a prisoner of war: no privacy,[35] but identification with others always problematic; and sexual love, by all accounts, out of the picture altogether—or, as Australian Ray Parkin described a conversation he had with friends after a year of captivity: 'We have all decided that Sex is out and Hunger is King.'[36] And then there is the additionally off-putting problem of Richardson's 'harrowing moral and stylistic vulgarity', as Watt puts it in a moment of unusual rhetorical extravagance (*RN* 219). But the greatest sticking point with Richardson's fiction is this question of pseudo-realism, or Watt's apprehension that the apparent

33. Samuel Johnson, 'The New Realistic Novel', in Samuel Johnson, *The Major Works*, ed. Donald Greene (Oxford: Oxford University Press, 2008), 176.
34. Watt, 'The Humanities on the River Kwai', 243, 251.
35. Rivett's profound pleasure in finding a bamboo grove in which he could write without fear of surveillance and interruption—'a little bamboo clump... where I can write undisturbed', 'a private haven'—reads like unconscious parody of Richardson's heroines in those closets that Watt considered part prototype for Woolf's 'room of one's own' and part 'forcing house of the feminine sensibility' (*RN* 188). As Rivett explained in this reprinted extract from his, so to speak, written-to-the-moment journal, 'one of our first needs, if and when we escape, will be to get right away into the country somewhere where we'll hardly see another man from one day's end to another' (*Behind Bamboo*, 222).
36. Parkin, *Into the Smother*, 53.

realism of a book like *Pamela* 'confuses the differences between reality and dream more insidiously than any previous fiction' (*RN* 205).

We see here the most negative interpretation on Watt's part of what J. Paul Hunter, writing of the eighteenth-century booksellers, describes as 'the fundamentally shrewd analysis of human desire that made the publishing industry, for three centuries, the central vehicle for broad-scale human communication'.[37] And when, in *Licensing Entertainment*, his important book on the 'rise' of the novel in the different sense of how this formerly risqué form achieved social respectability, William B. Warner calls the *Pamela* publishing sensation a 'media event', the continuity becomes clearer between the popular novel of private experience that Richardson had helped to inaugurate and what Watt cast as the self-flattering but fantastical Hollywood responsible for *The Bridge on the River Kwai*, a film in which 'historical and political and psychological reality became infinitely plastic to the desires of the audience'.[38] In the context of Richardson, Watt identified 'adolescent wish-fulfilment' as one of the degradations to which the novel as a form has always been prone (*RN* 202); in the context of *The Bridge on the River Kwai*, he wrote of the 'childish' rejection of the reality principle.[39]

That popular film continued what the eighteenth-century novel had begun was demonstrably on Watt's mind in the years leading up to the publication of *The Rise of the Novel*. In September 1955, Theodor Adorno, now back in West Germany after his wartime exile in California, wrote to Watt soliciting a contribution to a volume of essays he proposed to edit on mass culture for his famous Institute for Social Research. Watt's handwritten note in the margin of Adorno's letter indicates that he had either replied or intended to reply with the offer of something along the lines of 'from Richardson's P. to 20c. Hollywood'.[40] Although the proposed essay seems never to have materialized, perhaps it would have been an amplification of Watt's passing observation in *The Rise of the Novel* that 'in the Hollywood film, as in the type of popular fiction which Richardson initiated, we have an unprecedentedly drastic and detailed Puritan censorship in conjunction with a form of art which is historically unique in its

37. Hunter, *Before Novels*, 61.
38. Warner, *Licensing Entertainment*, 176–230. Watt, '*The Bridge over the River Kwai* as Myth', 201.
39. Watt, '*The Bridge over the River Kwai* as Myth', 204.
40. Letter from T. W. Adorno to Ian Watt, dated 1 September 1955, Stanford University Special Collections, SC401-ACCN 1994-106, Box 1, Folder 'Adorno'.

concentration on arousing sexual interests' (*RN* 171). We can say more confidently, on the basis of Adorno's letters to Watt, that Adorno took the significance of *The Rise of the Novel* to be its implied argument about the origins of modern mass culture in the eighteenth-century novel; in later years Watt came to suppose that the reason why Adorno admired the book when he read a draft back in California (a work of 'genius', Adorno apparently thought it) was because, although Watt had not known this at the time, Adorno and Max Horkheimer had been thinking along some similar lines in their recent *Dialectic of Enlightenment*.[41] Watt thanks Adorno in the acknowledgements of *The Rise of the Novel*, and, although we cannot know if Watt was correct in believing that Adorno liked the book mainly because it supported arguments that he had also advanced, obvious parallels can be found in the depth of their pessimism about what they considered the debasing effects of mass culture, and what Watt elsewhere called its 'supreme objective': 'that total (and sickening) collusion of two "I's", the hero's and the audience's, as they jointly throw down the gauntlet to reality—and triumph'.[42] 'Much has been written against the mass media,' Watt wrote in his unfinished final book *Myths of Modern Individualism*, 'and their capacity to corrupt human values has no doubt been exaggerated, but... not by a great deal' (*MMI* 269).

Aside from these initially unconscious echoes of the Frankfurt School in Watt's attack on commercial pseudo-realism in *The Rise of the Novel*, there are more domestic literary-critical influences as well. These are especially pronounced in Watt's denunciations of mass-market fantasy as 'childish' and 'adolescent', which suggest the equally-but-differently stern influences of the interwar Cambridge English Faculty: debts to Q. D. Leavis and Ivor Richards are also declared in the book's acknowledgements. Although Watt shook off the most sententious trappings of Leavisite criticism, F. R. Leavis's characteristic language of 'maturity' survives, *mutatis mutandis*, in the Richardson sections of *The Rise of the Novel*, as does some of the moralized sociology of Q. D. Leavis's ground-breaking *Fiction and the Reading Public* (1932), in which she had attacked the bestsellers of her day as 'wish-fulfilment or opportunities

41. In fact an earlier letter from Adorno (19 November 1953) to Watt, again soliciting an essay, paraphrases the significance of Watt's work in exactly this way. Stanford University Special Collections, SC401-ACCN 1994-106, Box 1, Folder 'Adorno'. On Watt's description of his dealings with Adorno, see Watt, 'Flat-Footed', 55–6.
42. Watt, 'Samuel Richardson', 13.

for emotional orgies'.[43] 'The forms of emotional debasement that concerned the *Scrutiny* writers were daydreaming, sentimentality, and the exaltation of material luxuries,' writes Christopher Hilliard, in a summary that recalls Watt's treatment of *Pamela*.[44] (The Leavisite influence may once have been strong: a fellow prisoner described Watt's views back then as 'the Gospel according to St Leavis'.[45]) And the Richards of *Practical Criticism* (1929), with his memorable mockery of students who mistake their own cultural illiteracy for a failure of communication on the poet's part, seems particularly relevant to Watt's acerbic handling of egotistical thinking.[46] More broadly, his serious if sceptical interest in mass culture in the first place reminds us that this was someone educated at Cambridge during the famously pink 1930s, and, as the slightly younger Raymond Williams recalled, the undergraduate culture at Cambridge was markedly sympathetic to the decade's left politics, with its 'very large' Socialist Club, to which Williams and Watt both belonged.[47]

Cyril Connolly attributed the anti-romantic 'new realism' of mid-century writing to 'the deflationary activities of the Cambridge critics (Richards, Leavis)', and Watt was among the obvious heirs to this tradition.[48] But what we find in Watt's reading of Richardson is something more widespread at mid-century than Cambridge influence; as Scottish novelist and wartime intelligence worker Muriel Spark also wrote in the 1950s, 'emotional immaturity... is a requisite of every best-seller'.[49] Published in the same year and by the same publisher as *The Rise*

43. Q. D. Leavis, *Fiction and the Reading Public* (London: Chatto & Windus, 1939), 89. Unsurprisingly, she casts the growth of literacy as the decline of literary taste; her turning point is Edward Bulwer-Lytton ('best-sellers before Lytton are at worst dull, but ever since they have almost always been vulgar' (164)).
44. Hilliard, *English as a Vocation*, 171.
45. Alexander, *Sweet Kwai*, 193.
46. Witness Richards's dry introduction of the student who found John Donne's 'At the Round Earth's Imagined Corners' incomprehensible: 'A reader unacquainted with the rules for attendance at the Day of Judgment next claims our interest...' (I. A. Richards, *Practical Criticism: A Study of Literary Judgment* (San Diego: Harcourt Brace Jovanovich, 1929), 45).
47. Williams, *Politics and Letters*, 41. On Watt's attraction to left-wing politics in the 1930s, see Goody, 'Watt, War, and Writing', 223–4. Goody writes that, although he and Watt were drawn to Leavis as undergraduates, a 'value system' proposing that 'the world was to be saved by a proper reading of D. H. Lawrence' was 'not altogether consistent with our own political stance' (232).
48. Cyril Connolly, *Enemies of Promise* (Chicago: University of Chicago Press, 2008), 73.
49. Muriel Spark, 'Daughter of the Soil', in Muriel Spark, *The Golden Fleece: Essays*, ed. Penelope Jardine (Manchester: Carcanet, 2014), 152.

of the Novel, Richard Hoggart's classic anatomy of working-class culture, *The Uses of Literacy*, also advanced a scathing attack on what Hoggart took to be the moral superficiality of mid-century popular culture.

As in the passage that I quote as an epigraph to this chapter, Hoggart's arguments about the 'improper appeals and moral evasions' of mass culture resemble Watt's in content if not in their somewhat overblown tone. Many of Hoggart's remarks on popular fiction and film there might have come from Watt's account of *Pamela*. 'Presumably most writers of fantasy for people of any class share the fantasy worlds of their readers,' Hoggart wrote: 'They put into words and intensify the daydreams of their readers, often with considerable technical skill.'[50] Hoggart lamented the disappearance of moral resilience in a culture he thought was falling under the spell of an undiscriminating populist individualism. According to Hoggart, a middlebrow modernity 'depreciates the value of a fine application of intellectual gifts, the courage to take unsentimental and unpopular decisions, a disciplining of the self. The word "discipline", for example, is almost unusable in popular writing, except in a derogatory sense; it suggests "pushing people around", the Armed Services, "being got at", and is rejected out-of-hand.'[51] There are frequent references to wartime service in *The Uses of Literacy*; Hoggart himself spent six years in the army, fighting in North Africa and Italy. Their contemporary (and, like Watt and Hoggart, a war veteran) Leslie Fiedler made the point most explicitly when he described how mass culture presents 'a dream of human possibilities to starved imaginations everywhere', or, as he wrote elsewhere, supplies 'prefabricated, masturbatory dreams'.[52]

And, although this is potentially a somewhat circular claim, perhaps some of Watt's disgust with the hypertrophied ego that he found in Richardson may have come from or been reinforced by his reading of Conrad—a potentially circular claim, inevitably, because it is impossible to know whether that distaste was an outcome or a cause of his affinity for Conrad. We might think here of the isolating dreams of wealth and celebrity of Conrad's Almayer, whose shadow casts on the walls of his Malayan hovel a human figure blown up to an ironically 'heroic size': Watt calls Almayer 'a Borneo Bovary' (*C.* 51), a vulgarized version of Flaubert's heroine now that 'the will and the poetry which

50. Hoggart, *The Uses of Literacy*, 209. 51. Hoggart, *The Uses of Literacy*, 187.
52. Leslie Fiedler, 'Introduction: No! In Thunder', in Fiedler, *Collected Essays*, i. 229.

inspire Emma Bovary have dwindled into Almayer's dream of enviable consumer status' (*C.* 52).[53] Implying the same link between commodity culture and literary fantasy suggested in his discussion of Richardson, Watt's reading of *Almayer's Folly* focuses on the sheer unreality of the love affair between Almayer's beautiful daughter Nina and her brave Dain, remnants from 'popular romance, whose heroes and heroines require a world which offers that unconditional freedom which is the essence of individual wish-fulfillment' (*C.* 45–6).

All the same, what is no less apparent in Watt's distaste for what he took to be the corrosive individualist fantasies of modern mass culture—aside from the influence of Adorno, of the Leavises, of Richards, even of Conrad—is the impact of an institutional consciousness predicated on the subordination of the individual to collective ends. When Watt attacks fantasies of the omnipotent self, we find a sobering institutional consciousness that had survived a catastrophic series of lived institutional failures. Such failures had taken Watt as a young officer from poorly defended Singapore into the prisoner-of-war camp in the first place, when the soldiers were ordered to surrender at Singapore because their highest command had put them into a position where there was no alternative left, and, in the words of former prisoner Ronald Searle, 'years of inept, incoherent and chaotic political and military mismanagement had reached a logical conclusion'.[54] As Durnford wrote of being told to put down arms, 'there are very few occasions in war when you can employ the Nelson touch or do a "Rupert of the Rhine". The amount of Beau Gestes who capture forts single-handed or escape from blazing cities in fully-victualled yachts is small in number compared with those who go on obeying orders.'[55] Ordered to surrender, the soldiers did. But the same acquiescence to collective ends would prove essential in captivity, and vastly more useful than trying to imitate Beau Geste and other heroes of popular adventure stories. Now the institutional discipline that almost got them killed as soldiers in a lost battle would end up saving their lives as prisoners. On the Burma–Thailand Railway, Watt wrote, 'all our circumstances were hostile to individual fantasies; surviving meant accepting the intractable realities which surrounded us, and making sure that our fellow prisoners accepted them too'.[56]

53. Joseph Conrad, *Almayer's Folly* (London: Penguin, 1976), 128.
54. Searle, *To the Kwai—and Back*, 58.
55. Durnford, *Branch Line to Burma*, 21.
56. Watt, '*The Bridge over the River Kwai* as Myth', 205.

Suffering like a Heroine

The literary models appropriate to the prison camp are not, in any case, such manly popular heroes as the dashing legionnaire Beau Geste. A subterranean theme throughout *The Rise of the Novel* is the identification of male authors with their women characters. 'Defoe's identification with Moll Flanders was so complete that... he created a personality that was in essence his own', Watt contended, and his 'hypothesis of the unconscious identification' is advanced again when he turns to Richardson and moves between the identification of authors with characters and the identification of readers with characters (*RN* 115). Among the reasons why Watt thought Richardson was historically so important to start with was that 'there had never before been such opportunities for unreserved participation in the inner lives of fictional characters as were offered by Richardson's presentation of the flow of consciousness of Pamela and Clarissa in their letters' (*RN* 201); this ultimately 'makes possible the novel's role as a popular purveyor of vicarious sexual experience and adolescent wish-fulfilment' (*RN* 202).

But—crucially—Watt presents a completely different aspect of Richardson's solicitations of identification when he turns to *Clarissa*, a novel that goes far beyond inviting the reader to identify uncritically with Pamela's fairy-tale vindication. At the risk of stating the most obvious point about *Pamela* and *Clarissa*, these are both narratives of imprisonment. *Pamela* is perhaps too easy a target of mockery for Watt because of the social benefits that the heroine reaps from her erotic Stockholm syndrome ('I was loth to leave the House. Can you believe it!—What could be the Matter with me, I wonder!'[57]), but Watt evidently finds it impossible to dismiss Clarissa's paralysing state of captivity. In fact, his effort to account for the utterly desolating impact of *Clarissa* is among the moments in *The Rise of the Novel* when his own war experience shows through most powerfully. Even his preliminary classification of *Clarissa* alongside *Middlemarch* and *The Portrait of a Lady* as a book about 'the all but unendurable disparity between expectation and reality that faces sensitive women in modern society, and *the difficulties that lie before anyone who is unwilling either to be used, or to use others, as a means*' is, to say the very least, a peculiarly war-haunted reading of

57. Richardson, *Pamela*, 244.

the supposedly 'domestic' novel (*RN* 225; emphasis added). Here, Watt may have been half-remembering Graham Greene's 1947 essay on *The Portrait of a Lady*—Watt admired Greene, who was among Conrad's most obvious successors—in which Greene argued that, for James's heroines, 'you must betray or, more fortunately perhaps, you must be betrayed'.[58] If so, Watt has turned Greene's moral melodrama into zero-sum choices that are more social than spiritual. His definition of the domestic novel here comes very close to suggesting that women's traditional experience of subjugation and disenfranchisement emblematizes all the moral and social predicaments of an individualistic modernity. To the extent that people are able actually to make choices, they get to choose only between using others or being used by them.

So, while Watt's reading of Richardson is, as I have suggested, explicitly 'about' identification, and how the presentational realism of the epistolary novel solicited the reader's identification as no prior narrative form had ever done, his treatment of the 'much more complicated psychological and literary world' (*RN* 214) of *Clarissa* is itself an identificatory reading. Watt takes with an unguarded seriousness the hopeless conditions under which Clarissa is forced to choose among differently destructive pseudo-options. He insists early and often that Richardson seems to have felt 'a deep personal identification with the opposite sex' (*RN* 153), only then to reveal, when he gets to *Clarissa*, an identification with the heroine's disempowerment such as to rival Richardson's. Explaining the appeal of fictional character in her own influential feminist account of the rise of the novel, Catherine Gallagher writes that the novel 'stimulates sympathy because, with very few exceptions, it is easier to identify with nobody's story [the story of a fictional character] and share nobody's sentiments than to identify with anybody else's story and share anybody else's sentiments'.[59] Watt's identification with Clarissa confirms this idea and yet also points to something more intimate.

And the surprising outcome is itself an insistently feminist reading of the novel. Watt emphasizes the ruthless and predatory qualities of an entitled aristocratic masculinity: 'a sport that had no closed season and where the quarry was human and feminine' (*RN* 215). He notes both

58. Graham Greene, 'The Portrait of a Lady', in Graham Greene, *Collected Essays* (London: Vintage, 2014), 49.

59. Catherine Gallagher, *Nobody's Story: The Vanishing Acts of Women Writers in the Marketplace, 1670–1820* (Berkeley and Los Angeles: University of California Press, 1994), 172.

the impossibly high stakes, or 'absolute dependence', of women on 'their marriage choice' (*RN* 222) and the miserable situation of unmarried women under eighteenth-century capitalism, with their 'tragic dependence' on the charity of male family members for mere subsistence whereas they once would have been 'economically useful members of a large family household by right of birth' (*RN* 146). He describes how Clarissa's victimization at the hands of Lovelace and her own tyrannical male relatives is underwritten by all the institutions of eighteenth-century public and private life, and by the 'abject legal status' (*RN* 142) of women like Clarissa against 'the power of all the forces which deny her sex their just equality with men' (*RN* 224), not least the 'concealed and self-righteous sadism' of middle-class morality (*RN* 223) and 'the barbarity which lies below the genteel veneer of rakery' (*RN* 227). Finally, he links male dominance with outright cruelty. 'Sadism is, no doubt, the ultimate form which the eighteenth-century view of the masculine role involved: and it makes the female role one in which the woman is, and can only be, the prey' (*RN* 231). At first glance, a male critic of the 1950s is not an obvious source of such forthright feminist commentary. Where is it coming from?

An answer is suggested by Hynes's survey of modern combatant writing, *The Soldiers' Tale* (1997), where he compares prisoner-of-war narratives to women's war stories because 'they tell the story of the *other* side of war, where human beings suffer but do not fight'.[60] (Hynes's own wartime career as an aviator with over a hundred Pacific missions and the Distinguished Flying Cross represents an outstanding record of courage in the more traditional style.[61]) Seen in that light, it requires no speculative leap of the imagination to see why the terminal foreclosure of all Clarissa's options could feel painfully authentic, rather than feverishly melodramatic, to a reader who had undergone the horror, which was unique among the Allied prisoners to those captured in Asia, of an imprisonment psychologically unmitigated by the dream of escape from what Watt described as the Burma–Thailand Railway's 'narrow and confused landscapes'.[62] This terrifying environment was also a desperately claustrophobic one. 'Escape for a POW is both a practical and a psychological refuge,' writes military historian

60. Hynes, *The Soldiers' Tale*, 232; emphasis in original.
61. Samuel Hynes, *Flights of Passage: Recollections of a World War II Aviator* (New York: Penguin, 2003).
62. Watt, 'Bridges over the Kwai', 217.

R. P. W. Havers, discussing how the inmates of the Japanese prison camps were denied that emotional resource: 'Escape, in whatever form, is the single decisive expression of self-determination that a prisoner can make.'[63] But for the Far East prisoners 'there was nowhere to go', as Hynes writes, and 'if there is nowhere to go, how can one be an agent in one's own imprisoned life?'[64]

To cast this predicament in the language of the eighteenth-century novel, the prisoner in Asia must learn to suffer like a heroine, to paraphrase Ann Radcliffe's villainous Montoni, one of the century's many gaolers of women.[65] (These men are such conventional villains of eighteenth-century fiction that one of the first things we learn about Catherine Morland's father in Jane Austen's parodic *Northanger Abbey* is that 'he was not in the least addicted to locking up his daughters'.[66]) Obviously there are many unjustly persecuted men in the eighteenth-century novel, from Fielding's Thomas Heartfree and Oliver Goldsmith's Dr Primrose to William Godwin's Caleb Williams. Jonathan Lamb has shown the centrality of the scriptural book of Job to eighteenth-century British culture, and Patrick Parrinder suggests in his history of the English novel that Job was 'perhaps the most influential of all devotional texts in seventeenth and eighteenth-century English culture'.[67] Indeed, the eighteenth-century novel is so concerned with ingenious psychological traps and tortures that Fielding even opens his (it has often been said) most Richardson-inspired novel, *Amelia*, with the metafictional boast that the 'Accidents' and 'Distresses' that are to befall Amelia and her feckless husband Billy Booth 'were some of them so exquisite, and the Incidents which produced these so extraordinary, that they seemed to require not only the utmost Malice, but the utmost Invention which Superstition hath ever attributed to Fortune'.[68] Importantly, however, the suffering of the incarcerated Booth is substantially a

63. Havers, *Reassessing the Japanese Prisoner of War Experience*, 33.
64. Hynes, *The Soldiers' Tale*, 250.
65. 'I can endure with fortitude, when it is in resistance of oppression', announces Radcliffe's Emily St Aubert. Her captor Montoni replies: 'You speak like a heroine...we shall see whether you can suffer like one' (Ann Radcliffe, *The Mysteries of Udolpho* (Oxford: Oxford University Press, 1998), 381).
66. Jane Austen, *Northanger Abbey* (London: Penguin, 2003), 15.
67. Jonathan Lamb, *The Rhetoric of Suffering: Reading the Book of Job in the Eighteenth Century* (Oxford: Clarendon Press, 1995). Patrick Parrinder, *Nation and Novel: The English Novel from its Origins to the Present Day* (Oxford: Oxford University Press, 2006), 58.
68. Henry Fielding, *Amelia*, ed. Martin C. Battestin (Oxford: Clarendon Press, 1983), 15.

consequence of his own actions, if not shortcomings, whereas Amelia, like so many other persecuted eighteenth-century heroines, suffers wholly undeservedly in what Hunter beautifully sums up as the 'cramped spaces of oppression' in which these fictional women live.[69] But nowhere even in the eighteenth-century British novel is there another imprisonment as irretrievably hopeless as Clarissa's.

Saved among Watt's papers is an admiring note he received from a woman reader of a late essay he had written about the experience of the Far East prisoners, and I think she got to the heart of the matter when she speculated that Watt's real subject in the essay was the brave endurance that would once have been thought honourable only in women. Watt's scribbled note in the margin reads: 'Perhaps, still?'[70] The disjunction between active and passive courage runs throughout former prisoners' writings. Describing the early days of their captivity after the fall of Singapore, Eric Lomax writes of the struggle to contain 'our bitter young energy' and come to terms with 'the overriding, dominant feature of POW life: constant anxiety, and utter powerlessness and frustration'.[71] At the other end of the war, Allied bombers overhead led Ian Denys Peek to reflect ruefully on the 'short distance between them and us, and they are free and fighting while we are prisoners and passive'.[72] 'Better have died in the excited streets | when death could still be choice. Who chose | the armistice prolonged,' Watt asked in an unpublished poem dated to 1943 in Chungkai.[73] The poem presents a contrast between brave service in 'the excited streets' of collapsing Singapore and protracted suffering in a Thai prison camp that is easy to see in the traditional gendered terms of individual agency and passive victimization. As historian Joan Beaumont writes, prisoners of war are 'problematical' figures because cultures typically value the same qualities in their servicemen: 'physical bravery, controlled aggression, machismo', whereas the prisoner is necessarily 'powerless, a victim, passive'.[74] Instructively, when the former prisoner of war 'Van Waterford'

69. Hunter, *Before Novels*, 272.
70. Card from Mrs Irma Y. Johnson to Ian Watt postmarked 8 May 1973, Stanford University Special Collections, SC401-ACCN 1990-131, Box 30, Folder 'Kwai: Recent Correspondence'.
71. Lomax, *The Railway Man*, 72.
72. Peek, *One Fourteenth*, 579.
73. Ian Watt, 'Dying in the Summer: Chung'Kai 1943', Stanford University Special Collections, SC401-ACCN 1994-106, Box 22, Folder 'Jap. Stuff Misc'.
74. Joan Beaumont, *Gull Force: Survival and Leadership in Captivity, 1941–1945* (Sydney: Allen & Unwin, 1988), 2.

(Willem F. Wanrooy) considers the miserable plight of civilian internees of the Japanese in his survey of different forms of Far East incarceration, he finds that women coped better psychologically with their imprisonment than their male counterparts. Drawing a conclusion from this finding that is rather bleaker in its implications than he probably intends it to be, he supposes that 'the traditional self-sacrifice and resignation expected of women aided them in the internment situation'.[75]

Still, if Watt's reading of what it means for Clarissa Harlowe to suffer like a heroine begins as a feminist reading of a liberal–humanist complexion, albeit a little surprising in coming from this mid-century source, it is also the case that the liberal problematic of being 'an agent in one's own imprisoned life', to borrow Hynes's evocative phrase, becomes somewhat secondary in Watt's account of the novel. Increasingly, Watt understands Clarissa's situation to be desperate in excess even of the cruel and insurmountable forces arrayed around her, because Richardson's attention to her psychological vulnerability produces a theme of self-splitting that Watt finds 'starker, less reticent, and, perhaps, even more revealing' than her persecution at the hands of others (*RN* 225). '*Clarissa* ... will never squeeze a tear from posterity,' Watt's former mentor Q. D. Leavis had confidently pronounced in the early 1930s, taking for granted the obsolescence of Richardson's sentimental mode in order to make a wider point about the historical contingency of literary taste; she, too, thought that the worst feature of popular fiction was its solicitations of identification but believed that the emotional rot set in only in the nineteenth century.[76] Her husband agreed about Richardson's contemporary irrelevance: early in *The Great Tradition*, we are told that *Clarissa* is 'a really impressive work'—very high praise from Leavis—but 'it's no use pretending that Richardson can ever be made a current classic again'.[77] Watt acknowledges the unfashionability of *Clarissa*, and yet considers this 'a more modern novel in a sense than any other written in the eighteenth century' because of its 'exploration of the private and subjective aspects of

75. Waterford, *Prisoners of the Japanese*, 59.

76. Q. D. Leavis, *Fiction and the Reading Public*, 156. Bulwer-Lytton serves again as her historical marker: fiction before Lytton 'keeps the reader at arm's length, and does not encourage him to project himself into the life he reads of by identifying himself with the hero or heroine' (235).

77. F. R. Leavis, *The Great Tradition: George Eliot, Henry James, Joseph Conrad* (London: Penguin, 1983), 13.

human experience' (*RN* 220). Perhaps *Clarissa* felt more rather than less relevant for critics like Watt in the years after the Leavises' consignment of Richardson to oblivion.[78]

In fact, Watt finds *Clarissa* shatteringly powerful not simply because of the heroine's victimization but also because of how it reveals Richardson's distinctively modern sense of subjectivity as destructively splintered. By virtue of being what they are, neither Clarissa nor Lovelace can know what she or he wants, perhaps because, Watt speculates, of their 'ultimate and no doubt pathological expression of the dichotomisation of the sexual roles in the realm of the unconscious' (*RN* 231). Of course it is true that Pamela reproaches her 'perfidious Traitor' of a 'treacherous, treacherous Heart' when she realizes that she has fallen in love with Mr B—and Watt wrote elsewhere that he found Pamela's mixed and contradictory motives 'wholly credible and consistent with any adequately complex notion of human behaviour'—but Richardson's happy ending allows the novel to set aside the inner conflicts it has dramatized.[79] In contrast, *Clarissa* pursues Richardson's sense of inner contradiction all the way to Clarissa's death, with what Watt admires as its 'overpowering sense of waste and defeat...combined with the fortitude she displays in facing it', and 'the horror and the grandeur' of the novel's devastating conclusion (*RN* 216).

Triumphantly, Watt wrote that Clarissa Harlowe 'is the heroic representative of all that is free and positive in the new individualism' (*RN* 222); and 'she proves that no individual and no institution can destroy the inner inviolability of the human personality' (*RN* 225). However, there is a very much darker, and also less confidently articulated, side to his reading when he wonders if the psychic horror of *Clarissa* is really that the seemingly inviolate individual is always on the point of disintegration, and that Clarissa and Lovelace ultimately do not need external forces to destroy them when their own unacknowledged desires can annihilate them both with such suicidal efficacy (*RN* 228–34). Clarissa senses this self-destructiveness: 'for don't you see, my dear', she asks Anna

78. The major Richardson scholar of the day also wondered if *Clarissa* was more timely at mid-century: 'Lovelace's insane persistence' and his 'elaborate contrivances' no longer feel so melodramatic when 'the age of the atomic bomb is in no position to deny that a life of obsessive drives and intricate techniques may assume this febrile quality, or that a protracted nightmare of this kind could begin in dull and stodgy Harlowe Place' (Alan Dugald McKillop, *The Early Masters of English Fiction* (Lawrence, KS: University of Kansas Press, 1956), 72–3).

79. Richardson, *Pamela*, 249. Watt, 'Samuel Richardson', 9.

Howe, 'that we seem all to be *impelled*, as it were, by a perverse fate which none of us are able to resist?—and yet all arising (with a strong appearance of self-punishment) from ourselves?'[80] It may generally be true that the humanist critic has sought 'to efface the contingency of events; he also wants a sturdy, reliable image of man', as Warner wrote in his deconstructive study of *Clarissa*, but Watt is not as useful an example of this as we might expect.[81]

Character, Watt wrote elsewhere, is 'nearly as intractable as circumstance, and equally unlikely to be transformed in accordance with our wishes': and no one 'should be judged and found wanting by standards derived from the unsupported modern dogmas that full self-knowledge is possible and that it can deliver us from the ignominious fate of being what we are' (*C.* 340). Imprisoned by temperament in a more tragic way than a character like Moll Flanders, whose 'resilient selfhood' is 'confident and indestructible' (*RN* 131), Clarissa cannot be other than the divided thing she is, and what she is condemns her to her fate; the same is true of self-destructive Lovelace, compelled by psychic forces he cannot understand to act against his highest impulses and even his own best interests. This is why 'their experience partakes of the terrifying ambiguity of human life itself', as Watt abruptly ends his discussion of Richardson—'concludes' is scarcely the right word for it (*RN* 238). 'This passage is a fine example of the humanist sublime' was Warner's rather sardonic verdict back in 1979: 'for, while it apparently simply talks about a book, it dignifies the very idea of Man'.[82] But Watt's writing is not really given to pompous sublimity, and Richardson is the only subject on which his usual laconic understatement gives way to this loaded and inscrutable emotional register.

Thus, when Watt writes opaquely of 'the frightening reality of the unconscious life' in *Clarissa* (*RN* 235), for example, or of 'thoughts and emotions of a kind that cannot issue in speech, and are hardly capable of rational analysis—the flux and reflux of Clarissa's lacerated sensibility' (*RN* 266), we are some distance away from the naively positive and positivist interpreter of individualist autonomy Watt is often taken to be. Most recently, he has made his appearance in the conventionally reduced form, albeit in an extremely sophisticated iteration of it, in

80. Richardson, *Clarissa*, 333.

81. William Beatty Warner, *Reading 'Clarissa': The Struggles of Interpretation* (New Haven: Yale University Press, 1979), 220.

82. Warner, *Reading 'Clarissa'*, 245.

Joseph Slaughter's important discussion of the novelistic shapes taken by the idea of the person in formulations of human-rights law shortly after the Second World War. Of course I believe that Watt might have made a more historically telling appearance here not as the 'apprentice literary critic' Slaughter designates him than as someone whom existing human-rights law had failed so signally to protect when the international conventions meant to safeguard captured personnel were violated wholesale in the Far East.[83] Clifford Kinvig has found that the Japanese handling of prisoners of war systematically flouted all but one of the seventy-three articles of the Geneva Convention dealing directly with the treatment of prisoners; the exception was Article 76, which was, deplorably enough, on prisoners' right to honourable burial.[84] This must be about as impoverished a human right as the one that allows Clarissa to organize her own funeral once all her other escape routes have been closed off.

In any case, Watt's uncharacteristically fraught reading of *Clarissa* implies a more troubled thinker of individualism than we have come to consider him on the basis of his better-known interest in Defoe. This major commentator on novelistic individualism was more sensitive by far to the vulnerability of that so-called individual to unforeseen depredations from within as well as without. The coming chapter describes how he and the other prisoners found a way of living with the knowledge of these destructive forces without being annihilated by them. I propose that Watt found the literary corollary of collective and psychological recovery in the stoical sociability of Fielding.

83. Joseph Slaughter, *Human Rights, Inc: The World Novel, Narrative Form, and International Law* (New York: Fordham University Press, 2007), 46.
84. Kinvig, 'Allied POW's', 45.

4

Chaos in the Social Order: Fielding and Conrad

'Having known real chaos in the social order, at the Fall of Singapore, for example, I recognise the horror of chaos more than some of you may; and I'm sure that at the social and political level Shakespeare believed in that order.'

Ian Watt, undergraduate lecture on *Troilus and Cressida* (undated)[1]

'Things are not allowed to become unduly emotional, although we often know that Fielding feels very strongly indeed.'

Claude Rawson, *Henry Fielding* (1968)[2]

Fielding is 'an easier novelist to live with than Richardson', according to Alan D. McKillop in his 1956 survey of the field not yet known as the rise of the novel, and many readers of *The Rise of the Novel* have sensed the lapse of momentum in its closing chapters, when Watt turns from Richardson to Fielding, and from 'realism of presentation' to 'realism of assessment'.[3] This feeling of lower critical urgency has typically been understood as Watt's perceived devaluation of Fielding. As early as 1961, in his classic *The Rhetoric of Fiction*, Wayne C. Booth used Watt as an example of an able reader who was nonetheless incapable of appreciating Fielding's self-consciously fictive mode. According to Booth, Fielding can never match up to Defoe and Richardson because 'Watt's

1. Ian Watt, 'Shakespeare's Wisdom: An Approach', Stanford University Special Collections, SC401-ACCN 1994-106, Box 23, Folder 3.
2. C. J. Rawson, *Henry Fielding* (London: Routledge & Kegan Paul, 1968), 7.
3. McKillop, *The Early Masters of English Fiction*, 133. Watt and McKillop reviewed each other's books respectfully in consecutive issues of *Modern Philology* (55/2 (November 1957), 132–4, and 55/3 (February 1958), 208–10).

all-pervasive assumption is that "realism of presentation" is a good thing in itself'.[4] Booth casts Watt's explicit disavowals of any such claim in *The Rise of the Novel* as merely a perfunctory protest, Watt's 'repeated demurrer'.[5] Robert Alter pursued a similar line in his 1968 study of Fielding when he suggested that one side effect of Watt's 'canonization' of formal realism was 'to excommunicate' fiction like Fielding's.[6] Thirty years on, the otherwise sympathetic Joseph Frank (a former colleague of Watt) repeated the old consensus on Watt's 'implied disparagement of Fielding': 'Watt does his best to be fair to Fielding, but continual comparison with the inventors of "formal realism" puts the more traditionally literary Fielding at a disadvantage.'[7] Fielding scholar Jill Campbell comes closest to Watt's expressed intentions when she writes of Watt's 'decorous appearance of fairness in his respective treatments of Richardson and Fielding, granting to each what belongs to each'.[8]

As far as Watt's private views are concerned, he called himself a 'Fielding-ite' in a 1980 letter to W. R. Irwin: 'I consider myself to be one despite what some other people say.'[9] With that in mind, this chapter argues that there may be a more profitable way to think about Watt's attitude to Fielding, and the palpable lowering of the critical temperature that attends the discussion of his fiction in *The Rise of the Novel*, than to discount Watt's categorical statements as merely pro forma disclaimers. There may be a reason, after all, why his analysis of Fielding reads so differently from his plainer fascination with Defoe's hard-minded entrepreneurs, his unease with *Pamela*'s saleable wishful thinking, or his identification with the self-condemned Clarissa. Reading his discussions of group consciousness and shared values in Fielding and Conrad alongside ideas of prison-camp community, this chapter proposes that what these novelists offer Watt is a defence of social order that is no less necessary for being psychologically so constraining. As Watt once put it in a public lecture on Jane Austen,

4. Wayne C. Booth, *The Rhetoric of Fiction* (Penguin: Harmondsworth, 1991), 41.
5. Booth, *The Rhetoric of Fiction*, 41.
6. Robert Alter, *Fielding and the Nature of the Novel* (Cambridge, MA: Harvard University Press, 1968), 25.
7. Frank, 'The Consequence of Ian Watt', 503.
8. Jill Campbell, *Natural Masques: Gender and Identity in Fielding's Plays and Novels* (Stanford: Stanford University Press, 1995), 121.
9. Letter to W. R. Irwin dated 1 February 1980, Stanford University Special Collections, SC401-ACCN 1990-131, Box 18, Folder 'IAUPE 1980'.

'without being overtly anti-social, how very little we like paying the price that social life exacts!'[10]

'The adaptation of the individual to society'

Watt draws a shorthand distinction between *Clarissa* and *Tom Jones* when he describes how their initially similar female plots diverge. In both novels, the heroine's mercenary family tries to force her into an economically useful marriage with a sexually repulsive man—Solmes, Blifil—but, 'whereas Richardson depicts the crucifixion of the individual by society, Fielding portrays the successful adaptation of the individual to society' (*RN* 270). The tension between the relative claims of the self and the group goes to the heart of the prison-camp experience, and, discussing Watt's dislike of what he took to be the individualist fantasies of mass culture, I have already suggested that their wartime experience compounded in critics like him a reluctant but genuine institutional-mindedness. As I shall argue, Watt's powerful feeling for group identity and normative, sometimes even deeply traditional, standards helps to explain his otherwise puzzling inclusion in *The Rise of the Novel* of Fielding, who, with implications described most comprehensively by Michael McKeon in *Origins of the English Novel*, jeopardizes the book's main argument about the rise of the novel as the rise of formal realism and individualism.

Due allowances can be made first for the most prosaic reason why Watt's treatment of 'realism of assessment' is relatively slight: when he had to shorten his manuscript for publication he edited the material on Fielding significantly (there was to have been a second chapter on *Tom Jones*), and cancelled chapters on Laurence Sterne and Tobias Smollett. With that abandoned prospectus in mind, Irving Howe was more correct than he could have known when, in his otherwise laudatory review, he described the unsatisfactory final section of *The Rise of the Novel* as 'by comparison, incomplete'.[11] Watt came to regret his decision to cut from the second half of the manuscript when he found that doing so had left the book vulnerable to being thought

10. Ian Watt, 'Jane Austen and the Tradition of Comic Aggression', Fall Honors Lecture, Washington University in St Louis, 22 September 1982, Office of Public Affairs, Assembly Series Administrative Records, University Archives, Department of Special Collections, Washington University Libraries.

11. Howe, 'Criticism at its Best', 146.

'rather more simpleminded in its advocacy of "realism of presentation" than it might have been otherwise'.[12] To Watt's mind, Fielding and the novelists who learned from him were performing no less important a role in the novel's development by emphasizing social and moral consensus over the individualistic and interior perspectives of Defoe and Richardson. As Watt's epilogue makes explicit, the reason why he admired Austen over the writers whom he had discussed at greater length earlier in the book was his view that she had managed to give her characters an absorbing inner life while still maintaining an intelligently distanced and civic-minded wisdom, or what he had described as Fielding's realism of assessment.

But the example of Fielding inevitably shows up the troublesome slipperiness of the concept of realism. To incorporate Fielding into *The Rise of the Novel*, the term needs to be able to accommodate meanings that are almost contradictory. So, whereas realism in the context of Defoe and Richardson means—or at least purports to mean—a form of unselective-seeming representation, the verisimilitude produced by accumulated circumstantial detail, Fielding's realism means something almost entirely evaluative. One definition speaks to perspective as an individual narrative situation, intimate but necessarily limited; the other sees it as a considered attitude towards the world in the light of shared kinds of wisdom. Realism is no longer a descriptive principle, but a normative one: 'a kind of control or discrimination, a depth of understanding', in Ronald Paulson's fine gloss on Watt's terminology.[13] Even the highly critical Alter was doing no more than replaying Watt's terms when he wrote that 'Fielding's decision to avoid the grossness of exhaustive realism generates in his novels another kind of realism, which is essentially social and moral in nature'.[14] But this was exactly what Watt meant by 'realism of assessment': shared standards, self-consciously adopted even in the face of alternatives such as those Richardson had made available with his famous new species of writing. This is less 'realism' in any literary or technical sense than realism in its semi-moralistic everyday usage, where to be 'realistic' is to temper our desires and expectations, to recognize and work within the limitations imposed by inhospitable circumstances instead of kicking against the pricks.

12. Watt, 'Serious Reflections on *The Rise of the Novel*', 4.
13. Ronald Paulson, *The Life of Henry Fielding* (Oxford: Blackwell, 2000), 146.
14. Alter, *Fielding and the Nature of the Novel*, 43.

To put it another way, Watt attributes to Fielding a 'realism' that he later attributes to Conrad, whose fiction, we are told early in *Conrad in the Nineteenth Century*, 'is mainly concerned with how to maneouvre among intolerable and yet intractable realities' (*C.* 8). This morally pragmatic Conrad can be seen, for example, in Watt's reading of the much-analysed 'destructive element' passage in *Lord Jim*. ('It seems to be a universal principle in criticism that the more interpretation a passage has had, the more it shall be given' (*C.* 325).) Jim has survived the immediate disgrace of deserting his ship, but he is tormented by his own memory of an act of cowardice irreconcilable with a self-image anchored in the heroic aspirations he has derived from fiction. Marlow consults his friend Stein on what they see as Jim's unforgiving romanticism:

> 'A man that is born falls into a dream like a man who falls into the sea. If he tries to climb out into the air as inexperienced people endeavour to do, he drowns—*nicht wahr?*... No! I tell you! The way is to the destructive element submit yourself, and with the exertions of your hands and feet in the water make the deep, deep sea keep you up.'[15]

Watt argues that Stein's cryptic injunction about submitting yourself to 'the destructive element' is absolutely nothing to do with following your bliss or embracing some proto-counter-cultural form of romantic oblivion. Properly understood, the passage means exactly the opposite. Watt looks back to Conrad's less ambiguous previous draft in which the opening line is 'A man that is born is like a man who falls into the sea'—nothing about dreams there—and finds a parable about playing whatever unlucky hand you have been dealt:

> Of course you don't like being thrown into the sea, that is, into the reality where you find yourself; but if you try and escape into the air, into unreality, you will merely drown; so your only chance of survival is to force yourself to accept the reality which surrounds you, and use it to keep your head above water and go on living. (*C.* 329)

Only later does Watt consider how the final section of *Lord Jim* arguably legitimizes the protagonist's romanticism: after all, Jim never actually has to learn to accommodate his circumstances, since the novel's plot instead accommodates Jim to make him 'a genuine hero of romance' (*C.* 346). Like Conrad, Fielding appeals to the hard-minded

15. Conrad, *Lord Jim*, 154; ellipsis in original.

side of Watt, to the extent that both novelists become even more anti-idealistic than many would consider them.

One of the main conclusions that Watt explicitly drew from his years of imprisonment was the need to temper individual aspirations and expectations. 'It isn't only on the walls of the Sorbonne that we can see the slogan "It is forbidden to forbid"', he told an audience at Stanford in 1971, describing the difficult necessity of submitting to institutional demands: 'It is written on all individuals at birth, in the form "It is forbidden to forbid me".'[16] Explaining why that sense of entitlement is as destructive as it is attractive takes him back to the prison camps of the Burma–Thailand Railway, and specifically to an early breakdown of discipline at Chungkai:

> It's probably true that at the beginning of our captivity many of us thought that at last the moment had arrived for revolt, if not against the Japanese, at least against our own military discipline and anything else that interfered with our individual liberty. But then circumstances forced us to see that this would be suicidal. We were terribly short of food, clothes, and medicine; theft soon became a real threat to everyone; and so we had to organize our own police.[17]

The disciplinary order that suppresses 'individual liberty' is initially resisted but finally supported ('our own police') because it offers everyone's best hope of survival. It is difficult not to think that he had his time as a junior officer at Chungkai in mind when he wrote of the treatment of hostility towards ships' officers in Conrad's fiction: 'On the one hand this kind of hostility is universal, and undoubtedly effective in cementing in-group cohesion; on the other hand it may go so far as to endanger the existence of the larger group to which they belong and on which they depend' (*C.* 102–3). Or, as he wrote of the prison camp, although 'it was easy to blame our terrible lack of food, clothes, and drugs on our own superior officers', 'it was soon brought home to us, however, that we absolutely needed a strict organization, and that the only possible form of it was a military one'.[18]

Pausing on the crisis situation at the Chungkai camp can give us some idea of what Watt believed was at stake in this reluctant subordination of self. I have already suggested that his manner in speaking of his wartime experiences can be understated, and the situation at

16. Watt, '*The Bridge over the River Kwai* as Myth', 206.
17. Watt, '*The Bridge over the River Kwai* as Myth', 206.
18. Watt, 'The Liberty of the Prison', 519.

Chungkai was, in fact, sometimes utterly desperate. Because of the vast size of Chungkai, where at times up to 10,000 prisoners were held, its camp culture is recorded more fully than most. Numerous eyewitnesses left reports of this breakdown of morale, and they help us to see why Watt cared so much about the restoration of social order that he identified approvingly with Fielding and then Conrad.

What these eyewitnesses describe is little short of anarchy—and Watt himself used the word in a manuscript draft of this lecture, although, characteristically, he excised it from the public version. The breakdown of ordinary social standards, civilian or military, was nearly total. Pricelessly scarce medicines were stolen to sell for private profit; the sick and dying were stripped of their possessions where they lay; the bodies of those who had died in the night were looted; and graves were secretly reopened in case the dead still had anything on their corpses worth robbing. The camp's apparently very capable commanding officer, Colonel Cary Owtram, established the internal police force in response to what his memoirs describe as 'a very low moral code in operation'.[19] 'No one knew how long it might be before we were released, and life is very dear,' he explains: 'Any man of weak character was liable to be influenced by the temptation now placed before him, knowing that his only chance of life lay in more and better food, and food cost money.'[20]

One veteran who described the collapse of discipline especially vividly was Captain Ernest Gordon of the 93rd (Argyll and Sutherland) Highlanders. (The original 'thin red line' of the Crimean War, this Scottish regiment had borne the brunt of the fighting in Malaya.) Like Watt, Gordon was an officer at Chungkai, and his account is rather more expressive than Watt's cool summary of what must have been an extremely frightening period in the camp's history. 'In Changi the patterns of army life had sustained us,' Gordon wrote, but the move north to undertake hard labour in the dreadful conditions at Chungkai, followed by a terrifying first outbreak of cholera, saw an end to the self-protective military solidarity of the early phases of captivity:

As conditions steadily worsened, as starvation, exhaustion and disease took an ever-increasing toll, the atmosphere in which we lived became poisoned by selfishness, hate and fear. We were slipping rapidly down the slope of

19. Owtram, *1000 Days on the River Kwai*, 49.
20. Owtram, *1000 Days on the River Kwai*, 49.

> degradation...Existence had become so miserable, the odds so heavy against survival, that, to most of the prisoners, nothing mattered except to survive. We lived by the law of the jungle, 'red in tooth and claw'—the law of the survival of the fittest. It was a case of 'I look out for myself and to hell with everyone else'.
>
> This attitude became our norm. We called it 'The Ladder Club'. Its motto was 'I've got the ladder up, Jack. I'm all right.' The weak were trampled underfoot, the sick ignored or resented, the dead forgotten. When a man lay dying we had no word of comfort for him. When he cried we averted our heads... Everyone was his own keeper. It was free enterprise at its worst, with all the restraints of morality gone.[21]

The 'ladder club' and its variants (such as 'a ladder job' or 'got your ladder') were universal idioms in the prison camps, according to an unpublished essay that Watt co-authored in the late 1940s with another former prisoner, Henry Fowler. They attributed the phrase's ubiquity to its ability 'to describe an aspect of human nature seen very clearly in the bad times'.[22]

In the war memoir of another Scottish prisoner, Lance-Corporal Donald Smith (like Gordon, a future clergyman), this collapsing camp is 'Chungkai, Chungkai. The place where the Englishmen come to die.'[23] An inmate driven insane on the Burma–Thailand Railway chants this couplet over and over again: even aside from minds giving way under intolerable stress, dementia as an organic consequence of pellagra (niacin deficiency) or cerebral malaria was a familiar but frightening feature of the camps. Seventy years later, one veteran still remembered its victims with horror: 'even now as I write, I feel my hair crawling at their screams and laughter.'[24]

Like Watt, the young officer Smith had been taken prisoner at the fall of Singapore with the 18th Division, and something of his experience can be inferred from the fact that he was demobilized weighing only six stone and with his eyesight permanently destroyed by malnutrition. Wounded on the railway, Smith was sent disabled down country to Chungkai in an ostensible reprieve from the hard labour that was killing him, but he left at the first opportunity when he saw that Chungkai 'was no hospital camp, but a dark, tragic burial-ground',

21. Gordon, *Miracle on the River Kwai*, 87–8; ellipses added.
22. H.W. Fowler and I. P. Watt, 'Japanese—Prisoner of War Language', Stanford University Special Collections, SC401-ACCN 1994-106, Box 24, Folder 4.
23. Donald Smith, *And All the Trumpets* (London: Geoffrey Bles, 1954), 105.
24. Twigg, *Survivor on the River Kwai*, 176.

peopled by 'broken-down skeletons of what had once been Allied soldiers [who] terrified me by their strange looks and dumb, silent suffering'.[25] Prisoners oust the disabled Smith by force from his precarious edge of vacant sleeping platform; they make it plain how much they grudge his pitiful rice ration; the water bottle he needs to survive is stolen the moment he puts it down. These are the conclusions Smith reached after only a single day and night at Chungkai:

> This was a vile, wicked place where men who had once marched shoulder to shoulder in a common cause could strip their very comrades and leave them for dead. There was no good Samaritan in Chungkai. Men passed by their brothers on the other side of the way, their heads averted. I had never believed that I could become so bitter as I was that night as I lay down to sleep.[26]

Smith records that, even in his debilitated state, he took the potentially suicidal decision to let himself be returned sick to the railway rather than 'set foot in that accursed camp again'.[27] His memoir suggests that it was less painful to confront what the Japanese were doing to the prisoners than what fear and need had led the prisoners to do to each other.

This is all rather a far cry, then, from Watt's scrupulous but rhetorically low-key account of Chungkai ('theft soon became a real threat to everyone'). It is nonetheless entirely in keeping with how other eyewitnesses describe prison camps when whatever vestigial social cohesion that has survived capture breaks down under the brutalizing pressures of sickness and starvation. Compared to their Japanese counterparts, the German Stalags were much less cruel places for Western prisoners of war, as evidenced by a mortality rate among American prisoners around twelve times lower there than for their compatriots in the Far East.[28] (However it is salutary to be reminded that more Americans died in German captivity than at either Pearl Harbor or on D-Day, given how relatively little their experience features in American

25. Smith, *And All the Trumpets*, 101, 102.
26. Smith, *And All the Trumpets*, 105.
27. Smith, *And All the Trumpets*, 108.
28. The relative survivability of German camps applied only to Western prisoners. Their death rate of around 58%, amounting to 3.3 million deaths, indicates the categorically different experience of Soviet prisoners (Frank Biess, *Homecomings: Returning POWs and the Legacies of Defeat in Postwar Germany* (Princeton: Princeton University Press, 2006), 3). For a useful summary of the mistreatment of prisoners on the Eastern Front by both German and Soviet armies, see MacKenzie, 'The Treatment of Prisoners of War', 504–12.

war memory.[29]) A Darwinian vocabulary informs William V. Spanos's account of the German camp where he was imprisoned in the final year of the war. The prison camp was 'like a jungle, in which everyone was a prey', Spanos writes: this was 'an infernal space, where the brutal and degrading reality of the cage prevailed' because 'the deprivation not simply of human rights but also of the basic amenities of civilized life—sanitation, clothing, and bodily nourishment, above all, food—had reduced all too many of them to instinctual life, to the elemental condition of biological survivors'.[30] Spanos found no trace of fellow feeling among his comrades, now lone competitors: 'hunger dehumanized us, turned our inner selves into single-minded wills committed to nothing more than survival, even at the expense of each other.'[31]

In fact, it is instructive to compare the dystopian description of Chungkai offered by Gordon and Smith, and the similarly Darwinian accounts of many other wartime prison camps, not with the professorial poise with which Watt spoke almost thirty years later, but with the description he gave in 'The Ways of Guilt'. This rendering of events is more overtly literary, but it was written when the events being described would have been painfully fresh in Watt's mind:

> Theft of every kind, and selfishness of every kind, had increased violently. Everywhere hunger and fear silenced or confused the voices of the past, confronting us everyday with choices that could be easily resolved in terms of 'my life or yours', blinding us with the insidious priorities of survival.
>
> There were a few who yielded completely, gang-robbers who stole a sick man's only blanket off his body at night, knowing he would be too weak to resist, and that someone would be glad to buy a blanket without asking questions. Perhaps a cry went down the hospital hut, but the thief always escaped; it was murder, but everyone had his own troubles. When a man died no possessions of any kind were ever found on him: no one discovered who it was that snatched a gold ring or a good shirt off the body before it was cold. Slowly we were forced to learn the new code of hunger and fear: all round us, every day, we could see the weakest going to the wall as the ruthless grew sleek, and the conclusion was powerful to corrupt.[32]

Watt said nothing quite like this in his public comments on the camps. Still, it is newly clear what sort of social dissolution he had in mind

29. Clifford G. Holderness and Jeffrey Pontiff, 'Hierarchies and the Survival of Prisoners of War during World War II', *Management Science*, 58/10 (October 2012), 1875.
30. Spanos, *In the Neighborhood of Zero*, 66.
31. Spanos, *In the Neighborhood of Zero*, 86.
32. Watt, 'The Ways of Guilt'.

when he wrote of *Robinson Crusoe* that Defoe's castaway is pure fantasy because in real life what has happened to people when the cultural supports have been kicked away is 'at best uninspiring': 'At worst, harassed by fear and dogged by ecological degradation, they sank more and more to the level of animals' (*RN* 88).

'Defoe disregarded two important facts: the social nature of all human economies, and the actual psychological effects of solitude'; Crusoe's sense of freedom from other people would be 'disastrous for human happiness' (*RN* 87). By avoiding the 'actual economic effects and psychological effects' of solitude, Defoe 'make[s] his hero's struggles more cheering than they might otherwise have been' (*RN* 89). Or, as Watt put it even more bluntly in an essay on *Robinson Crusoe* written only a few years after demobilization, the fact that Crusoe 'turns his forsaken estate into a triumph' is no less than 'a flagrant unreality'.[33] 'An inner voice continually suggests to us that the human isolation which individualism has fostered is painful and tends ultimately to a life of apathetic animality and mental derangement,' he wrote, but, given what he had witnessed as a young man, Watt hardly needed his 'inner voice' to tell him so (*RN* 89). The demoralizing story of breakdown that Defoe avoids in *Robinson Crusoe* is far closer to what Watt had known at first hand, and no distance at all from accounts by other veterans of how people, stripped of 'the basic amenities of civilized life', are brought down to 'the elemental condition of biological survivors'. 'Darwinists call it survival of the fittest, don't they? What that means is survival of the most selfish bastards imaginable,' Reg Twigg remembered: 'Helping yourself was paramount; helping a mate was risky; helping anybody else was a luxury nobody could afford.'[34] Russell Braddon recalled feeling that even his first months of imprisonment had already changed him: 'the old Braddon was the nicer one . . . the present Braddon was probably not nice at all. I nevertheless faced up finally to the fact that what I had become was, if I were to survive, what I would stay.'[35]

So the real surprise, then, is that prisoners nonetheless managed to reassemble an almost tolerable society from this very low point. Another former prisoner of war, captured in Libya in 1942, English economist R. A. Radford argued that 'the social institutions, ideas and

33. Ian Watt, '*Robinson Crusoe* as a Myth', *Essays in Criticism*, 1/2 (April 1951), 107.
34. Twigg, *Survivor on the River Kwai*, 150, 154.
35. Braddon, *The Naked Island*, 121.

habits of groups in the outside world are to be found reflected in a Prisoner of War Camp. It is an unusual but a vital society.'[36] Some camps had to work harder than others to achieve this social equilibrium, or, as medical historian Charles Roland more clinically describes their achievement, 'a successful reversion to a primitive level of existence', when 'a condition of relative balance resulted, morbidity stabilized, and mortality rates fell'.[37] The impulse towards collective rehabilitation and the restoration of order can be felt in Watt's feeling for Fielding and for the 'realism of assessment' for which he made him stand. To borrow John Richetti's eloquent description of the differences between Fielding and the introspective mode that he rejected, Fielding represents a turn away from a way of thinking that 'overvalues an isolated and aberrant individuality'; his novels are ultimately 'affirmations of community and defenders of a neglected sense of connection and tradition'.[38]

Affirmations of Retrospect

In 1959, Ernest Gordon wrote to Watt after reading his 'Bridges Over the Kwai', an essay on David Lean's film that appeared in different versions in *Partisan Review* and the BBC magazine the *Listener*. Gordon's criticism was not of Watt's understated treatment of the prisoners' appalling conditions—characteristically, Watt had said little about them, although Gordon was about to publish the account from which I have quoted—but with the pessimistic conclusions that Watt had drawn from the fragility of the prisoners' solidarity. An interesting post-war figure in his own right, Gordon was by now also resident in the United States as Dean of the Princeton University Chapel; a friend of Martin Luther King and his family, he was strongly committed to the Civil Rights movement, perhaps in keeping with the practical Christianity that he outlined in his prisoner-of-war memoir. In the memoir, Gordon recounts how he had been converted to Christianity on the

36. Radford, 'The Economic Organisation of a P. O. W. Camp', 189.
37. Charles G. Roland, 'Stripping Away the Veneer: P. O. W. Survival in the Far East as an Index of Cultural Atavism', *Journal of Military History*, 53/1 (January 1989), 79.
38. Richetti, *The English Novel in History*, 121.

Burma–Thailand Railway by witnessing or hearing of acts of selflessness and courage there, 'stories of self-sacrifice, heroism, faith and love'.[39]

There is no indication in his letter to Watt that they knew each other beforehand, but they would have had a fairly similar war experience (aside from Gordon's religious conversion) as British junior officers in some of the same camps at the same time: Changi on Singapore, and Chungkai and Kanchanaburi in Thailand. They both later contributed to a book titled *Beyond Hatred* (1969), edited by Guthrie Moir, a prisoner friend of Watt's. What motivated Gordon's letter was the wish to mitigate the bleakness of Watt's conclusion, which I have already quoted in part: 'that survival, always a selfish business, gets more so when it is difficult; and that the greatest difficulties of the task are the result not of any exceptional cruelty or folly but only of the cumulative effects of man's ordinary blindness and egotism and inertia.'[40] This was surely not the whole story, Gordon wrote a little reproachfully in his otherwise appreciative letter, since some people showed themselves able to rise above their terrible conditions in inspirational ways.[41]

Gordon's published account of his captivity insists upon this transcendence of a hunger-induced individualism. As much a spiritual autobiography as a war memoir, his book recounts how he and those around him redeemed themselves from the Darwinian squalor of the camp by developing out of a few tentative acts of kindness some sense of corporate responsibility. 'And this is what the Christian faith is all about,' Gordon gently sermonizes in his contribution to Moir's volume: 'The love of God in Christ, and through the Holy Spirit in the community of love, brings men together in the one family.'[42] But from the theological point of view, what is most telling about Gordon's effort to explain how this agnostic young soldier became a believing Christian, and ultimately an ordained minister, is its emphasis on very materially human interventions. Gordon is concerned not with faith but with works, and he advances an altogether ecumenical ideal of fellowship and solidarity as a conscious antidote to the lonely misery

39. Gordon, *Miracle on the River Kwai*, 113.
40. Watt, 'Bridges over the Kwai', 218.
41. Letter from Ernest Gordon dated 14 September 1959, Stanford University Special Collections, SC401-ACCN 1994-106, Box 25, Folder 'Bridge—Correspondence'.
42. Ernest Gordon, 'No Hatred in My Heart', in Guthrie Moir (ed.), *Beyond Hatred* (Philadelphia: Fortress Press, 1970), 20.

and division of dog-eat-dog. Indeed, he writes uncharacteristically scathingly of the religious sectarians of his puritanical Scottish childhood who 'regarded themselves as God's anointed' in their 'grey, sunless abode of the faithful where everybody was angry with everybody else'.[43] In that respect, Gordon's memoir recalls the broad-minded Christian fellowship one finds in Fielding—fellowship, that is, as opposed to the more schismatic, and perhaps more easily faked, forms of religious enthusiasm that Fielding invariably derided, as when in *Tom Jones* the hypocrite Captain Blifil (whose prior association with what the novel calls 'the pernicious principles of Methodism' already damns him) sets out 'with great learning' to prove to Allworthy 'that the word *charity* in Scripture nowhere means beneficence or generosity'.[44] In *Joseph Andrews* the benevolent Parson Adams denounces 'the detestable Doctrine of Faith against good Works... for surely, that Doctrine was coined in Hell, and one would think none but the Devil himself could have the Confidence to preach it'.[45] Gordon's version of Christianity follows the same lines as Allworthy's response to Blifil's self-interested sophistry: 'there is one degree of generosity (of charity I would have called it) which seems to have some show of merit, and that is, where, from a principle of benevolence and Christian love, we bestow on another what we really want ourselves; where, in order to lessen the distresses of another, we condescend to share some part of them, by giving what even our own necessities cannot well spare'.[46]

With its insistence on the final triumph of charity and fellowship, Gordon's is the kind of prisoner-of-war memoir that might be taken to provide support for Terrence Des Pres's claim, in his controversial book about the concentration-camp survivor, that, however prevalent social atomization becomes in extreme conditions, total dissolution is intrinsically a temporary condition even there: 'A war of all against all must be imposed by force, and no sooner has it started than those who suffer it begin, spontaneously and without plan, to transcend it.'[47] Writing about the Nazi concentration camps and the Soviet gulags, Des Pres finds that 'survival is an experience with a definite structure, neither random nor regressive nor amoral': 'the most significant fact about their [the survivors'] struggle is that it depended on fixed activities:

43. Gordon, *Miracle on the River Kwai*, 131.
44. Henry Fielding, *Tom Jones* (Oxford: Oxford University Press, 1996), 373, 81, 81.
45. Henry Fielding, *Joseph Andrews and Shamela* (London: Penguin, 1999), 113.
46. Fielding, *Tom Jones*, 82–3.
47. Des Pres, *The Survivor*, 142.

on forms of social bonding and interchange, on collective resistance, on keeping dignity and moral sense alive.'[48]

Needless to say, Des Pres's claim about the non-arbitrary and fundamentally explicable nature of survival—that people survive in inhuman conditions by spontaneously improvising some form of social order—feels less believable when it turns into the argument that the will to sociality is a biological imperative, an instinct hardwired in the human animal. 'How comforting', Stephen Greenblatt mordantly commented in his review of Des Pres's *The Survivor*.[49] (Whether or not he had read the book, Watt saved a clipping of Greenblatt's review.) But if we set aside the quasi-biological determinism to which it leads, Des Pres's more plausible general argument about the utility of social organization in the camps is borne out not only by the prisoners in Europe with whom Des Pres is concerned but to some degree by prisoners of the Japanese as well.

For sure, these reports are seldom as wholeheartedly affirmative as that of Gordon, as we shall see, and it is obviously important to keep in mind that Gordon's memoir has a marked Christian tendency, if not an agenda as such. Particularly in his readings of Conrad, Watt insists on the need to resist grasping at the happier moral of people's fundamental goodness as a way of overwriting an unsettling experience that points in exactly the opposite direction. Thus, for example, Conrad may have summed up a whole code of redemptive values as 'the sense of reality, vigilance, and duty', but Watt felt that institutional life, in the form of his experience at sea, would have shown Conrad something altogether different about people's attitude towards social obligation: 'No one knew better than Conrad that actual human behaviour reveals solidarities that are at best irresolute and only occasionally conscious' (*C.* 81).[50] Regardless of what Conrad's narrators claim, what actually happens in Conrad's novels proves that solidarity 'seems to operate fully only in moments of acute crisis; and most of its manifestations are wayward, fragile, and impermanent' (*C.* 116). 'Fidelity is the supreme value in Conrad's ethic, but it is always menaced and often defeated or betrayed,' he wrote (*C.* 6), and, although Conrad's Marlow reverentially describes in *Lord Jim* 'an obscure body of men held together by a

48. Des Pres, *The Survivor*, v, vii.
49. Stephen Greenblatt, 'The Survivor: Life in the Death Camps', *San Francisco Review of Books*, 2 (May 1976), 13.
50. Conrad, *The Nigger of the 'Narcissus'*, 98.

community of inglorious toil and by fidelity to a certain standard of conduct', even the most rudimentary summary of that novel—the consequences of Jim abandoning his post when overcome by self-protective fear—abundantly demonstrates that Conrad never underestimated, in Watt's words, 'the strength of the various forces which are arrayed against solidarity, and especially of the almost universal and continuous power of individual egoism' (*C.* 109).[51]

The basis of Gordon's argument with Watt was the fact that individual egotism did not prove 'universal and continuous' in the camps. But it could surely be claimed with equal justification that the near-ubiquity of individualism in its rawest forms is attested to by the literally life-changing effect on Gordon of encountering just a few acts of unselfish decency when it was no longer to be looked for. In a section of *Conrad in the Nineteenth Century* titled 'The Affirmations of Retrospect', Watt described how Conrad idealized people from his time at sea, and there is 'an obvious discrepancy between his nostalgic affection for his sailor comrades and what he has actually shown them doing in the narrative' (*C.* 120). Watt's verdict on Conrad's idealizations of comradeship is this: 'From a distance of months or years, a few special moments may stand out whose absolute quality almost obliterates all those other unremembered moments which brought the commoner message that as usual no one has quite come up to snuff' (*C.* 122).

But a familiar paradox of the prison camp is that self-interest may itself dictate solidarity. Or, as Watt explained, again ostensibly with reference to Conrad, 'throughout history . . . individuals are driven by circumstances into the traditional forms of human solidarity' and solidarity is 'derived from the economic necessities to which men find themselves involuntarily but inexorably exposed'.[52] Watt's reading of Conrad's sea fiction stresses that 'all those on board share an immediate mutual dependence in which everyone's survival is continuously at stake' and reminds us of 'our utter, but usually forgotten, dependence on the labors of others' (*C.* 116, 125). 'We exist only in so far as we hang together,' argues Marlow in *Lord Jim*, explaining why Jim experiences his desertion of the Patna as so disastrous a betrayal.[53] To the extent that Jim is rehabilitated, it is thanks to 'courage, work, and self-

51. Conrad, *Lord Jim*, 37.
52. Watt, 'Joseph Conrad: Alienation and Commitment', 14.
53. Conrad, *Lord Jim*, 162.

discipline', Watt writes (*C.* 339). Traditional values prevail in Conrad just as they would prevail in the prison camps—although only just.

Conrad saw that 'dependence on others was a necessary condition for the very existence of the individual self' (*C.* 33), and what the prisoners describe substantially accords both with Watt's Conradian perspective and with Des Pres's claim that 'solidarity becomes power in proportion to the degree of disciplined order'.[54] In 1943, while the Allied prisoners confronted the second year of their captivity, American psychologist Abraham Maslow was publishing his famous, but individualistic, hierarchy of needs that made human relationships (love, belonging, esteem) stand on the broader base of physiological imperatives already met. On the other side of the world, the Burma–Thailand Railway had flipped the pyramid over, for only when social belonging became possible could basic needs be addressed—not 'met', for they never were—better than they could be under the prevailing misery of dog-eat-dog.

Without suggesting, then, that such awed memories as Gordon's of prisoners pulling together in the deeply adverse circumstances of the Burma–Thailand Railway are largely 'the affirmations of retrospect', we more usually find a marked uncertainty in former prisoners' recollections about the relative dominance of antisocial feelings within their camp cultures, or what one of Watt's friends in captivity remembered as 'the personal tugs-of-war in the darkest days of the railway between altruism and self-preservation'.[55] According to Graham Hough: 'There was comradeship, there was mutual help; but a degree of insensibility to anything but your own situation was, I suppose, a necessity for survival.'[56] To dwell on the disintegration of morale could be taken as a betrayal of fellow veterans, however, and the earlier the memoir, the greater the reticence on this matter. 'In such a struggle for survival, there were, inevitably, selfishness, racketeering, meanness and injustice,' wrote the journalist Rohan Rivett in the virtually instantaneous memoir he published in the autumn of 1945; but there was also, he immediately adds, 'the unbeatable courage and optimism and the sterling loyalty to comrades with which the vast majority faced starvation, disease and persecution'.[57]

54. Des Pres, *The Survivor*, 121.
55. Alexander, *Sweet Kwai*, 1.
56. Hough, 'Prisoners', 8.
57. Rivett, *Behind Bamboo*, ix.

'Only group cohesion could have ensured group survival,' writes Clifford Kinvig, even though 'the squalor and oppression of the situation did encourage... an attitude of *sauve qui peut*'.[58] The veterans tended to take this more qualified line that altruism was virtually out of the question, but cooperation saved their lives. 'It cannot be too strongly stressed how, in those days, the individual had to subordinate his desires to society rules if that society were to survive,' Russell Braddon wrote:

> The three things that could, at any time, kill us all off were work, disease and starvation.
>
> To overcome the murderous effects of the almost impossible tasks set us by the Japanese, team work was required to the nth degree. Only split-second timing and simultaneous effort by a squad of sick men could enable them to lift huge dredge cups on to railway trucks—and, having lifted them, to deposit them so gently that fingers and limbs were not severed. Only rigid self-discipline could keep latrines un-fouled so that the maggots did not breed round them and the disease-carrying fly increase its numbers. Only a faithful adherence to the rules could ensure that the tiny quantity of food which came into the camps would keep everyone alive: and that the limited water available would slake one's thirst, keep one clean and wash one's eating irons. All those things were managed. The prisoner-of-war life of those four years was an object lesson in living together.[59]

Or, as he put it more succinctly in a later work: 'Over a period of almost four years we prisoners of war had built for ourselves, out of a chaos of disease and starvation and degradation and brutality, a society that was good.'[60] What the prisoners assembled was a kind of simulacrum of ordinary life even in the absence of ordinary amenities. Durnford ended up at Chungkai after the restoration of order and was astonished to find people playing bridge in the evenings, or discussing literature, or paying formal visits to their friends' huts, with all the 'civilised urbanities and absurdities'.[61] They remind him of 'shipwrecked sailors suddenly found in more agreeable circumstances'.[62] The protagonist of Australian prisoner Leslie Greener's novel *No Time to Look Back* (1951) marvels at the peculiarity of a camp society in which 'We have nothing, yet we have everything like a little world. We exist on a starvation diet, yet we go out to lunch. We have hardly a shirt to our backs and we live in hovels, yet we go visiting, we have theatres,

58. Kinvig, *River Kwai Railway*, 96.
59. Braddon, *The Naked Island*, 117.
60. Braddon, *End of a Hate*, 22.
61. Durnford, *Branch Line to Burma*, 126.
62. Durnford, *Branch Line to Burma*, 127.

churches.'[63] Lest it all become too self-congratulatory, another character interjects: 'And we never know if to-morrow isn't zero day for us all to get our throats cut.'[64] This protective imitation of normalcy in the face of deadly threat must surely have been at the back of Watt's mind when, in the context of Conrad, he defined civilization as 'a structure of behaviour and belief which can sometimes keep the darkness at bay' (*C.* 250).

'That so many people should have died seemed obvious enough, considering our conditions of life,' Watt once wrote of the Japanese prison camps: 'What was difficult to understand was rather how so many managed to survive.'[65] Of course he knew that they survived through the construction of the society they improvised out of chaos. The structure of recovery is identical with the one he projected onto the importance—positive and negative—of Defoe in *The Rise of the Novel*, where Watt ends his reading of *Robinson Crusoe* by arguing that it marks the point at which traditional solidarities have been undone with such devastating comprehensiveness that new allegiances must come into being:

> Defoe's story is perhaps not a novel in the usual sense since it deals so little with personal relations. But it is appropriate that the tradition of the novel should begin with a work that annihilated the relationships of the traditional social order, and thus drew attention to the opportunity and the need of building up a network of personal relationships on a new and conscious pattern; the terms of the problem of the novel and of modern thought alike were established when the old order of moral and social relationships was shipwrecked, with Robinson Crusoe, by the rising tide of individualism. (*RN* 92)

If the catastrophic 'shipwreck' of civilization at Chungkai makes it clearer what Watt would have meant when he attributed a fundamentally fantastical quality to Defoe's robust Robinson Crusoe, whose selfhood survives so bravely the degradations imposed by his environment, it is clearer, too, what he meant when he wrote of Fielding that his worldliness finally 'brought [the novel] into contact with the whole tradition of civilised values' (*RN* 288); this, he later claimed, was 'the ultimate aim of "realism of assessment"'.[66] Watt praises Fielding for giving the novel 'something that is ultimately even more important than

63. Leslie Greener, *No Time to Look Back* (London: Gollancz, 1951), 34.
64. Greener, *No Time to Look Back*, 34.
65. Watt, 'The Liberty of the Prison', 515.
66. Watt, 'Serious Reflections on *The Rise of the Novel*', 12.

narrative technique—a responsible wisdom about human affairs' (*RN* 288). Fielding has 'a true grasp of human reality, never deceived or deceiving about himself, his characters or the human lot in general' (*RN* 288). By rejecting Richardson's inwardness, Fielding 'converts the novel into a social and indeed into a sociable literary form' (*RN* 285). Watt did not have terms of approbation stronger than these. Watt's intellectual and moral acceptance of Fielding's values may have been such that he had relatively little to say about them. The problems Defoe and Richardson's ideas of selfhood raised were far more unsettling, but they were also much more compelling as a result.

The language in which he praises Fielding prefigures the language in which, only two years after the appearance of *The Rise of the Novel*, he would praise another favourite eighteenth-century writer, the more pessimistic Samuel Johnson, for his 'steady awareness of mankind's limitations'.[67] Watt sees the resistance to unrestrained individualism (or, say, 'free enterprise at its worst, with all the restraints of morality gone', as Gordon had put it in his account of the disorder at Chungkai) as the great strength of Fielding's world view, with its belief that 'society and the larger order which it represents must have priority' (*RN* 271). 'Restraint' is as important a concept for Watt as it had been for Conrad in *Heart of Darkness*: 'a quality which is not usually needed in modern society, where all necessary sanctions on conduct are supplied externally' (*C.* 227).

'The power of doing what we please'

Fielding's anti-individualism is obviously not simply a matter of style, or of the opposite of 'realism of presentation', but also of attention at the level of argument to individualism's potentially corrosive human effects. In his 1958 essay on *Tom Jones*, William Empson argued that after *Joseph Andrews* 'Fielding set himself up as a moral theorist... because he decided he could refute the view of Hobbes, and of various thinkers prominent at the time who derived from Hobbes, that incessant Egotism is logically inevitable or a condition of our being'.[68] Fielding's engagement with selfishness is especially marked in the books most

67. Ian Watt, 'Dr Samuel Johnson after 250 Years', *Listener*, 24 September 1959, 478.
68. William Empson, 'Tom Jones', *Kenyon Review*, 20/2 (Spring 1958), 224.

explicitly about crime, *Jonathan Wild* (1743) and *Amelia* (1751). Here, criminality and individualism are linked as strongly as in Defoe's fiction, only from a completely different moral perspective. Early in *Amelia* we meet Jonathan Thrasher, a corrupt Justice of the Peace who is a legal ignoramus but comprehensively 'well versed in the Laws of Nature':

> He perfectly well understood that fundamental Principle so strongly laid down in the Institutes of the learned Rochefoucault; by which the Duty of Self-love is so strongly enforced, and every Man is taught to consider himself as the Centre of Gravity, and to attract all things thither. To speak the Truth plainly, the Justice was never indifferent in a Cause, but when he could get nothing on either Side.[69]

Not long afterwards, Fielding has Billy Booth voice his own disgust for cynical individualism, in a conversation with the fallen Fanny Mathews about the provocatively amoral arguments of Bernard Mandeville (here, unambiguously, 'Man-devil'):

> 'I look upon the two Words you mention [Virtue and Religion], to serve only as Cloaks under which Hypocrisy may be the better enabled to cheat the World. I have been of that Opinion ever since I read that charming Fellow *Mandevil*.'
>
> 'Pardon me, Madam,' answered *Booth*, 'I hope you do not agree with *Mandevil* neither, who hath represented human Nature in a Picture of the highest Deformity. He hath left out of his System the best Passion which the Mind can possess, and attempts to derive the Effects or Energies of that Passion, from the base Impulses of Pride or Fear. Whereas, it is as certain that Love exists in the Mind of Man, as that its opposite Hatred doth, and the same Reasons will equally prove the Existence of the one as the Existence of the other.'[70]

In an even more negative vein, Fielding connected individualism and crime through the disgusted mockery of antisocial ideas of distinction in *Jonathan Wild*. The triumph of the individual means that everyone else must suffer for his solitary good: 'Lastly, when I consider whole Nations extirpated only to bring Tears into the Eyes of a GREAT MAN, that he hath no more Nations to extirpate, then indeed I am almost inclined to wish that Nature had spared us this her MASTERPIECE, and that no GREAT MAN had ever been born into the World.'[71] Famously, Alexander the Great was said to weep because there were no more

69. Fielding, *Amelia*, 21. 70. Fielding, *Amelia*, 114–15.
71. Henry Fielding, *Jonathan Wild* (Oxford: Oxford University Press, 2008), 43.

worlds to conquer; to borrow the phrasings of *Amelia*, Alexander is among 'all the Heroes who have ever infested the Earth', and it would be no cause for grief should such heroes be 'hanged all together in a String'.[72] The gang-master, thief-taker protagonist Jonathan Wild is likened to such heroes as Alexander throughout, and Newgate turns out to be 'a Castle very far from being an improper, or misbecoming Habitation for any GREAT Man whatever'.[73] To these novels' attacks on a ruinous and aggrandizing individualism, we might even add *Shamela* (1741), which Tom Keymer has argued is not 'a reactionary attack on plebeian adventurism' but a denunciation of 'enterprise culture' and 'the corrupt and pharisaical entrepreneur'.[74]

In his powerful autobiographical travelogue *The Journal of a Voyage to Lisbon* (1755), the dying Fielding wrote of the social and economic havoc caused by 'the vague and uncertain use of a word called Liberty': 'commonly understood [as] the power of doing what we please'.[75] Paulson writes of this final work that its 'general theme... is degeneration', a reflection of the deepening social pessimism born of Fielding's years as a magistrate, when he saw at close quarters the loose weave of the social fabric.[76] Along with 'the heroic struggles for human betterment which he conducted as a magistrate under the most adverse personal circumstances', Watt names Fielding's *Journal* as the place where Fielding's 'moral qualities' (which Watt names as his 'dignity and generosity') are most apparent (*RN* 287).

In the last-ditch journey to Lisbon to save his life, Fielding's physical dependence upon those around him—his helplessly immobile body is mere 'dead luggage... incapable of any bodily motion without external impulse'—can only have enhanced the acuteness of his perceptions of human vulnerability and the problem of self-interest.[77] The *Journal* is full of dismay at how enterprising individuals take amoral advantage of the dependency of others, such as the greedy innkeeper Mrs Francis of Ryde and her fellows on the coast who profit from the need of those caught offshore, or in even worse circumstances: 'they are so far from taking any share in the distresses of mankind, or of being moved with any compassion for them, that they look upon them as blessings

72. Fielding, *Amelia*, 359. 73. Fielding, *Jonathan Wild*, 124.
74. Tom Keymer, *Richardson's* Clarissa *and the Eighteenth-Century Reader* (Cambridge: Cambridge University Press, 1992), 25.
75. Henry Fielding, *The Journal of a Voyage to Lisbon* (London: Chiswick Press, 1892), 121, 122.
76. Paulson, *Henry Fielding*, 322. 77. Fielding, *Voyage to Lisbon*, 94.

shower'd down from above; and which the more they improve to their own use, the greater is their gratitude and piety.'[78] Watt would have known this phenomenon of old. Another former prisoner recalled the 'exorbitant profit' made by prisoners who found themselves in better circumstances than others, and supposed that while no one would 'object to them making a degree of profit for their trouble...there is something immoral in their greed for exorbitant profit from their position of advantage over our helplessness'.[79]

This kind of entrepreneurship is a recurrent feature of Fielding's *Journal*. As he waits, both chair-bound and ship-bound, for wind enough to move the boat forward, Fielding finds that Kent boatmen take advantage of the ability to name their own prices for supplying passengers immobilized on their ships off the coast. Darker forms of exploitation are implied, however, by the 'monsters' who are 'triumphing... in the miseries of those, who are, in many circumstances at least, their fellow-creatures, and considering the distresses of a wretched seaman, from his being wrecked to his being barely wind-bound, as a blessing sent among them from above, and calling it by that blasphemous name'.[80] Perhaps social disorder is always lamentable when it is seen from above, Fielding's usual social perspective; it may, after all, be an ominous symptom of threat to one's own class privilege. What makes the *Journal* so affecting, though, is that Fielding is seeing disorder as if from below, having become through his sickness and fragility the underdog he had previously championed on more patrician principles. Hearing the watermen of Rotherhithe uproariously ridicule his failing body—disfigured by dropsy and paralysed by gout, Fielding knows that it is 'a spectacle of the highest horror'—Fielding describes the episode as 'a lively picture of that cruelty and inhumanity, in the nature of men, which I have often contemplated with concern; and which leads the mind into a train of very uncomfortable and melancholy thoughts'.[81]

The sobering conservatism of Fielding is not an uncritical acceptance of the hierarchical status quo. Nor is what emerges in the recollections of prisoners of war as they describe their painful efforts to remake a society in the camps any unreflective embrace of hierarchical discipline in the old style. On the contrary, memoirs describe how efforts by senior officers to cling to their old power and privileges were mockingly

78. Fielding, *Voyage to Lisbon*, 84.
79. Peek, *One Fourteenth*, 200–1.
80. Fielding, *Voyage to Lisbon*, 85.
81. Fielding, *Voyage to Lisbon*, 46.

nicknamed 'Aldershot of the jungle' and 'The Imperial War Museum'.[82] The prisoners' point is that solidarity requires discipline, and discipline commits officers to not pulling rank for privilege or asking for more than others have.

Against unthinking observance of hierarchy, submission to the social order for the collective good is 'necessary'—here Watt is ostensibly ventriloquizing Conrad—in 'a world where nobody works or accepts any social constraint willingly' (*C.* 111). Because, of course, things could have been much worse for Watt, as he explained in 'The Liberty of the Prison', because, while prisoners of war are typically taken individually and lost in the anonymous mass of prisoner-strangers, 'we had our own old social organization as some sort of basis for communal life'.[83] The deadly predicament of the Asian civilian labourers brought home every day to the Allied prisoners what was at stake: as one English prisoner recalled: 'With no organisation to bind them together, and no one to speak up for them, their society has disintegrated until nobody has the will to do anything.'[84]

But, if banding together was a strategy for literal survival, it was a strategy for psychological salvation too. 'Role-playing is safer than idleness', Alexander explained, 'and make-believe morale better than demoralisation'.[85] Watt also wrote of 'rather an innocent schoolboy world—the world of the public surface that we felt free to elaborate, rather than the inner private world that was still full of nameless fears'.[86] This was the mock society that Durnford and Greener described, with its recreational card games and churchgoing. The cost was that subjective feelings had to be subordinated or simply denied. 'Looking back I can see that there were whole ranges of emotion that were taboo,' Watt wrote, although of course he never elaborated what those emotions were.[87] We can infer something, perhaps, from his comments on Conrad: 'although the sceptical mind knows that all ideological structures are really illusions, they may in practice be necessary restraints upon human egoism, laziness, or despair' (*C.* 248).

82. Durnford, *Branch Line to Burma*, 44, 166. In an intriguing quantitative study, survival rates among US prisoners during the Second World War were found to decline the closer the camp environment corresponded to military hierarchies. Holderness and Pontiff, 'Hierarchies and the Survival of Prisoners', 1873–86.

83. Watt, 'The Liberty of the Prison', 519.

84. Peek, *One Fourteenth*, 252–3.

85. Alexander, *Sweet Kwai*, 72.

86. Watt, 'The Liberty of the Prison', 526–7.

87. Watt, 'The Liberty of the Prison', 527.

Adam Piette's important survey of British Second World War writing *Imagination at War* (1995) explicitly rules out consideration of prisoners of war, but Piette captures sharply the way in which those who lived through the period experienced the disparity between social and emotional life: 'The public stories stressed vital resistance, public heroism, stoic good humour; the private stories are stories about broken minds, anaesthetized feelings, deep depression and loss of any sense of value.'[88] One prisoner summed up how he had schooled his emotional habits in order to survive:

> Adapt, alter, redirect thoughts, suppress emotions, control temper, twist and distort your personality to accommodate circumstances forced upon you, to create a defensive shell, to be part of a bond of *togetherness* with those around you. For it was that bond, loyalty *to* each other and concern *for* each other, that forged a tough shield of mutual protection. Without it you were too vulnerable—you could simply fall apart.[89]

Watt's attitude is similarly utilitarian: that, when life itself is at stake, the 'inner private world' populated by 'nameless fears' assuredly cannot help you, whereas 'the world of the public surface' just might. The narrative equivalent is the cool, ironic distance of a Fielding as an antidote to what Richetti sums up as 'the interminable analytic sessions' of the psychological fiction that reached its first shattering apotheosis in *Clarissa*.[90] Rawson captures well this combination of self-suppression and deep feeling when he writes that 'things are not allowed to become unduly emotional, although we often know that Fielding feels very strongly indeed'. This is why, as McKillop said, Fielding is 'an easier novelist to live with'.

Modern Augustans, Modern Memory

'Fielding's plot invites the reader to detachment, and thence to conscious assessment,' Watt wrote in an essay looking back at *The Rise of the Novel* a decade later.[91] He views this tendency towards distanced evaluation

88. Adam Piette, *Imagination at War: British Fiction and Poetry 1939–1945* (London: Papermac, 1995), 5.
89. Peek, *One Fourteenth*, 666; emphasis in original.
90. Richetti, *The English Novel in History*, 122.
91. Watt, 'Serious Reflections on *The Rise of the Novel*', 15.

as a positive social force, despite the fact that it leaves Fielding's position open to the charge 'that it's conformist, cautious, cold; too much superego and too little id'.[92] This maps directly onto his prison-camp sense of 'the world of the public surface' as dismissal of and protection against 'the inner private world that was still full of nameless fears', as well as onto his more sceptical ruminations on institutional consciousness in Conrad, where he speculates that 'solidarity may be only the code of those whom experience has brought into an un-protesting conformity with the attitudes of their group' (*C.* 351). But the same accusations of coldness and conformism proved the underlying ground of his approval in an essay on the Augustans, where he praised their characteristic 'civic sense', their 'equable, independent, and wide-eyed self-command': they are 'skeptical, observant, worldly wise... rational, polite, controlled'.[93] Watt ends this essay with a major claim, but he articulates it only in a self-consciously anticlimactic style that mimics the restraint being described:

> Actually one of the constants in Augustan writing is a sense of the cost of preserving civilization. Deeply committed to social order, the Augustans made the necessary sacrifices with open eyes. Johnson and Pope would have agreed with [theologian] William Law when he wrote that 'our *Imaginations* and *Desires*... are the greatest Reality we have'. The public good, in their view, required man to discipline the impulses of his imagination and his passions.[94]

The claim initially suggests a reading of eighteenth-century culture through Freud, who, in the paragraph immediately prior, is said to 'have made us aware of how deeply traditional civilization arose from psychological and social repression'.[95] In *Beyond the Pleasure Principle*, Freud wrote of 'the instinctual repression upon which is based all that is most precious in human civilization'; in *Civilization and its Discontents*, he argued that 'it is impossible to overlook the extent to which civilization is built up upon a renunciation of instinct, how much it presupposes precisely the non-satisfaction... of powerful instincts'.[96] Watt is suggesting that you can care as deeply about the preservation of the social order as the eighteenth-century anti-individualists did

92. Watt, 'Serious Reflections on *The Rise of the Novel*', 19.
93. Ian Watt, 'The Augustan Age', in Watt, *The Literal Imagination*, 27, 27, 32.
94. Watt, 'The Augustan Age', 36; ellipsis in original.
95. Watt, 'The Augustan Age', 36.
96. Freud, *Beyond the Pleasure Principle*, 50. Freud, *Civilization and its Discontents*, 51–2.

only if you know from your own emotional reality what that social order is asking you to give up.

'The replacement of the power of the individual by the power of a community constitutes the decisive step of civilization,' Freud wrote.[97] Arguing against what he saw as the modern critical tendency to make too much of 'the more unsettling and nihilistic side of their vision' (*C.* 167), Watt wrote of the similarities between Conrad and Freud as contemporaries who were looking for a route out of the predicament they had identified:

> Freud had a much deeper belief in systematic thought than Conrad, but they shared much the same vision of how they should direct their moral energies: they saw that culture was insecurely based on repression and restraint, and yet what seemed most worth their effort was to promote a greater understanding of man's destructive tendencies, and at the same time support the modest countertruths on which civilisation depends. As against the more absolute negations of Rimbaud and Nietzsche, or the equally absolute transcendental affirmations of Dostoevsky or Yeats, both Freud and Conrad defend a practical social ethic based on their fairly similar reformulations of the Victorian trinity of work, duty, and restraint. (*C.* 166–7)

Notwithstanding his own lack of conviction about 'systematic thought' when it came to literature, all Watt's writing is shot through with a relatively uncritical acceptance of psychoanalysis in its broadest outlines, probably reflecting Freud's impact on the generation who came of age intellectually between the wars.[98] Still, Watt's renunciatory reading of the eighteenth century may have less to do with the diffusion of psychoanalysis than with the curious topicality that recent history had given the Augustans' worldly and ironic perspectives.

Like Watt a junior officer during the Second World War, Paul Fussell presents the closest comparison. Universally known in modern literary studies for his dark classic *The Great War and Modern Memory* (1975), he was, in fact, already a very distinguished scholar of Augustan literature before that, as the author or editor of numerous books on topics

97. Freud, *Civilization and Its Discontents*, 49.

98. Broad outlines, that is, because Watt was sceptical about more programmatic uses of psychoanalysis: on the one hand, 'we may agree that, out of the whole gamut of human behaviour in general, very little, if any, is wholly rational and conscious'; on the other hand, psychoanalytic criticism often entails 'the discovery of nonliteral meanings to support whatever conceptual apparatus is being applied', and 'you either believe in night journeys and primal scenes or you don't' (*C.* 239).

ranging from Samuel Johnson to eighteenth-century theories of prosody. But the book that helps to explain how he became so compelling a critic of modern war literature is his intensely sympathetic treatment of conservative irony in *The Rhetorical World of Augustan Humanism* (1965). To understand that 'rhetorical world', Fussell argued there, it is necessary to appreciate the death-haunted atmosphere that brought it into being, a pervasive sense 'of horror, and shock, and fear'.[99] Perhaps the ironic and civic stoicism of the Augustans felt newly timely for those who had experienced the Second World War: 'Indeed, the power and . . . the fury of Augustan humanist expression suggests ideas of actual wartime conditions,' and Fussell devotes a whole chapter to these writers' surprisingly insistent use of military metaphors.[100] 'The human being is essentially a failure,' Fussell paraphrases: 'He must operate as a social and public creature only because he is too frail and incomplete to exist by himself.'[101] Evident throughout the book is Fussell's sympathy with the fear and anxiety underlying the protective sociability of the Augustans, and their belief that 'the life of solitude is ultimately anti-human'.[102]

The veterans Fussell and Watt emphasize that Augustan writers thought they knew what anarchy looked like, and that these writers believed they were living through the breakdown of the once-accepted values and norms that kept society together. Even though he writes that many eighteenth-century fears were 'blown out of all proportion', J. Paul Hunter asks us to take them seriously nonetheless:

> They share the same urgent fear that something valuable (they are often not sure what) is being lost in the brave new world. Tradition is the most common name for it in belletristic texts, but other terms describe it equally well: family coherence, community values, cultural loyalty, shared ethical standards, human dignity, heritage, honor, integrity, continuity. It may be wise ultimately not to choose among these terms. All of them meant, to the persons who defended them then, much the same thing: a loss of familiarity most often expressed as the waning prestige of religion. Fading religious values may have been only a metaphor for a lost sense of balance or for a lost explanation of human history, and perhaps it does not matter much what we call either the loss or the fear.

99. Paul Fussell, *The Rhetorical World of Augustan Humanism: Ethics and Imagery from Swift to Burke* (Oxford: Clarendon Press, 1965), 290.
100. Fussell, *The Rhetorical World of Augustan Humanism*, 21. See the chapter titled 'Moral Warfare: Strategy and Tactics', 139–70.
101. Fussell, *The Rhetorical World of Augustan Humanism*, 53.
102. Fussell, *The Rhetorical World of Augustan Humanism*, 32.

But it is important that we take seriously the feelings themselves and allow dignity to the structure of belief that sponsored them, however we feel about the beliefs themselves.[103]

Watt's corresponding worries about individualism had no religious underpinning; in his unfinished final book he joked that the concern with the afterlife in the Don Juan story 'is rather uncongenial for those who, like myself, and Lord Chesterfield, make their main concern about death not "to be buried alive"' (*MMI* 115). Still, much of what Hunter says of the Augustans' beleaguered values—cultural continuity, shared moral norms, human dignity, heritage, and honour—would have resonated powerfully as the opposite of individualism.

These are the values that Watt found in Fielding, so he might well have been, as he professed, a 'Fielding-ite'. Alter writes that Fielding's 'literary method works on the tacit assumption of a community of values', but Fielding 'creates rather than reinforces shared outlooks, for Fielding is clearly aware that in his age the community of values, like the community of men, has lost much of the wholeness it may once have had'.[104] There is darkness and anger even in the sunniest of Fielding's novels. We see this in, for example, the emphasis on degradation and suffering in the ostensibly comic *Joseph Andrews*, where prospects of help from others are chronically uncertain. (Or: 'Common Charity, a F—t!' as Mrs Tow-wouse declares when she wishes to evict from his apparent deathbed the stripped and battered Joseph.[105]) In *Tom Jones*, perhaps, the most engagingly arranged of plots compensates for as well as attests to a fundamental sense of moral disorder, but it is still far distant from 'old Harry Fielding's hearty Englishness', as Alter sums up one common mid-century underestimate of this writer: 'all right for the casual entertainment of readers who relish foaming English ale, cheery English inns, plump and blushing English wenches, crackling hearthfires, mutton on the spit, and the occasional rousing interlude of a two-fisted free-for-all'.[106] Watt always took Fielding far more seriously than this. In his afterword to a 1966 reprint of *Joseph Andrews*, for example, we find that Fielding's Cervantic road narratives are not opportunities for good-hearted manly romping but, startlingly, 'a way of mirroring the full range of the world's selfishness, brutality, and stupidity'.[107]

103. Hunter, *Before Novels*, 243–4.
104. Alter, *Fielding and the Nature of the Novel*, 45.
105. Fielding, *Joseph Andrews*, 93.
106. Alter, *Fielding and the Nature of the Novel*, 4.
107. Ian Watt, 'On Reading *Joseph Andrews*', in Watt, *The Literal Imagination*, 118.

Because Alter was concerned with Fielding's technical importance, he found it noteworthy that 'Watt's desire to be fair-minded ultimately reduces him to praising Fielding in oddly nineteenth-century terms for his "wisdom"'.[108] But it is difficult to suppose that Watt would have found this a troubling complaint. This is not only because he treats Fielding 'as a great humanistic writer rather than as a novelist', as McKillop saw in his review of *The Rise of the Novel*, but because, and as Daniel Schwartz shrewdly noted in 1983, something much like wisdom was central to Watt's project as a critic.[109] With mocking apology, Watt told a 1978 lecture audience that he was 'properly ashamed to thus affront your sophistication with such fly-blown terms as wisdom and truth; but they are—and not very obscurely—part of my overt concern in *The Rise of the Novel*'.[110] 'Watt enacts in his criticism the argument that a literary critic must also be an experienced, mature, judicious observer of human behavior,' Schwartz writes: 'Watt judges behavior and motives from the stance of his own rational, humanistic, and egalitarian impulses'.[111]

From an altogether different perspective, David Hirsch had already noted this propensity to judge in *The Rise of the Novel*. His inexplicably bad-tempered 1969 essay 'The Reality of Ian Watt' denounces Watt first for misreading John Locke, and then for not needing Locke anyhow when what is 'real' depends finally on Watt's own judgement:

> when Watt comes to speak about realism in the novel he can speak of it only as a feeling or a belief or an intuition. That is to say that Watt, who represents himself as a wholly objective critic, is in truth a most subjective critic. This subjectivity is concealed beneath such stylistic subterfuges as authoritative expletives and declarations of reality, and by appeal to a supposedly universal emotional and intellectual response by a mysterious 'we'. But who has given Watt the authority to declare reality?[112]

Hirsch exaggerates on the 'supposedly universal', but he is entirely correct to suggest that Watt either presupposes or attempts to create a community of readers who will share his sense of what is plausible and

108. Alter, *Fielding and the Nature of the Novel*, 6.
109. Alan D. McKillop, '*The Rise of the Novel: Studies in Defoe, Richardson, and Fielding*, by Ian Watt', *Modern Philology*, 55/3 (February 1958), 209.
110. Watt, 'Flat-Footed', 62.
111. Daniel R. Schwartz, 'The Importance of Ian Watt's *The Rise of the Novel*', *Journal of Narrative Technique*, 13/2 (Spring 1983), 66.
112. David H. Hirsch, 'The Reality of Ian Watt', *Critical Quarterly*, 2/2 (Summer 1969), 178.

acceptable. Yet it is hard to imagine Watt finding this a wounding line of attack, given his declared conviction that 'literary criticism is essentially a social rather than a philosophical activity'.[113]

In conclusion, the 'wisdom'—as he was perfectly happy to call it—of writers like Fielding mattered to Watt as an antidote to what he saw as an increasingly impoverished individualism. On the famous opening of Rousseau's *Confessions* ('Whether Nature did well or ill in breaking the mould in which she formed me...'), he recounted: 'I once heard an eminent devotee of Augustan literature comment on the passage, "Isn't it enough to ruin your whole day?"' (*MMI* 177). 'Since the brave days of the Romantics', he wrote elsewhere, 'the idea of existence as essentially an escape by the individual to realise his private dream had been widely diffused and progressively debased both in literature and in life' (*C.* 52). His anti-Romanticism is a distaste for 'the developing imperatives of Romantic individualism, with its Faustian ideal of absolute liberation from religious, social, and ethical norms in the pursuit of experience' (*C.* 163), and, above all, for the dissemination of 'antirational and anti-collective attitudes'.[114]

Of course, it is not a controversial claim to suggest that the main thread running through Watt's scholarly career is the relationship between individualism and the novel. But he was no cheerleader for individualism, and became increasingly outspoken about what he considered its politically and socially incapacitating effects. Although they were published at spaces of roughly twenty years apart, his three monographs *The Rise of the Novel, Conrad in the Nineteenth Century*, and *Myths of Modern Individualism* were all conceived at the beginning of his career. Research for the Conrad book had begun in 1955, two years prior to the publication of *The Rise of the Novel*, although it was published twenty-two years after it, while the first essay on Robinson Crusoe as a 'myth' of modern individualism alongside Faust, Don Juan, and Don Quixote, the subject of the book left unrevised at Watt's final illness, was published back in 1951. If one reads the books in the order of their writing, though, it is impossible not to notice their increasingly forthright pessimism about the socially damaging effects of individualism, and these apprehensions explain better than anything his admiration for Fielding, the great misfit in *The Rise of the Novel.*

113. Todorov, *Literature and its Theorists*, 116.
114. Watt, 'The Humanities on the River Kwai', 234.

Perhaps, Watt surmised, 'writers of great literature' all believe in 'various traditional moral values, such as selflessness, courage, resolution, kindness, and intellectual realism'.[115] In *Conrad in the Nineteenth Century*, he wrote of Conrad's concern with the 'values of courage, tenacity, honour, responsibility and abnegation' (*C.* 7), and argued that his novels show 'a moral strength and sanity that remains unrivalled in the literature of our century' (*C.* 25). Finally, he wondered in the coda to his unrevised final work if the only redeeming cultural values to set against the 'current perversions of modern individualism' might 'all turn out to be anti-individualist: a sense of history, an absolute ethic of right and wrong, awareness of the rights and feelings of others, discipline . . . ' (*MMI* 271).

115. Ian Watt, *Joseph Conrad: Nostromo* (Cambridge: Cambridge University Press, 1988), 79.

5

Realist Criticism and the Mid-Century Novel

'The eighteenth-century novel is formally most like our own, under comparable pressures and uncertainties, and it was in the deepening understanding of the relations between individuals and societies that the form actually matured.'

Raymond Williams, *The Long Revolution* (1961)[1]

'And so strong was the general air of collapse that, when the task of the novel resumed in post-war conditions, it resembled the task of beginning all over again.'

Malcolm Bradbury, *The Modern British Novel* (1993)[2]

Writing in an issue of the journal *Eighteenth-Century Fiction* from 2000 devoted to *The Rise of the Novel*, W. B. Carnochan attributed Watt's staying power to the fact that this is 'a book people can actually read'.[3] Carnochan returns to Watt's much-annotated typescript pages in order to describe the labour that produced his unusual clarity, as if to say that this work on the writer's part is as essential for the production of readable criticism in the twenty-first century as it was in the 1950s. Three years later Gerald Graff named Watt among the critics from whom academic novices should take courage: 'scholars who wrote with lucidity and wit' and reached 'the top of the profession'

1. Raymond Williams, *The Long Revolution* (Peterborough, Ontario: Broadview Press, 2001), 305.
2. Malcolm Bradbury, *The Modern British Novel* (London: Penguin, 1993), 221.
3. W. B. Carnochan, '"A Matter *Discutable*": *The Rise of the Novel*', *Eighteenth-Century Fiction*, 12/2 (2000), 181.

without ever sacrificing the approachability of their writing.'[4] Needless to say, Carnochan's and Graff's emphasis on this aspect of Watt's criticism implies a judgement on the unreadability of much academic prose.

But if there is a transhistorical drive behind their use of Watt as exemplar, where good scholarly writing from the 1950s remains recognizably good writing still, there is also an importantly historical dimension to Watt's style. In *The Rise of the Novel* an interest in realism gets advanced at the level of critical style by a kind of writing analogous to Watt's own definitions of realism in fiction, 'formal realism' and 'realism of assessment'. Watt's critical writing is precise and concrete, but it also appeals in a worldly way to the values (in Daniel Schwartz's words, 'rational, humanistic, and egalitarian') that Watt assumes his readers share. Looking back at the mid-century, we find among critical and creative writers alike a pronounced discomfort with what they saw as verbal abstraction in the service of mystification. Philosopher Colin McGinn writes that a 'new mood' unites mid-century writers with the British logical positivists, with their 'clarity, tough-mindedness, descriptive accuracy, attention to linguistic fact, down-to-earthness, anti-obscurantism, celebration of the ordinary, respect for common sense, hatred of pretentious nonsense'.[5] Meanwhile, some critics felt that something had gone wrong even in the language of humanistic enquiry. Graham Hough worried that literary complexity had 'often been met by making the language of criticism itself as impenetrable to ordinary modes of apprehension as the language of poetry is alleged to be. To much of what has been said about poetical discourse in the present century it is impossible to attach any meaning at all.'[6] Watt made a similar point about 'ordinary modes of apprehension' when he emphasized the importance of accessibility in criticism to his undergraduates at Stanford: 'Literature, unlike the mysteries of faith and physics, is not invisible to the unassisted naked eye. On the contrary, it is visibly there; it would still be there if there were no professors to teach it.'[7]

William Empson had also studied with I. A. Richards at Cambridge, but, although Richards influenced them both as critics, a different aspect

4. Gerald Graff, *Clueless in Academe: How Schooling Obscures the Life of the Mind* (New Haven: Yale University Press, 2003), 124.
5. Colin McGinn, 'Philosophy and Literature in the 1950s: The Rise of the "Ordinary Bloke"', in Zachary Leader (ed.), *The Movement Reconsidered: Essays on Larkin, Amis, Gunn, Davie, and their Contemporaries* (Oxford: Oxford University Press, 2009), 130.
6. Hough, *Image and Experience*, 123.
7. Watt, 'Writing about Literature', 3.

of Richards's work resonated in their writing for decades, Richards's advocacy of Basic English. Neither Watt nor Empson was ever an actual believer, but it had a kind of ironized utility for them both as a touchstone. While Basic was meant to become a standard point of entry for English as a Second Language, many of Empson's more biting pronouncements are concerned with native speakers of an advanced kind: writers and critics. 'Practice in turning their own stuff into Basic really would be the kindest education in style you could give them, even if it made them realise how often they are talking nonsense,' he wrote in an essay for a 1973 Festschrift for Richards: 'To pretend that it could possibly make them use the language worse than they do already sounds to me farce.'[8] Recalling the link between clear thinking and clear writing on which his wartime BBC colleague George Orwell had based 'Politics and the English Language', Empson argued that 'to get a thing said fully in Basic may be a training in thought', and that for English speakers to know Basic 'might make them a bit less easily deceived by nonsense written in bloated English'.[9] In 1954, he declared his intent to Janet Adam Smith, literary editor of the *New Statesman*: 'I have to read so much Mandarin English Prose now, especially in literary criticism, and am so accustomed to being shocked by its emptiness, that I feel I must do otherwise at all costs.'[10]

Watt's essays give an even stronger sense of his commitment to the plain style. Critical writing should convey 'the notion that it is the product neither of a card index nor of a divine oracle, but of a putative human being communicating with other human beings'; and there ought to be more 'exceptions to the rule that "scholarly" usually means "unreadable" and "readable" usually means "wrong"'.[11] In another essay he joked that, although 'all more or less specialised pursuits have their own vocabularies; plumbers make a nice distinction between a coupling and a union', 'the vocabulary of criticism should be as common sense as possible in its attempt to achieve clarity and accessibility of statement':

8. William Empson, 'The Hammer's Ring', in Empson, *Argufying*, 221.
9. William Empson, 'Basic and Communication', in William Empson, *The Strengths of Shakespeare's Shrew: Essays, Memoirs and Reviews*, ed. John Haffenden (London: Bloomsbury, 2015), 164. William Empson, 'Basic English and the Modern World', in *The Strengths of Shakespeare's Shrew*, 175.
10. William Empson, *Selected Letters*, ed. John Haffenden (Oxford: Oxford University Press, 2006), 222.
11. Watt, 'Serious Reflections on *The Rise of the Novel*', 5, 6.

The effect of long words is a little like that which Fowler attributes to the exact pronunciation of French words in English conversation: 'the greater its success as a *tour de force*, the greater its failure as a step in the conversational progress; for your collocutor, aware that he could not have done it himself, has his attention distracted whether he admires or is humiliated.'

Any literary criticism whose effect is to humiliate the reader (and I've seen some cases where that seemed its only intention), seems to me to defeat its primary purpose, which is, I take it, to be part of a conversation among lovers of literature. In that sense, the critic's concern for a common orientation with his reader towards literature should produce a style of discourse which is fraternal; that is, discourse whose rhetoric implies the common and equal possession of shared interests and feelings.[12]

To write accessibly is sociable good manners, and a vote of confidence in literary criticism as a place where the possibility of democratic consensus can, if only rhetorically, be assumed.

One defining quality, then, of a body of mid-century criticism is its commitment to transparency in fields otherwise inclined towards 'pretentious jargon or bogus sentiment', in the contemporary words of the great émigré art critic Ernst Gombrich: 'I have striven sincerely to avoid these pitfalls and to use plain language even at the risk of sounding casual or unprofessional.'[13] As in *The Rise of the Novel*, the critical style follows the theme in Gombrich's classic *The Story of Art* (1950). This is, among other things, a book about ('formal') realism and empiricism, and Gombrich unmistakably approves of those artists who 'tried to explore the visible world', arguing that the major artistic watersheds came when the artist 'decided to have a look for himself instead of following the old prescription' and 'began to rely on what he saw' rather than on pre-existing traditions.[14] (Watt may not have known this argument when he was writing *The Rise of the Novel*, but he cites it in *Conrad in the Nineteenth Century* (C. 171).)

For these writers, critical language goes wrong when it is merely ventriloquizing pre-existing formulae and feelings, Gombrich's 'pretentious

12. Watt, 'Flat-Footed', 68.
13. E. H. Gombrich, *The Story of Art* (London: Phaidon, 2006), 7.
14. Gombrich, *The Story of Art*, 377, 66, 67. Obviously much more could be said about the Jewish–German Gombrich and the 1940s. See, for example, the final chapter of his classic children's book *A Little History of the World*, in which he recalls his experiences in anti-Semitic Vienna, his war work in England translating German broadcasts into English, and his realization that the Holocaust had actually happened. E. H. Gombrich, *A Little History of the World*, trans. Caroline Mustill (New Haven: Yale University Press, 2005), 273–84.

jargon or bogus sentiment'. These second-hand descriptions were what Orwell denounced as 'readymade' language in his classic denunciation of writing produced not by 'picking out words for the sake of their meaning', but by 'gumming together long strips of words which have already been set in order by someone else'.[15] Most famously, Orwell cast political writing as the truly dangerous violator of everyday referential norms, but in the same essay he also identified 'art criticism and literary criticism' as academic disciplines culpable for whole bodies of writing in which 'it is normal to come across long passages which are almost completely lacking in meaning.'[16]

So this chapter describes how the 'plain style' became so important at mid-century, and asks why a hyper-referential realism should have entered criticism in so self-conscious and sustained a way in exactly the same years as it dominated Britain's literary fiction. Thinking about Watt's writing in a specifically literary context—in a period when criticism could imagine, even assume, a non-academic readership—helps us to see what was unique to the literary conditions of the mid-century. It offers a different way into a critical topic that has been familiar to scholars of twentieth-century fiction since the 1960s: the so-called return to realism in the novels of the 1940s and 1950s. Up to this point, I have been treating Watt's criticism the way we ordinarily treat creative rather than critical writing, unpacking the biographical and historical contexts that helped to make it possible; this chapter reads Watt's concern with realism—qua transparency, concreteness, empirical observation, and the appeal to normative values—explicitly in the context of his British contemporaries' work in the novel.

The Return of the 'Real'

That British fiction after the war was characterized by a 'return to realism' was first argued in Rubin Rabinovitz's influential 1967 study *The Reaction against Experiment in the English Novel, 1950–60*, and the claim was shored up by numerous surveys of what up until the early twenty-first century was easily the least critically fashionable phase of modern

15. George Orwell, 'Politics and the English Language', in *The Complete Works of George Orwell*, xvii, ed. Peter Davison assisted by Ian Angus and Sheila Davison (London: Secker & Warburg, 1998), 426.
16. Orwell, 'Politics and the English Language', 424–5.

British writing. Bernard Bergonzi, for example, substantially echoed Rabinovitz's view in *The Situation of the Novel* (1970). Here, the post-war novel's characteristic realism is less a positive choice than a symptom of depletion: the novelist 'has inherited a form whose principal characteristic is novelty, or stylistic dynamism, and yet nearly everything possible to be achieved has already been done'.[17] (Perhaps tellingly, only a few pages earlier Bergonzi takes exception to what he considers Watt's overemphasis in *The Rise of the Novel* on 'a relation between the novel and philosophical empiricism'.[18]) Bergonzi offered a more enthusiastic account of early post-war fiction when he looked back in *Wartime and Aftermath* (1993), however, and in his survey of the modern British novel published in the same year, Malcolm Bradbury argued that the mid-century novel had certainly indicated 'a return to an older concept of fiction, to realism, materialism, empiricism', although he thought earlier critics had underestimated the extent to which realism had been a feature of modern British fiction all along.[19]

As the literally negative characterization of realism in Rabinowitz's title suggests—'the reaction against experiment' makes realism merely a refusal of something else—critics have often understood the assertively realist strand of mid-century writing as fundamentally reactionary, a movement (or, indeed, The Movement) reflecting a widespread sense among writers of the 1950s that modernist fiction had inflated the importance of the inner life at the expense of the social and material world. In the wider European context, this argument is most familiar from Georg Lukács's 'The Ideology of Modernism' (1957), a document itself so comprehensively of its time that its denunciation of modernist individualism might not be wholly reducible to the politics of the Iron Curtain. Without minimizing the importance of the backlash against modernism as such (or, more precisely, against a radically antisocial and obscurantist modernism of the mid-century's symptomatic exaggeration), we might supplement that canonical story by considering how the period around the Second World War made realism not merely the customary generational revolt against immediate literary predecessors or simply a default position for second-tier novelists, but a positive and self-conscious decision.

17. Bernard Bergonzi, *The Situation of the Novel* (London: Macmillan, 1970), 19.
18. Bergonzi, *The Situation of the Novel*, 15.
19. Bradbury, *The Modern British Novel*, 279, 281.

The mid-century re-energizing of realism obviously touches on matters of primarily literary-historical interest such as the relationship between mid-century writing and the end of modernism, but it had considerable moral and political as well as literary urgency in its own time. Although one could disagree with sociolinguist Deborah Cameron's attribution of Movement writers' prescriptivist attitudes to language to the socially insecure conformism arising from their non-elite backgrounds—the 'verbal hygiene' she describes demonstrably pre-existed and exceeded the Movement—it is certainly true at mid-century that 'putting language to rights becomes a surrogate for putting the world to rights'.[20] Anxieties about language in this period are substantially anxieties about something else. Even the attack on modernism is frequently a way of articulating fundamentally political worries, motivated by a war-haunted feeling that modernist individualism had come to look less like the emancipation it had once promised than a validation of debilitating atomization. 'We live, as we dream—alone,' Conrad's Marlow had announced in a famous line from *Heart of Darkness*, but, as Watt pointed out, surely no writer had tried as strenuously as Conrad to mitigate the condition he had diagnosed.[21] I have already quoted Watt's claim that 'the dominating question in Conrad' is 'alienation, yes, but how do we get out of it?'

By the late 1940s, individualization is represented as an imprisonment—as in the title of Patrick Hamilton's tragicomic *The Slaves of Solitude* (1947). In a boarding house in the middle of the war, the Nazi-sympathizing Mr Thwaites and his German housemate Vicky Kugelmann bait the novel's intelligent and likable spinster heroine almost to the point of nervous collapse. What is most telling about *The Slaves of Solitude* is how explicitly it ties social fracture to problems of language, for Hamilton's novel is primarily concerned with what John Mepham identified as 'bad talk'.[22] The chief weapon of Miss Roach's tormenters is their peculiar idiolect: they can speak only in phrasings that are sometimes excruciatingly banal, littered with ersatz medievalisms and obsolete slang, and sometimes ominously oblique and insinuating.

20. Deborah Cameron, '"The Virtues of Good Prose": Verbal Hygiene and the Movement', in Leader (ed.), *The Movement Reconsidered*, 142.
21. Conrad, *Heart of Darkness*, 33.
22. John Mepham, 'Varieties of Modernism, Varieties of Incomprehension: Patrick Hamilton and Elizabeth Bowen', in Marina MacKay and Lyndsey Stonebridge (eds), *British Fiction after Modernism: The Novel at Mid-Century* (Basingstoke: Palgrave, 2007), 67.

'Be sporty, old thing... You must learn to be sporty, Miss Prude,' spurts Vicki in the colloquialisms of twenty years earlier, as she flirts with Miss Roach's American serviceman admirer.[23] Meanwhile, Mr Thwaites's archaisms keep sliding from merely foolish and irritating to aggressive: 'And what of my Lady of the Roach?', he asks Miss Roach about her plans for the day: 'She goeth, perchance, unto the coffee-house... there to partake of the noxious brown fluid with her continental friends?'[24] Importantly, Miss Roach, the 'English Miss', as the bullies nickname her, in a slight against her supposed lack of sophistication, is not only a good liberal humanist and committed social democrat but the only major character in the novel whose words mean no more nor less than they are intended to mean. Instructively, the linguistically fastidious Miss Roach is an assistant in a publishing house, and words are her work.

Much of Hamilton's fiction is concerned with misuses of language. In his oddball pre-war satire *Impromptu in Moribundia* (1939), the inhabitants of the planet Moribundia think only in the language of advertising, while the grotesque comedy of *Mr Stimpson and Mr Gorse* (1952) depends substantially on the unrelieved awfulness of the characters' witlessly automatized verbal mannerisms. The novel's funniest set pieces include a colonel's gullible and snobbish widow, besotted by the conman Gorse, writing in her diary in a pseudo-literary style ('Whither shall I turn? What woman, ever, was in such woeful or wildering pass? Shall I or shall I not? Do I or do I not? Yes or no? Aye or Nay?') and a retired Army Major (Staff) attempting to compose his annual Armistice poem: 'Mention of Passchendaele, he felt, would be most inspiring... Next to Passchendaele, the Major was tremendously anxious to use Ypres. But here, when it came to rhyming, he was totally stumped.'[25] But it is in his novels set during the war that Hamilton outlines with diagrammatic clarity the mapping of politics on to verbal style that will dominate the early post-war period: bad speech is opaque, and it goes with fascist politics, while good speech is precise and unambiguous, and a reliable index of authenticity and political intelligence.

The Nazi politics of the German Vicki Kugelmann are implied rather than definitively shown—a *Kugel* is a bullet—and Mr Thwaites's

23. Patrick Hamilton, *The Slaves of Solitude* (New York: New York Review of Books, 2007), 129.
24. Hamilton, *The Slaves of Solitude*, 66.
25. Patrick Hamilton, *Mr Stimpson and Mr Gorse*, in Patrick Hamilton, *The Gorse Trilogy* (London: Black Spring, 2007), 435, 287.

Nazi sympathies are unambiguous. In Hamilton's wartime *Hangover Square* (1941), too, the most verbally impenetrable character, the narcissistic Netta, is a fascist sympathizer. What Hamilton's fiction shows is verbal expression going politically wrong: language becomes second-hand mannerism; it comes unmoored from ordinary common-sense meanings not for modernism's exuberantly defamiliarizing aesthetic effects, but rather to advance bullying political ends. The transparency of language has become a categorically new interest, and what happens to verbal communication in Hamilton's claustrophobic wartime pubs and boarding houses is, his novels imply, merely mimicking what is happening in the political world outside.

In this insistence on a link between bad speech and unspeakable politics, the under-read Hamilton is a wholly representative mid-century figure. He is among those novelists whose insistence on realist concreteness in the early post-war period can be seen as a way of dramatizing and contradicting the willed illegibility of war language, a particularly urgent matter in the new contexts provided not only by totalitarianism but also by the ugly and obscuring jargon of the democracies that fought them. Hamilton's own realist narrative style, with his deployment of a decisive and knowing narrator whose ideological and moral perspectives are always both legible and legitimate, suggests a way out of the linguistic ordeals his heroes and heroines are forced to undergo. While we are privy to and sympathize with the characters' inner lives and can reconstruct their almost journalistically specific environments as a result of the kind of circumstantial detail Watt cast as the hallmark of 'formal realism', Hamilton's perhaps outdated-seeming replay of what Watt called 'realism of assessment' means that we are never subjected to the protagonists' uncertainties about what the other characters are up to.

Some writers' responses, then, to the misuses of language—the development of perniciously anti-referential forms of language—were not portentous declarations about the difficulties of articulation but a renewal of realism, with its drive towards clarification and its belief in the possibility of rational communication. The effort to repair what these writers understood to be a war-broken relationship between words and things dominated mid-century prose. Particularly among those whose victimization had been abetted by fraudulent speech, notions of the inevitability of communicative failure seemed a gratuitous betrayal of their experience. 'According to a theory fashionable during those years, which to me seems frivolous and irritating, "incommunicability" supposedly was an inevitable ingredient, a life sentence inherent to the human condition,' Primo Levi wrote in *The Drowned and the Saved*: 'To say that it is impossible to communicate is false; one always can.'[26] 'Modern intellectuals quarrel a great deal about their communication difficulties and in the process talk a lot of pure nonsense, which would better remain unsaid,' wrote former political prisoner Jean Améry.[27]

Perhaps writers like Hamilton have fallen into obscurity because after modernism they might look exceedingly old-fashioned, as if they were trying to channel Austen in entirely the wrong century. Nevertheless, we might see them instead as the writers most responsive to the conditions of their post-war time. This pressing new attention to problems of reference means that Bradbury's virtually *Stunde Null* version of the mid-century British novel is nowhere near as extravagant as it initially sounds: 'so strong was the general air of collapse that, when the task of the novel resumed in post-war conditions, it resembled the task of beginning all over again.' Small wonder, then, that Raymond Williams should have speculated at mid-century that 'the eighteenth-century novel is formally most like our own'.

Prose and the Problem of Truthfulness

In the age of totalitarianism the possibility of language attaining a kind of independence acquired darker associations than it had for modernists in the 1920s. As the interwar period goes on, attention to the materiality of language mutates into a pervasive fear that language is somehow rotting, and, in its decay, is attaining zombie autonomy of a more ominous kind. This feeling of a threatened language animated many discussions of the endangered literary artist. In his Munich-era *Enemies of Promise* (1938), Cyril Connolly argued that the degradation of political discourse was destroying the integrity of linguistic reference. In terminology shadowed by the economic troubles of the 1930s, he singled out journalism as a major culprit in the depreciation (his metaphor) of language:

> The perfect use of language is that in which every word carries the meaning that it is intended to, no less and no more. In this verbal exchange Fleet Street is a kind of Bucket Shop which unloads words on the public for less than they

26. Levi, *The Drowned and the Saved*, 88–9. 27. Améry, *At the Mind's Limits*, 4–5.

are worth and in consequence the more honest literary bankers, who try to use their words to mean what they say, who are always 'good for' the expressions they employ, find their currency constantly depreciating.[28]

Distinguishing good writing from bad is a matter of the relative degrees of ownership the author takes over his or her words; as all economic crises remind us, it is because economic disasters are also social and moral ones that the metaphor works so effectively to speak of language in relation to our responsibilities to people we cannot personally know. Among the most treacherous of Connolly's 'enemies of promise' was the attraction of his generation's writers to political activism; the politically minded writer must avoid getting dragged into creativity-sapping activities in committees and on platforms. The writer's political mission, Connolly argued instead, is as 'a lie-detector who exposes the fallacies in words and ideals before half the world is killed for them'.[29]

Connolly's friend Christopher Isherwood had made a similar point about what he considered the contemporary depreciation of language in *Mr Norris Changes Trains* (1935), the first of his novels set during Germany's catastrophic collapse. The vocabulary of economic crisis represents both a public language legitimizing political dishonesty and an unaccountable culture industry that licenses political irresponsibility:

The murder reporters and the jazz-writers had inflated the German language beyond recall. The vocabulary of newspaper invective (traitor, Versailles-lackey, murder-swine, Marx-crook, Hitler-swamp, Red-pest) had come to resemble, through excessive use, the formal phraseology of politeness employed by the Chinese. The word *Liebe*, soaring from the Goethe standard, was no longer worth a whore's kiss. *Spring, moonlight, youth, roses, girl, darlings, heart, May*: such was the miserably devalued currency dealt in by the authors of all those tangoes, waltzes, and fox-trots which advocated the private escape.[30]

Here, the perceived emptying-out of language haunts both political engagement ('traitor, Versailles-lackey...') and the attempt to escape from politics ('Spring, moonlight...'). Among all the novelists of the 1930s, Isherwood has always been admired for the conversational lucidity of his prose—'a camera with its shutter open', as in the famous opening of *Goodbye to Berlin* (1939)—and in comments like these it

28. Connolly, *Enemies of Promise*, 10–11. 29. Connolly, *Enemies of Promise*, 138.
30. Christopher Isherwood, *Mr. Norris Changes Trains*, in *The Berlin Novels* (London: Vintage, 1999), 108.

becomes clear why the pursuit of transparency was so high a priority for him.[31]

Or we might call it the pursuit of 'purity of diction', after the title of a symptomatic mid-century critical work by an author whom Watt as departmental chair appointed to a professorship at Stanford. (As an undergraduate he had brought Isherwood to speak to his College literary society: decisions made in the course of institutional life betray our own critical preferences and prejudices as visibly as our writing does.) A book about the undervalued grace of eighteenth-century English poetry, Donald Davie's *Purity of Diction in English Verse* (1952) argues that 'pure diction can be found where a poet has tried to revivify the dead metaphors of studied conversation or artless prose'.[32] In keeping with the conversational ordinariness of much mid-century literary language, Davie shows eighteenth-century poetry taking on qualities of good prose. This is prose in a descriptive rather than a pejorative sense, following what Northrop Frye, also writing in the 1950s, called 'the antique snobbery about the superiority of metre which has given "prosy" the meaning of tedious and "prosaic" the meaning of pedestrian'.[33] But prose can have positive connotations as well. We might think here of dissident Milan Kundera's admiring definition of 'prose' as denoting 'the concrete, everyday, corporeal nature of life', or Margaret Doody's praise for this 'ultimate literary vernacular, the expression of the demotic, the democratic'.[34]

Both Kundera and Doody mean 'prose' in the ordinary sense—they are writing about the novel—but draw upon the word's richer range of associations: the empirical, the contemporary, the material, the lived, the everyday, and the un-sublime. This is the kind of writing that dominates the late 1940s and 1950s in an assertively politicized way. According to Orwell, now perhaps the period's most canonical spokesperson, his was an age that not only 'forces' politics upon writers, but in doing so 'raises in a new way the problem of truthfulness'.[35] To Orwell's

31. Christopher Isherwood, *Goodbye to Berlin*, in *The Berlin Novels*, 243.
32. Donald Davie, *Purity of Diction in English Verse* (London: Chatto & Windus, 1952), 32.
33. Northrop Frye, *Anatomy of Criticism: Four Essays* (Princeton: Princeton University Press, 1990), 71.
34. Milan Kundera, *The Curtain: An Essay in Seven Parts*, trans. Linda Asher (New York: HarperCollins, 2008), 8. Doody, *The True Story of the Novel*, 187.
35. George Orwell, 'Why I Write', in *The Complete Works of George Orwell*, xviii, ed. Peter Davison assisted by Ian Angus and Sheila Davison (London: Secker & Warburg, 1998), 320.

mind, political and literary imperatives were inextricably connected under the banner of truthfulness. Had he been writing in an earlier era, Orwell supposed, he could have been the kind of writer only too ready to surrender to the strictly aesthetic pleasures of language—of the 'ornate' and the 'merely descriptive' for their own sake—but 'as it is, I have been forced into becoming a sort of pamphleteer'.[36]

'The art of prose is bound up with the only régime in which prose has meaning, democracy,' Jean-Paul Sartre announced in an obscure but historically indicative declaration of 1948: 'When one is threatened, the other is too.'[37] For Sartre, 'prose' means truthful articulation of a kind that cannot exist under a dictatorship; and perhaps the combination of verbal obscurity here with his own blind spots about dictatorship ironically confirms his point. In any case, the fundamental distinction he draws is not the usual one between prose and poetry—Sartre explicitly exempts poetry from discussions of political writing—but between prose and lying. Less cryptically, he explained that 'prose is, in essence, utilitarian', because 'its substance is by nature significative—that is, the words are first of all not objects but designations for objects'.[38]

'The solid world exists, its laws do not change', Winston Smith reminds himself: 'Stones are hard, water is wet, objects unsupported fall toward the earth's centre.'[39] In his famous discussion of the corrosive effects of power on language, Orwell argued that to write well is to think well, and that clarity of expression 'is a necessary first step towards political regeneration'; with that in mind, it was high time to take a stand against the 'swindles and perversions' of bad writing.[40] His examples

36. Orwell, 'Why I Write', 319.
37. Jean-Paul Sartre, *What Is Literature? and Other Essays* (Cambridge, MA: Harvard University Press, 1988), 69.
38. Sartre, *What Is Literature?*, 34, 35. The tendentiousness of this 1940s figuration of the prose/poetry distinction is exposed by how easily it was reversed. 'A poem is, so to speak, a democratic state, whereas a prose discourse—mathematical, scientific, ethical, or practical and vernacular—is a totalitarian state. The intention of a democratic state is to perform the work of state as effectively as it can perform it, subject to one reservation of conscience: that it will not despoil its members, the citizens, of the free exercise of their own private and independent characters. But the totalitarian state is interested solely in being effective, and regards the citizens as no citizens at all; that is, regards them as functional members whose existence is totally defined by their allotted contributions to its ends; it has no use for their private characters, and therefore no provision for them' (John Crowe Ransom, 'Criticism as Pure Speculation', in Donald A Stauffer (ed.), *The Intent of the Critic* (Princeton: Princeton University Press, 1941), 108).
39. George Orwell, *Nineteen Eighty-Four* (New York: Signet, 1977), 81.
40. Orwell, 'Politics and the English Language', 421, 425.

of bad writing are obviously expressive of the totalitarian 1940s: real verbs such as '*break, stop, spoil, mend, kill*' should replace 'pretentious diction' along the lines of '*exploit, utilize, eliminate, liquidate*' in order to say what is being done to real bodies.[41] In *The Abolition of Man* (1943), C. S. Lewis—a writer to whom Orwell had a predictably conflicted attitude—had already noted the connection between contemporary euphemism and the transformation of human beings into un-persons: 'Once we killed bad men: now we liquidate unsocial elements.'[42] His famous list of rules includes avoiding cliché and periphrasis, but for Orwell the most important quality of good prose is concreteness, a quality most dangerously lost from political writing. 'As soon as certain topics are raised, the concrete melts into the abstract.'[43]

'The concrete melts into the abstract': Watt offered advice of exactly the same kind as Orwell's for wireless listeners in the winter of 1950–1. Instructively enough, Watt's series of Forces broadcasts on the BBC's Light Programme was titled 'Plain English'. In a talk with the altogether leading title of 'Concrete or Abstract?' broadcast early in 1951, Watt summed up a typical lesson: 'I said there were two things to watch in abstract words; one was—watch yourself; the other—watch other people when they use them. But there's another—and it's the most important of all. Don't use them at all unless you really have to.'[44] He returned to the need for absolute precision in the final talk, 'Every Word Has a Meaning'. 'There's nothing more annoying than people who always exaggerate, always use a stronger word than they should. Using too weak a word may be not quite so bad; but its [*sic*] worth avoiding all the same.'[45]

Watt's dislike of overblown language was so total that it compelled the one substantial criticism he made of Conrad. Conrad may have tried to convey 'not only the immediacies of his subject, but their perspective in the whole tradition of civilization', but 'the actual prose in

41. Orwell, 'Politics and the English Language', 423–4.
42. C. S. Lewis, *The Abolition of Man* (Las Vegas: Lits, 2010), 43. Orwell deplored the politically reactionary thrust of Lewis's Christian apologism, but nonetheless admired his dystopian novel *That Hideous Strength* (1945), which fictionalizes ideas from *The Abolition of Man*.
43. Orwell, 'Politics and the English Language', 423.
44. Ian Watt, 'Concrete or Abstract?' Forces Educational Broadcast, 1951. This talk was broadcast on 23 January 1951 on the BBC's Light Programme. Stanford University Special Collections, SC401-ACCN 1990-131, Box 41, Folder 'BBC: Past'.
45. Ian Watt, 'Every Word Has a Meaning', Stanford University Special Collections, SC401-ACCN 1990-131, Box 41, Folder 'BBC: Past'.

which some of the loftier elements of this perspective are conveyed, however, is a good deal more grandiloquent than we can today happily stomach'; he complains in the same essay of Conrad's 'somewhat portentous magniloquence'.[46] Not at all surprisingly, Watt admired the 'fine intensity' with which Orwell 'demonstrated the necessary connections among literature, language, and the collective life', and like many writers of this moment shared Orwell's scepticism about the social unaccountability of linguistic grandeur.[47] 'It is better to renounce revealed truths, even if they exalt us by their splendor', wrote his contemporary Levi, in a passage that reminds us of the relationship between his career as a writer and his background in applied science: 'It is better to content oneself with other more modest and less exciting truths, those one acquires painfully, little by little and without shortcuts, with study, discussion, and reasoning, those that can be verified and demonstrated.'[48]

Verification and demonstration reflect attitudes toward the external world and they are also ways of talking about it. In *Politics and the Novel*, a work exactly contemporary with *The Rise of the Novel*, Irving Howe wrote of *Nineteen Eighty-Four* that the concrete and unadorned prose style disparaged by 'many readers' of Orwell as 'drab or uninspired' 'would have been appreciated by someone like Defoe, since Defoe would have immediately understood how the pressures of Orwell's subject, like the pressures of his own, demand a gritty and hammering factuality'; for Orwell, Howe went on, 'things took on reality . . . only as they were particular and concrete'.[49] One reason why Orwell's spare prose and insistent materiality would have been recognizable to Defoe is that mid-twentieth-century writers like Orwell were, with differing degrees of self-consciousness, replaying a conversation about language from centuries earlier, from a moment when, as Ryan Stark puts it, 'a group of experimental philosophers—by creating a new understanding of style, and of language in general—brought about a paradigm shift in the English rhetorical tradition'.[50] Writing of Defoe's 'readability'

46. Ian Watt, 'Conrad Criticism and *The Nigger of the "Narcissus"*', in Watt, *Essays on Conrad*, 68, 65.
47. Watt, 'Winston Smith: The Last Humanist', 225.
48. Primo Levi, 'Afterword', trans. Ruth Feldman, in Levi, *The Reawakening*, 229.
49. Irving Howe, *Politics and the Novel* (New York: Horizon Press, 1960), 237, 242.
50. Ryan J. Stark, 'Language Reform in the Late Seventeenth Century', in Tina Skouen and Ryan J. Stark (eds), *Rhetoric and the Early Royal Society: A Sourcebook* (Leiden: Brill, 2015), 94. Watt would have inherited this view of the Royal Society, but see also Brian Vickers,

(*RN* 104), Watt attributed the 'simple and positive quality of Defoe's prose' (*RN* 102) to his Dissenters' academy. This style is traditionally associated with the linguistic reforms of the Royal Society, which, as Thomas Sprat famously put it in his 1667 work of institutional propaganda, was attempting a 'return back to the primitive purity, and shortness, when men deliver'd so many *things*, almost in an equal number of *words*. They have exacted from all their members, a close, naked, natural way of speaking; positive expressions; clear sense.'[51] This may have been the passage that Connolly had in mind when he identified the writer as the 'honest banker', with a quantity of words denoting a quantity of objects. Indeed, Defoe is among the writers Connolly names when he identifies a period of exemplary prose 'at the end of the seventeenth and the beginning of the eighteenth century': 'when words expressed what they meant and when it was impossible to write badly.'[52]

Taking the Side of 'Things'

Among the distinctive features of mid-century fiction and criticism, then, is a half-conscious reprise of the empirical climate that Watt and others saw as a critical factor in the emergence of the novel, and a recasting of the eighteenth century through the mid-century's own preoccupations with and understanding of realism. Writing of Defoe, John Richetti points out that the word realism comes ultimately from the Latin *res*, 'a thing', and Paul Hunter relates the eighteenth-century novel's empiricism to the practice of 'occasional meditation':

> Diarists learned to 'meditate' on earthly objects by imitating the printed meditations of figures like Robert Boyle, Edward Bury, and John Flavell, who encouraged readers to observe all the details of everyday life and preserve their thoughts on everything. Bury, for example, himself meditated on such objects as snails, toads, apples, falling leaves, and 'a Tuft of green Grass'.[53]

Watt was extremely interested in a mid-century counterpart to those diarists meditating on 'snails, toads, apples', the French poet Francis

'The Royal Society and English Prose Style: A Reassessment', in Brian Vickers and Nancy S. Streuver, *Rhetoric and the Pursuit of Truth: Language Change in the Seventeenth and Eighteenth Centuries* (Los Angeles: William Andrews Clark Memorial Library, 1985), 1–76.

51. Thomas Sprat, *History of the Royal Society* (Whitefish, MT: Kessinger, 2003), 113.
52. Connolly, *Enemies of Promise*, 11.
53. Richetti, *The Life of Daniel Defoe*, 191. Hunter, *Before Novels*, 200.

Ponge, whose Occupation-era *Le Parti pris des choses* (1942), 'Taking the Side of Things', is a collection of short prose poems each focusing on a particular object, either a living thing such as an oyster, a snail, or an orange, or an equally perishable manmade one—a cigarette, a loaf of bread.

In the light of my argument that criticism and creative writing were similarly concerned with empiricism at this moment, it seems especially significant that on the sole occasion Watt wrote about Ponge it was as a model for literary criticism. The occasion was an address to the Modern Language Association:

> I have always found my own attitude to literature, and to the institutional context with which that attitude coexists, much simpler, much more intuitive, and much less amenable to discussion or theoretical formulation, than it seems to be for most of my colleagues. If I look for an image that can bridge this gap between the public and the private and enable me to express something of my own sense of the prospects of English departments, I must go back some three decades, and to the Parisian left bank, where I found myself again after an absence of seven years in the army. In the talk I heard then, four new words struck me. I soon got tired of the first three: *Engagé. Authentique. Absurde*; but the fourth—*Les Choses*—seemed somewhat less fly-blown.[54]

Watt then describes a public lecture in which Ponge had 'circled amiably around his dislike of the common hyperboles about literature, his sense of being sickened at general theoretical and public propositions, and how in his own writing, finding it impossible to put the great literary subjects into words, he had determined, like a man at the edge of a precipice, to fix his gaze on the immediate object—a tree, the balustrade, the next step—and try to put that into words instead'.[55] Apparently Ponge ended his lecture by embracing the table in front of him because 'if I love it, it's because there's absolutely nothing in it which allows one to believe that it takes itself for a piano'.[56] Ponge's devotion to the particularity of objects through a language that allows the human being to 'express his fraternity with the objects of his world', in Watt's words, becomes a model for the kind of literary studies that Watt tries to practise. What is required is 'an intellectual recognition of just what I am modestly but directly attending to; an aesthetic appreciation of the object of

54. Ian Watt, 'On not Attempting to Be a Piano', *Profession* (1978), 13.
55. Watt, 'On not Attempting to Be a Piano', 13.
56. Watt, 'On not Attempting to Be a Piano', 13.

my attention for what it exactly is; a direct commitment of my feelings to that object; and lastly, perhaps incidentally, an attempt to express all of the first three things in words'.[57] Abstraction and systematization miss the point of reading, he avers, for 'it is the concreteness of literature which it is characteristic strength . . . the stubborn resistance of the particularities of the other'.[58]

'So long as I remain alive and well I shall continue to feel strongly about prose style, to love the surface of the earth, and to take a pleasure in solid objects and scraps of useless information,' Orwell had explained in 'Why I Write'.[59] In his admiring 1950 review of Orwell's posthumous work, E. M. Forster commended Orwell's love of 'small things', 'little immediate things'.[60] And so against the fraudulence of public language in Orwell's fiction are the truths of the material world, and Winston Smith's literally *felt* contradiction of the Party's claim to have improved people's lives: 'the mute protest in your own bones, the instinctive feeling that the conditions you lived in were intolerable and that at some other time they must have been different.'[61] But Ingsoc has abolished what the confected traitor Goldstein's book sums up as 'the empirical method of thought'.[62] Its success is evident when even Winston Smith proves so comprehensively schooled in abstraction that he cannot interpret empirical evidence. When he quizzes the old prole in a pub, for example, he fails to discern that the prole's private memories are actually supplying the information he wants. His question about top-hatted aristocrats—Party 'history' claims that only aristocrats wore top hats—has been answered by the old man's meandering reminiscences about wearing a top hat to a funeral. Winston does not pick up on this evidence that the Party has falsified the past once more.

Watt writes that Winston Smith 'finds himself defeated by the random but invincible concreteness of what the old man remembers', notwithstanding Winston's 'love of the particular'—and this is a phrase Watt uses with palpable approval no fewer than three times in a single paragraph, in support of his resoundingly humanistic assertion that 'Winston Smith is the only person in the novel who makes any sort of stand for the simple intellectual and moral values which, for over two

57. Watt, 'On not Attempting to Be a Piano', 13.
58. Watt, 'On not Attempting to Be a Piano', 14.
59. Orwell, 'Why I Write', 319–20.
60. E. M. Forster, 'George Orwell', in E. M. Forster, *Two Cheers for Democracy* (San Diego: Harcourt Brace, 1967), 61, 62.
61. Orwell, *Nineteen Eighty-Four*, 73.
62. Orwell, *Nineteen Eighty-Four*, 193.

millennia, have had the majority of the literate and the decent on their side'.[63] Watt could hardly sound much more like Orwell here, with that conversational ('any sort of stand') but uncompromising appeal to common values that are self-evident to 'the literate and the decent'. For Orwell and Watt, as for Jake's fictionalized Hugo in Iris Murdoch's mid-century debut *Under the Net* (1954), attention to the particular has become a moral matter. As Hugo explains: 'the movement away from theory and generality is the movement towards truth. All theorizing is flight. We must be ruled by the situation itself and this is unutterably particular.'[64] This passage probably explains why Murdoch is the solitary novelist discussed in George Watson's survey of British literary theory: 'If there is a connective thread, it lies in the Primacy of the Instance: the recognition that a theoretical claim is seen to be true only by testing it against known cases.'[65]

'The whole language is a machine for making falsehoods,' Murdoch's Hugo announces; Hugo believes that the most one can say truthfully of an experience at the time 'would be perhaps something about one's heart beating'.[66] Orwell's similar insistence on what Winston Smith knows through his body is profoundly characteristic of this period's particular style of political writing. In a phrase that would serve for many mid-century writers, Shoshana Felman argues that Albert Camus's *The Plague* 'offers its *historical eyewitnessing in the flesh*'.[67] In her famous essays on the Nuremberg Trials and their aftermath, British novelist Rebecca West would reflect on eyewitnessing in the flesh when she identified the chasm between the linguistic abstractions and the human experiences of totalitarianism. The first essay in West's series reports on the trial at Nuremberg of the major Nazi war criminals, but in the second, 'Greenhouse with Cyclamens II' (1949), she describes meeting a group of Berlin women living under the Soviet Occupation. 'To say in this room, "I was at the Nuremberg trial," would have meant nothing to any of these women, and, indeed, it would have presented them with an argument less developed than their own':

63. Watt, 'Winston Smith: The Last Humanist', 218, 221, 227.
64. Iris Murdoch, *Under the Net* (London: Penguin, 1982), 80.
65. George Watson, *Never Ones for Theory? England and the War of Ideas* (Cambridge: Lutterworth Press, 2000), 24.
66. Murdoch, *Under the Net*, 60, 59.
67. Shoshana Felman and Dori Laub, *Testimony: Crises of Witnessing in Literature, Psychoanalysis, and History* (New York: Routledge, 1992), 109; emphasis in original.

> There [at Nuremberg] men had made a formal attack on the police state. But here these women had incarnated the argument. They were discussing the matter with their bodies as well as their minds. Because it would not do if the wrong people read the letter to brother Hans in Cologne, the tired legs had to trudge down the tenement steps and up the street and over to the Western Sector and back, the old shoes letting in the water and rubbing the corns. Because the man from the Eastern Zone with a message from Grandmama in Magdeburg could not come to the granddaughter's home, lest the spy in the tenement should see him, she had to go a long way to meet him in a café where she was not known, and the fare and the price of the coffee left her short of what would have bought sausages for supper.
>
> By tired feet and leaking shoes, and by the watering of mouths over missed meals, these women had learned with their whole being that justice gives a better climate than hate.[68]

'Nuremberg' has turned into mere verbiage and cliché, and West believes that nothing she can say about the evil uncovered there can make totalitarianism feel real. Only by being forced to live in a police state that affects them at the level of wet feet can they comprehend what totalitarianism means. West's essay was first published in the same year as *Nineteen Eighty-Four* and shares its fierce empiricism. The most compelling argument against totalitarianism is an 'incarnated... argument', not actually verbal at all; that one best knows the wrongness of totalitarianism through one's own body, and even concrete description ('tired legs... old shoes... corns') will always come second to the dreary daily experiences to which it refers.

Haunting the Courtroom

Like Orwell, too, West keeps returning to the period's distinctively bad uses of language. Her Nuremberg essays appear in a volume of her journalism about legal trials, and even the least obviously political reports are concerned with the problem of a sinisterly automated speech. 'Mr Setty and Mr Hume', on a seedy 1949 torso murder, notes the significance of witnesses demonstrating a 'simple and economical use of language': people who 'said "no" and "about" instead of

68. Rebecca West, 'Greenhouse with Cyclamens II', in Rebecca West, *A Train of Powder: Six Reports on the Problem of Guilt and Punishment in our Time* (Chicago: Ivan R. Dee, 2000), 159.

"definitely no" and "approximately" ', and who, thanks to their plain speech, conjured up the literally material aspects of an otherwise baffling case: 'a trail of five-pound notes, a carpet, a prescription, a carving knife, a cup of tea, a piece of rope'.[69] Not surprisingly, West's attention to good and bad speech is even more explicit in her many reports on the Second World War and early cold-war treason trials. On one end of the political spectrum, she finds in *The Meaning of Treason* (1947) that the traitor John Amery's superior education (Amery's father was a well-regarded Conservative MP) has done nothing for his capacity to speak—or think: 'Words flowed from Amery's mouth in the conventional groupings of English culture, but he had no intelligence, only a vacancy round which there rolled a snowball of Fascist chatter.'[70] Her essay 'The Better Mousetrap' reports on the trial of Foreign Office radio worker William Marshall, who had been passing secrets to the USSR so ineptly that he looked to have been set up by the Soviets. For West, Marshall's all-encompassing political stupidity is reflected in his trite and formulaic expressions, as when he speaks of having 'exchanged cultural information on Moscow': 'This perfect specimen of *Daily Worker* English dashed and depressed the court. Such words would come naturally only to a young man who had taken a linguistic tan from exposure to the fierce rays of Communist prose.'[71]

Arthur Koestler outlined and ridiculed the features of that prose in the 1954 instalment of his memoirs, where he described how joining the Communist Party in the early 1930s had changed his language:

My vocabulary, grammar, syntax, gradually changed. I learnt to avoid any original form of expression, any individual turn of phrase. Euphony, gradations of emphasis, restraint, nuances of meaning, were suspect. Language, and with it thought, underwent a process of dehydration, and crystallised in the ready-made schemata of Marxist jargon. There were perhaps a dozen or two adjectives whose use was both safe and mandatory, such as: decadent, hypocritical, morbid (for the capitalist bourgeoisie); heroic, disciplined, class-conscious (for the revolutionary proletariat); *petit-bourgeois*, romantic, sentimental (for humanitarian scruples); opportunist and sectarian (for Right and Left deviations respectively); mechanistic, metaphysical, mystical (for the

69. Rebecca West, 'Mr Setty and Mr Hume', in West, *A Train of Powder*, 194.
70. Rebecca West, *The Meaning of Treason* (London: Reprint Society, 1952), 130.
71. Rebecca West, 'The Better Mousetrap', in West, *A Train of Powder*, 279.

wrong intellectual approach); dialectical, concrete (for the right approach); flaming (protests); fraternal (greetings); unswerving (loyalty to the Party).[72]

No judgement or selection is necessary when your sentences simply complete themselves. In *Nineteen Eighty-Four*, Orwell had called it 'duckspeak', and it is first named when Winston watches two Party members in apparent conversation:

Winston had a curious feeling that this was not a real human being but some kind of dummy. It was not the man's brain that was speaking; it was his larynx. The stuff that was coming out of him consisted of words, but it was not speech in the true sense: it was a noise uttered in unconsciousness, like the quacking of a duck.[73]

Among the many other mid-century non-fiction writers who remarked upon this kind of anti-language was Watt's friend Leslie Fiedler. Also in the context of Communism, Fiedler wrote of verbal automatism as 'ready-made epithets... released like a dog's saliva at the *ting* of a bell'.[74] His controversial reflections on the trial of the Rosenbergs for cold-war treason are in the same family as West's trial reportage in their attention to failures of expression reflecting more fundamental failures of thought. Outrageously, he argued that Ethel Rosenberg's letters showed her to be 'hopelessly the victim not only of her politics, but of the painfully pretentious style that is its literary equivalent'; the Rosenbergs were martyrs to neither their political convictions nor their Jewishness, but 'only to their own double talk, to a handful of banalities'.[75]

Orwell names it duckspeak, Fiedler understands it as Pavlovian drooling, and West uses similarly passive images of suntanning and snowballs; what their metaphors share is an alarm at the extent to which agency disappears the moment the speaker succumbs to readymade formulae. Hannah Arendt had frequent recourse to the image of Pavlov's dog around this time in *The Origins of Totalitarianism*, where she argued that 'Pavlov's dog, the human specimen reduced to the most elementary reactions, the bundle of reactions that can always be liquidated and replaced by other bundles of reactions that behave in exactly the same

72. Arthur Koestler, *The Invisible Writing: The Second Volume of an Autobiography: 1932–40* (London: Vintage, 2005), 32–3.
73. Orwell, *Nineteen Eighty-Four*, 55, 54.
74. Leslie Fiedler, 'Afterthoughts on the Rosenbergs', in Fiedler, *Collected Essays*, i. 39.
75. Fiedler, 'Afterthoughts on the Rosenbergs', 40, 44.

way, is the model "citizen" of a totalitarian state'.[76] In this instance, Arendt was speaking about the effects of the concentration camp ('such a citizen can be produced only imperfectly outside of the camps'), but he or she is the ideal of all totalitarian regimes: 'a world of conditioned reflexes, of marionettes without the slightest trace of spontaneity'.[77] Political true believers are 'robots' who 'can be reached by neither experience nor argument; identification with the movement and total conformism seem to have destroyed the very capacity for experience'.[78]

The image of the war criminal as automaton found famous expression in her subsequent reflections on 'the strange interdependence of thoughtlessness and evil' in her report on the trial of Adolf Eichmann.[79] 'The longer one listened to him, the more obvious it became that his inability to speak was closely connected with an inability to *think*', she remarked early in the book, describing Eichmann's recourse to stock phrases and clichés: 'No communication was possible with him, not because he lied but because he was surrounded by the most reliable of all safeguards against the words and the presence of others, and hence against reality as such.'[80] Novelist Muriel Spark had also attended the Eichmann trial—the backdrop to her novel *The Mandelbaum Gate* (1965)—and had been no less struck that he 'could only come out with these banal phrases, he never grasped the evil he had perpetrated'.[81] Spark's attention to the violence enabled by automated speech gives a deeply sinister edge to her 1960s fiction. A character in her war-set *The Girls of Slender Means* (1963) is likened to 'a speaking machine that had gone wrong', and the novel is full of characters thinking and speaking only in prefabricated phrases.[82] Most consequential is beautiful Selina, whose seemingly silly course of auto-suggestion ('Poise is perfect balance, an equanimity of body and mind, complete composure whatever the social scene') helps to condition her into the inhuman presence of mind required to steal another girl's dress from a burning hostel while her friends await their deaths by fire there.[83]

76. Arendt, *Origins of Totalitarianism*, 456.
77. Arendt, *Origins of Totalitarianism*, 456, 457.
78. Arendt, *Origins of Totalitarianism*, 363, 308.
79. Hannah Arendt, *Eichmann in Jerusalem: A Report on the Banality of Evil* (London: Penguin, 1994), 288.
80. Arendt, *Eichmann in Jerusalem*, 49.
81. Quoted in James Bailey, '"Repetition, Boredom, Despair": Muriel Spark and the Eichmann Trial', *Holocaust Studies*, 17/2–3 (Autumn–Winter 2011), 188.
82. Muriel Spark, *The Girls of Slender Means* (New York: New Directions, 1998), 41.
83. Spark, *The Girls of Slender Means*, 50.

Arendt places Eichmann's bad speech in the context of the 'language rule' ('itself a code name; it meant whatever in ordinary language would be called a lie') prevailing in Nazi Germany, whereby what was happening to Jews could never be named as such:

> The net effect of this language system was not to keep these people ignorant of what they were doing, but to prevent them from equating it with their old, 'normal' knowledge of murder and lies. Eichmann's great susceptibility to catch words and stock phrases, combined with his incapacity for ordinary speech, made him, of course, an ideal subject for 'language rules'.[84]

When, at the end of the book, Arendt reports upon Eichmann's hanging and notes that even on the gallows he was capable only of speaking in muddled clichés, she realizes that 'the lesson' of Eichmann and his trial consists of 'the fearsome, word-and-thought-defying *banality of evil*'.[85] Automated speech has gone from being bizarre and sinister to nothing short of evil itself. Arendt's 'task', writes Lyndsey Stonebridge, was to find a way 'of thinking in the wake of Eichmann's profound thoughtlessness'.[86]

'Eichmann's trial had made the activity of thinking, and its absence, newly and politically conspicuous.'[87] It is striking how many instances of empty, thoughtless political language are coming from mid-century writings about trials: Nuremberg, Eichmann, the cold-war spies. 'I find it a little uncanny to discover how my imagination has always haunted the courtroom,' mused Fiedler.[88] It is less uncanny than it might be, surely, given that Fiedler had been trained during the war as an interpreter for interrogating Japanese prisoners of war. As Allan Hepburn has shown in an important essay on Elizabeth Bowen's 1949 novel *The Heat of the Day*, questions of legality—punishment, complicity, culpability—were of powerful importance at mid-century.[89] Indeed, we might usefully see the renewed interest in novelistic realism in the light of what Hepburn identifies as the 'postwar perplexity about law' reaching back to the

84. Arendt, *Eichmann in Jerusalem*, 85, 86.
85. Arendt, *Eichmann in Jerusalem*, 252.
86. Lyndsey Stonebridge, *The Judicial Imagination: Writing after Nuremberg* (Edinburgh: Edinburgh University Press, 2011), 59.
87. Stonebridge, *The Judicial Imagination*, 62.
88. Leslie Fiedler, 'Introduction to the Second Edition of *An End of Innocence*', in Fiedler, *Collected Essays*, i, xix.
89. Allan Hepburn, 'Trials and Errors: *The Heat of the Day* and Post-War Culpability', in Kristin Bluemel (ed.), *Intermodernism: Literary Culture in Mid-Twentieth-Century Britain* (Edinburgh: Edinburgh University Press, 2009), 131–49.

fraudulent Russian show trials of the 1930s: a concern with authenticity, particularity, and truth-telling.[90] As the Soviet instance implies, any parallel between law and realism makes realism even more problematic because of the ease with which the appearance of authenticity can be conjured up through the procedures that were meant to underwrite it.

So it is less surprising than it might otherwise seem that legal procedures give *The Rise of the Novel* one of its foundational analogies for formal realism. Noting that realism has long-standing connotations of criminality ('Moll Flanders is a thief, Pamela a hypocrite, and Tom Jones a fornicator'), Watt insists that nonetheless 'the novel's realism does not reside in the kind of life it presents, but in the way it presents it' (*RN* 11). But here, too, we are haunting the courtroom, for Watt draws a telling juridical parallel to explain what he means by realism as a mode defined by 'particular individuals having particular experiences at particular times and at particular places':

> The novel's mode of imitating reality may therefore be equally well summarised in terms of the procedures of another group of specialists in epistemology, the jury in a court of law. Their expectations, and those of the novel reader coincide in many ways: both want to know 'all the particulars' of a given case—the time and place of the occurrence; both must be satisfied as to the identities of the parties concerned, and will refuse to accept evidence about anyone called Sir Toby Belch or Mr Badman—still less about a Chloe who has no surname and is 'common as the air'; and they also expect the witnesses to tell the story 'in his own words'. The jury, in fact, takes the 'circumstantial view of life' (*RN* 31).

Realism is, 'like the rules of evidence, only a convention' (*RN* 32), but Watt endorses Hazlitt's claim that the experience of *Clarissa* 'is like reading evidence in a court of Justice' (*RN* 34). The metaphor is particularly apt in this instance, of course, given that the text of *Clarissa* is a substitute for the legal remedies that its heroine will not pursue.

As Ros Ballaster observes, 'the role of the disinterested "jury member"' is 'the defining characteristic of the eighteenth-century reader for Ian Watt'.[91] We might attribute this quasi-legal understanding of the novel in part to the prevalence of notions of public redress in the 1940s and 1950s, the era of the Nuremberg and Tokyo War Trials and their successors. This is the modern era's 'juridical unconscious', in the title of Felman's study of the relationship between law and trauma, whereby, post-Nuremberg, the law has been recruited in an 'unprecedented and

90. Hepburn, 'Trials and Errors', 140. 91. Ballaster, *Seductive Forms*, 40.

repeated' way 'to cope with the traumatic legacies and the collective injuries' of historical events.[92] Felman's and Dori Laub's landmark *Testimony* explains the central importance of testimonial articulation to the representation of the Second World War, 'the watershed of our times'.[93] 'Testimony' itself, they remind us, is in the first instance a legal term that speaks to a 'crisis of truth' and 'a crisis of evidence'.[94]

Allegories of Imprisonment

Watt's 'The Ways of Guilt' is testimonial writing in this sense: with a powerful aura of the unresolved and incompletely processed, it also asks to be taken as verifiable truth: 'Every prisoner of the Japanese who worked on the railway in the summer of 1943 will recognise each detail I have set down below.'[95] The mid-century canon often insists like this upon truthfulness—not lifelikeness, but truthfulness. Witness the case of Camus's *The Plague*, in which the first-person narrator Dr Bernard Rieux turns the novel into quasi-omniscient narration in order to create the authority that a necessarily subjective and partial first-person narration lacks.[96] In the end, the novel has it both ways: when the protagonist Dr Rieux unveils himself as the novel's real narrator, he also attains the different authority of the testifying witness. The juridical language is the novel's own here too. 'Summoned to give evidence regarding what was a sort of crime, he has exercised the restraint that behooves a conscientious witness,' Camus's narrator writes: 'To be an honest witness, it was for him to confine himself mainly to what people did or said and what could be gleaned from documents.'[97]

Camus's novel asks many of the same questions as prisoner-of-war writings: about individualist amorality, the struggle for communitarian feeling, and the shoring-up of social order through rhetoric itself

92. Shoshana Felman, *The Juridical Unconscious: Trials and Traumas in the Twentieth Century* (Cambridge, MA: Harvard University Press, 2002), 2.
93. Felman and Laub, *Testimony*, xiv.
94. Felman and Laub, *Testimony*, 6.
95. 'As a relation to events, testimony seems to be composed of bits and pieces of a memory that has been overwhelmed by occurrences that have not settled into understanding or remembrance, acts that cannot be constructed as knowledge nor assimilated into full cognition, events in excess of our frames of reference' (Felman and Laub, *Testimony*, 5).
96. Camus, *The Plague*, 3.
97. Camus, *The Plague*, 301, 302.

('it was up to him to speak for all').[98] Like Defoe, and indeed like Watt, Camus is concerned with how people respond to catastrophe on the grand scale. On the one hand there is the perversely lonely quality of a communal suffering that chills your capacity to feel pity for others ('the plague had gradually killed off in all of us the faculty not of love only but even of friendship'). On the other, there is the competing pull towards discipline in order to stabilize a community falling apart in the face of mass death ('The thing was to do your job as it should be done'[99]). But at the level of style, too, the novel is connected to a legalistic kind of circumstantial realism, with its insistence upon reportage as a corrective to the 'epical or prize-speech verbiage' of public messages to the suffering city.[100] Avowedly fond of 'fine speech', the eloquent, sinister narrator of Camus's *The Fall* admits that 'style, like sheer silk, too often hides eczema'.[101]

'It is as reasonable to represent one kind of imprisonment by another, as it is to represent anything that really exists by that which exists not,' reads the epigraph of *The Plague*, quoting Defoe's *Serious Reflections on Robinson Crusoe*. The epigraph captures the ambiguous truthfulness of both books: acutely circumstantial, based on real events but not exactly real, allegorizing historical events and experiences (the German Occupation of France, the French Occupation of Algeria, Defoe's personal isolation) through fictional narrative. The reportage style as well as the substance owes much to Defoe's *Journal of the Plague Year*, with its blurring of the factual and the fictional.

> To some, these events will seem quite natural; to others, all but incredible. But, obviously, a narrator cannot take account of these differences of outlook. His business is only to say: 'This is what happened,' when he knows that it actually did happen, that it closely affected the life of a whole populace, and that there are thousands of eyewitnesses who can appraise in their hearts the truth of what he writes.'[102]

From Defoe, Camus takes the idea of 'vigilance': 'It may be proper to ask here, how long it may be supposed, Men might have the Seeds of the Contagion in them, before it discover'd it self in this fatal Manner; and how long they might go about seemingly whole, and

98. Camus, *The Plague*, 302.
99. Camus, *The Plague*, 41.
100. Camus, *The Plague*, 138.
101. Camus, *The Fall*, 5, 6.
102. Camus, *The Plague*, 6.

yet be contagious to all those that came near them?'[103] The important mid-twentieth-century difference, however, is that Camus has transformed vigilance into a linguistic category, as when the anti-capital-punishment activist Tarrou concludes that 'all our troubles spring from our failure to use plain, clear-cut language. So I resolved always to speak—and to act—quite clearly.'[104]

Among the other major fablers of the early post-war period, wartime naval officer William Golding also found Defoe an inspiration for war-set works like *Lord of the Flies* (1954) and *Pincher Martin* (1956). The destroyer on which Christopher Hadley Martin is sailing sinks off the Western Isles of Scotland, and he attempts to survive on a barren rock eating shellfish and collecting rainwater. The comparison with *Robinson Crusoe* is explicitly invited from the outset ('The first thing to do', thinks Christopher Martin, 'is to survey the estate'), while, Crusoe-like, Martin's plan for survival takes the rational, schematic form of a numbered catalogue of needs, priorities, and potential difficulties, with language itself becoming a form of domestication when he starts naming his surroundings.[105] 'I am busy surviving,' he tells himself: 'I am netting down this rock with names and taming it.'[106] As Richetti points out, to organize the external world mentally is a way of surviving for Robinson Crusoe, for 'enumeration is the beginning of practical knowledge, a laying out of what is available and of possibilities for survival'; or, as he writes elsewhere, for Defoe's characters, 'the exact apprehension of the world is a technique for survival and not an end in itself'.[107] As Martin waits there—not knowing that he is already dead—he recalls his ruthlessly individualistic past, which he revisits through a remembered anecdote about a Chinese delicacy, where a fish is buried in a tin until the maggots emerge from the corpse:

'The little ones eat the tiny ones. The middle-sized ones eat the little ones. The big ones eat the middle-sized ones. Then the big ones eat each other. Then there are two and then one and where there was a fish there is now one huge successful maggot. Rare dish.'[108]

103. Defoe, *A Journal of the Plague Year*, 189.
104. Camus, *The Plague*, 253, 254.
105. William Golding, *Pincher Martin* (London: Faber, 1956), 77, 81.
106. Golding, *Pincher Martin*, 86.
107. Richetti, *The Life of Daniel Defoe*, 191. John Richetti, 'Defoe as Narrative Innovator', in John Richetti (ed.), *The Cambridge Companion to Daniel Defoe* (Cambridge: Cambridge University Press, 2008), 131.
108. Golding, *Pincher Martin*, 136.

The cannibalistic anecdote reflects both Martin's selfishness and the self-destructive predicament to which it has led: he may be the top maggot, but his purpose is to be eaten. Like Defoe's characters, of whom Watt wrote that they all belong on Crusoe's island, or the character in Ballard's *Concrete Island* who is told that he was on an island long before he got to his present one, Martin comes to a similar realization: 'Because of what I did I am an outsider and alone.'[109]

Adding collectivity to similar concerns with survival, cruelty, and cannibalism is what makes *Lord of the Flies* read so much like a prisoner-of-war book. A war continues in the background; the children are evacuees whose plane has been struck; an atomic bomb has been dropped; and a uniformed officer in a military cruiser is finally responsible for the boys' rescue in what reads like a paradigmatic camp liberation scene, with filthy scarecrow prisoners and the mingled compassion, shock, and shame of the crisply dressed liberating officer. Levi describes the 'strangely embarrassed' Red Army soldiers who reached Buna-Monowitz in January 1945, who 'seemed oppressed not only by compassion but by a confused restraint': 'that shame we knew so well... the feeling of guilt that such a crime should exist'.[110] Among those dealing with the liberated camps in the Far East in September 1945, British officer Lieutenant-Colonel Nicholas Read-Collins reported to the Tokyo Tribunal that 'his first reaction on visiting the camps was that he was in another world and talking to people who had already died'.[111] Late in Ballard's *Empire of the Sun* Jim is almost at the point of collapse when liberation begins to look possible, and he is urged by a former stalwart of the expatriate community in Shanghai to show a bit of the national stiff upper lip ('Remember you're British'), which has Jim reflect that it is 'sad that he should have been so demoralized that all he could do to reassure Jim was to remind him that he was British'.[112] The scene is surely recalling the end of *Lord of the Flies* when the liberating officer remonstrates awkwardly with the young savages: 'I should have thought that a pack of British boys—you're all British, aren't you?—would have been able to put up a better show than that—I mean—.'[113]

On Golding's island the boys replicate the conflict between the will to order and the threat of disorder so central to prisoner-of-war

109. Golding, *Pincher Martin*, 181. 110. Levi, *The Reawakening*, 15, 16, 16.
111. Quoted in Russell, *Knights of Bushido*, 169.
112. Ballard, *Empire of the Sun*, 186, 187.
113. William Golding, *Lord of the Flies* (New York: Perigee, 1954), 201–2.

books. Among the victims is Simon, who seems, on the one hand, to be the portentous Christ figure of mid-century fiction but, on the other, reads as Jewish, with his profound Old Testament insights and his quasi-instinctive apprehension of the logics of persecution ('that ancient, inescapable recognition' when he looks at the demonic lord of the flies: 'Fancy thinking the Beast was something you could hunt and kill!').[114] The other victim of persecution is the rationalist Piggy ('We could experiment'), who works out how to make a smoke signal; there is no hope of Piggy surviving in a social environment that has turned its back on reason.[115] It is as if Golding is arguing that in this mid-century totalitarian dystopia in miniature an empiricist like Piggy is as 'inevitable' a casualty as the tragically insightful Simon. (There is no longer a word for science on Airstrip One either.)

Like Ballard and Camus, Golding reminds us how amenable was *Robinson Crusoe*, the novel that supposedly inaugurated the realistic tradition of prose fiction, to being rewritten as a fable. In language recalling summaries of the Royal Society style, Samuel Hynes claims that war writers are typically 'realists, adopting a common style that would come as close as language can to rendering the things of the material world as they are . . . a plain, naming vocabulary, describing objects and actions in unmetaphorical terms, appealing always to the data of the senses'.[116] Ballard's, Golding's, and Camus's prose insists on reportage, however extreme the limit-events it is used to report. All these mid-century writers' indebtedness to Defoe goes beyond content and into style—that plain, referential, anti-rhetorical language.

The referentiality and materialism of mid-century writing would come to look passé in the 1960s. Although Ballard's stock continued to rise, thanks to the marked postmodernity of much of his subject matter—virtuality, the media, the post-human, the melding of flesh and machine—mid-century realism would be treated as merely the work of a literary culture that had exhausted its fictional resources but persisted anyhow in the old style. In his famous essay 'The Literature of Exhaustion', John Barth could not have been clearer about the break between his generation of novelists and those of the immediately post-war period. Orwell had very famously written that 'Good prose is like a window pane', and Barth revived that metaphor when he distinguished between

114. Golding, *Lord of the Flies*, 138, 143.
115. Golding, *Lord of the Flies*, 130.
116. Hynes, *The Soldiers' Tale*, 25–6.

realism and postmodernism as the contrast between 'the Windex approach to language' and 'the stained-glass approach'.[117] But, if the renewed commitment to the fiction of concretely described things presented an easy target for the playfully self-referential writers who followed, it was also historically overdetermined. The return to realism was driven by a sense of moral accountability that was perhaps unprecedented in the novel's history. In the same years, the concern with truthtelling was conveyed with no less commitment in the critical writing of the novel's best readers. And so, in correspondence with Brigadier Toosey, Watt summed up what his profession meant to him: 'whatever other disadvantages it has, one is never selling oneself, or saying or writing things other than for what one believes to be the objective truth.'[118]

117. Orwell, 'Why I Write', 320. John Barth, *The Floating Opera and The End of the Road* (New York: Anchor, 1988), v.
118. Letter from Ian Watt to Brigadier Philip Toosey dated 19 January 1969, Stanford University Special Collections, SC401-ACCN 1994-106, Box 24, Folder 12.

Ian Watt in 1963, by the temporary School of English Studies at UEA. Students had borrowed the 'Watts Court' street sign from a Norwich alleyway of the same name.

6

The Prison-Camp English Department

'I don't like work—no man does—but I like what is in the work—the chance to find yourself. Your own reality—for yourself, not for others—what no other man can ever know. They can only see the mere show, and never can tell what it really means.'

Joseph Conrad, *Heart of Darkness* (1899)[1]

'I can almost believe that I came to Shepperton 30 years ago knowing unconsciously that one day I would write a novel about my wartime experiences in Shanghai, and that it might well be filmed in these studios. Deep assignments run through all our lives; there are no coincidences.'

J. G. Ballard, annotation to *The Atrocity Exhibition* (1990)[2]

In 1962 Watt left the University of California, Berkeley, where he had taught for ten years, to take up a new position as founding Dean of the School of English Studies at the University of East Anglia in Norwich. His appointment was made by the university's first Vice-Chancellor, Frank Thistlethwaite, a British scholar of American history who had known Watt ever since they were undergraduates together at Cambridge. At the moment of Watt's appointment, the University of East Anglia was due to admit its first students in the autumn of 1963, but so far had mainly a fiscal and civic rather than material status in the world. Watt's task was to imagine into existence English Studies at a university whose most important feature was precisely that it

1. Conrad, *Heart of Darkness*, 35.
2. J. G. Ballard, *The Atrocity Exhibition: New Revised Edition* (San Francisco: Re/Search, 1990), 11.

was new, and would not follow the pre-existing Oxbridge and Red Brick models.

Looking back almost forty years later, Thistlethwaite wrote that Watt's 'role in the founding of UEA was both powerful and beneficent and he is to be ranked among our principal founding fathers'.[3] He had given Watt the job of determining what 'English' should be, of appointing colleagues and designing a curriculum accordingly, and even of assisting with the architectural designs that would allow Watt's vision for the subject to be realized.[4] But this massive assignment was not Watt's first experience of humanities administration, for he had been among the founders of a 'university' in the Japanese prison camps. One conclusion he drew explicitly there was the need 'to accept the dull fact' that institutions matter, because 'the continuity of human affairs will not happen of itself'.[5] This concluding chapter considers how the unusual view Watt's earliest and most urgent experience as a humanities administrator gave him of English as a discipline carried over into the creation of one of Britain's then most distinctive universities for the study of literature. Although as a critic he resisted systematic theorizing about literature, Watt was driven in wartime to formulate, and in peacetime to institutionalize, a coherent programme for literary studies.

In her absorbing study of the recreational activities of British prisoners in the Second World War, Midge Gillies quotes George Haig's view that prisoners of war fall into 'one or more categories: escapers, creators, administrators, students and sleepers'.[6] Watt was an administrator of a special kind, since the administration with which he was concerned was of the 'university' that he helped to found at the Changi camp where Allied prisoners were held when Singapore fell. Some prison camps in Europe were places of extraordinary intellectual productivity; for example, Gillies describes Allied prisoners of the Germans sitting formal exams through distance learning.[7] Where highly advanced study is concerned, we might think of *Annales* historian Fernand Braudel drafting his panoramic multi-volume masterpiece *The Mediterranean and*

3. Frank Thistlethwaite, *Origins: A Personal Reminiscence of UEA's Foundation* (Cambridge: Frank Thistlethwaite, 2000), 27.
4. On Watt's architectural input, see Michael Sanderson, *The History of the University of East Anglia, Norwich* (London: Hambledon & London, 2000), 158–9.
5. Watt, 'The Humanities on the River Kwai', 251.
6. Midge Gillies, *The Barbed-Wire University: The Real Lives of Allied Prisoners of War in the Second World War* (London: Aurum, 2012), xvi.
7. Gillies, *The Barbed-Wire University*, 275–90.

the Mediterranean World in the Age of Philippe II (1949) in a camp near Lübeck. The picture was entirely different in the Far East, albeit with one astonishing exception. While he later dismissed the final product as 'worthless', the mere fact of prescriptivist philosopher R. M. Hare, captured at Singapore with his Indian regiment, writing an entire philosophical monograph in captivity on the Burma–Thailand Railway ('a page or two every few days') speaks to positively superhuman resilience.[8] Hare was an anomalous figure among the Far East prisoners, but Watt's friend John Durnford must have known of numerous productive incarcerations in Europe when he wrote sarcastically that the Japanese camps 'were not ideal places from which to take a correspondence course in law, aerodynamics or the humanities. No one emerged from them after three years with a postal degree.'[9]

In the first essay he published about his imprisonment, Watt refers in passing to the 'Changi University' as 'a fairly successful attempt to build up the system of organized study classes that are a regular feature of most prisoner-of-war camps', and he also mentions the almost prohibitively difficult revival of the university later in the war, when the railway was finished ('we had lost most of our books, and the Japanese would not allow us to write').[10] Watt never mentions his own leading part in these enterprises. However, we learn from the memoir of Stephen Alexander, one of Watt's 'students', that Watt and his friends Guthrie Moir and Henry Fowler were the 'instigators' of the 18th Division University in the spring and summer of 1942, which took shape when a forced work party outside the camp found books that had been abandoned at the fall of Singapore and Moir used them to create a library at Changi.[11]

The Changi enterprise appears also in John Coast's memoir, *Railroad of Death* (1946). Coast uses pseudonyms, perhaps because the very early date made him uneasy about naming other prisoners, but he alters his friends' names only so slightly that readers can identify everyone quite securely when they already know who these people are likely to be. Ian Watt has become Ian White:

> The English faculty was run by three friends of mine. Henry was the administrator of the faculty and one of the chief lecturers. Then we had a young and charming Professor of English from Raffles College, whose lectures on the

8. R. M. Hare, 'A Philosophical Autobiography', *Utilitas*, 14/3 (November 2002), 283, 282.
9. Durnford, *Branch Line to Burma*, xiii.
10. Watt, 'The Liberty of the Prison', 525.
11. Alexander, *Sweet Kwai*, 78.

19th century novel were amongst the most delightful one could wish for. And also there was Ian White. He was one of the brightest young men Cambridge had seen for some years. From the University he had won a double scholarship, one in England and one at the Sorbonne. He was an example of a very good brain in an equally robust body; there was little frail about him.[12]

Of course, to describe as a 'university' the ad hoc improvisation of informal, bookless, and predominantly oral learning that Watt and his friends initiated perhaps sounds exaggerated; and yet to say that what was created in the prison camps was not a university at all is to move too quickly over the question of what a university really is.

Even UEA was less a university than a funded concept when Watt took up his post. When it opened a little over a year later in 1963, its physical existence was merely as a cluster of portable temporary buildings on the site still known as University Village, ten minutes' walk from what became UEA's distinctive Denys Lasdun campus. Watt wrote of a first year in post during which 'much of our time is spent worrying about whether there will actually be a roof over our heads when the students arrive'; he had already left the university years earlier by the time its first permanent building was opened.[13] Intriguingly, the first candidate approached as a possible Dean of English Studies was Raymond Williams, in 1961; he instead took up his appointment at Cambridge that year. Thistlethwaite writes that Williams was 'sympathetic but did not feel drawn to it'.[14] But among all the products of interwar Cambridge who could have considered giving up their tenure elsewhere to create an English department from scratch, Watt would have found it easier than most people to imagine a university as something less sturdily material than the bright concrete of the future UEA. His wartime experience had shown him that learning could go on in incalculably more pressured and provisional settings than these.

Literature in History

In unconscious tribute to UEA's earliest years, 'Literature in History' has for decades been the core first-year English course there. The most

12. Coast, *Railroad of Death*, 45.
13. Ian Watt, 'The University of East Anglia: Some Notes on Progress', *Critical Survey*, 1/4 (Summer 1964), 247.
14. Thistlethwaite, *Origins*, 23.

distinctive feature of English Studies, UEA's first humanities department, was its founding as a single academic unit comprising both English and History. (UEA acquired a separate School of History only in 1994.[15]) Watt's sole-designed curriculum required all first-year English students to take courses in 'Historical Method' as well as 'Practical Criticism and Expository Writing'; the degree regulations that Watt wrote allowed students to emphasize either English or History after the first year if they wished, but made it impossible to specialize entirely in either subject. Reporting in 1964 on UEA's inaugural year, Watt was explicit about the opportunity that the university's newness had given him to institutionalize his view of English and History as substantially the same area of enquiry: 'Many people had thought about it; but the combination had not been formally instituted anywhere, presumably because it would have been virtually impossible where there were several separate departments and professors already established.'[16] More forthrightly, he wrote: 'At Norwich, English Studies means English History *and* English Literature. It would no doubt be generally agreed that anyone teaching English Literature ought to know a lot of English History, and vice versa. The two fields are complementary: literature both has a history and is a part of history; while history uses literature, and often is itself literature.'[17] His leadership of the School elicited many uncharacteristically direct statements of first principles of this kind: writing in August 1962, shortly after his appointment, he wrote that UEA would reflect 'the direction which I believe English studies in general should take; that is, developing the empirical tradition of

15. Sanderson, *History of the University of East Anglia*, 90.
16. Watt, 'The University of East Anglia', 248. Leavisite and Left-Leavisite versions of the English–History combination—that is, based more or less on 'criticism' and 'values' rather than the scholarship Watt had in mind—were in circulation decades earlier, as in L. C. Knights, 'The University Teaching of English and History: A Plea for Correlation' (1939), L. C. Knights, *Explorations: Essays in Criticism Mainly on the Literature of the Seventeenth Century* (London: Chatto & Windus, 1946). F. R. Leavis, 'Sketch for an English School' (1943), proposed a required paper on—rather inevitably—the seventeenth century, where students would study topics such as 'Church and State' and 'The Rise of Capitalism'. To the objection that this is History and not English, Leavis's defence is substantially a deflection: that students would also be required to achieve competence in practical criticism. F. R. Leavis, *Education and the University: A Sketch for an 'English School'* (London: Chatto & Windus, 1943), 48–65.
17. Watt, 'The University of East Anglia', 250.

English thought so as to combine literary criticism with historical and sociological scholarship'.[18]

This was a decisively new approach for a British university, but Watt appears to have been thinking along similar lines for decades. What emerges most powerfully from Alexander's account of studying in Watt's prison-camp English department is that his classes were not meant to supply merely a psychological escape or distraction from the protracted tedium of imprisonment. Rather, Watt apparently emphasized the miserable conditions that he and his 'students' shared in order to get them to consider the importance of historical and sociological context for literary studies.

We learned from Ian that literary works are not things to be enjoyed unthinkingly, but dissected and related not only to their own social background but to ours, too. Would Wordsworth have been so trusting of Nature if, instead of reclining above Tintern Abbey, he had been caught in the monsoon in the Malayan jungle? Would Dorothy have slept in William's sacramental hammock and mosquito net when he had had to paddle down a tropical river to report to the DC?[19]

This is a revealing insight into Watt's apparent belief in situational reading: the poet's social context matters, but so does the reader's. Accordingly, the ideological dimension of poetry that the prisoners' experience had laid bare was also fair game, and Alexander recalls Watt wondering 'was there not a class feeling in the more traditional kind of war poetry that invalidated it as art'.[20] Apparently Watt classed Byron on Waterloo as interested only in aristocrats; Henry Newbolt's schoolboy heroes must have been economically insulated young gentlemen; and poet Julian Grenfell contemplated the First World War trenches from the perspective of a country squire.[21] The only counterexample the students offered was 'The Private of the Buffs', the famous Victorian jingo poem about the Chinese execution of a young English private in the Opium Wars ('Yes, honour calls!—with strength like steel | He put the vision by. | Let dusky Indians whine and kneel; | An English lad must die.'[22]), to

18. Ian Watt, 'The Idea of an English School: English at Norwich', *Critical Survey*, 1 (Autumn 1962), 45.
19. Alexander, *Sweet Kwai*, 79.
20. Alexander, *Sweet Kwai*, 79.
21. Alexander, *Sweet Kwai*, 79.
22. Sir Francis Hastings Doyle, 'The Private of the Buffs', in Sir Francis Hastings Doyle, *The Return of the Guards and Other Poems* (London: Macmillan, 1866), 106.

which Watt pointed out that the hero may have been working class but 'the poet saddled him with colour prejudice'.[23]

Obviously it is problematic to have to rely on the single extended record that survives of Watt's wartime teaching; and it is hard to believe that a summary of our own views from a former student decades later would represent them as we would. Still, Alexander's account resonates very believably with what we know of Watt's interwar left politics and also of his Cambridge education, as when we find how I. A. Richards's work made it into the prison camps.

> 'Margaret are you grieving over Goldengrove unleaving?' intoned Ian Watt, and we were invited to guess the author of this and other poems, giving them a sort of points system of merit. I was impressed alike by the eclectic choice of poems and by the critical analysis applied to them, and it wasn't until much later that their provenance in I. A. Richards's *Practical Criticism* was revealed, and the book itself, with its fold-out appendices, made available to us.[24]

It seems almost too good to be true that, in conditions of such scarcity, the teaching mode should rely on 'practical' criticism.

But William Empson, another former student of Richards and also (more famously) a wartime university lecturer in difficult conditions in the Far East, had also turned to practical criticism as the necessary mode for an almost bookless English department. In his 1940 poem 'Autumn on Nan-Yüeh', parenthetically subtitled '(with the exiled universities of Peking)', Empson wrote about lecturing in the late 1930s in China's 'Temporary University' in flight from the Japanese. The poem reflects wittily on the business of lecturing without books, when 'the soul remembering' is no longer a Wordsworthian conceit but a pedagogical necessity thanks to the 'abandoned libraries' of the Far East:

> And men get curiously non-plussed
> Searching the memory for a clue.
> The proper Pegasi to groom
> Are those your mind is willing to.
> Let textual variants be discussed;
> We teach a poem as it grew.[25]

23. Alexander, *Sweet Kwai*, 80.
24. Alexander, *Sweet Kwai*, 82–3.
25. William Empson, 'Autumn on Nan-Yüeh', in William Empson, *Collected Poems* (London: Hogarth, 1984), 73.

Most of us could reassemble some poems from memory, particularly if they were short lyrics of the kind that had served as the basis of Richards's best-known interwar work. We could not necessarily remember them perfectly, hence Empson's joke about 'textual variants' (he was notorious for misquoting from memory even in more convenient circumstances).[26] Looking back at this period in the inaugural lecture he delivered on taking up his chair at Sheffield in 1953, Empson explained that 'the chief interest of this university teaching was that there were practically no books or lecture notes'.[27] Academics had crossed the Japanese lines 'with the clothes they stood up in and maybe some lecture notes; a fairly dangerous business, and you certainly couldn't take a library', but 'lectures went on sturdily from memory'.[28] It is in the nature of public occasions like inaugural lectures to invite high-flown humanist sentiment, but there is no reason to suppose that Empson was being insincere when he said that undertaking literary studies in his depleted wartime circumstances had been a useful experience because of its 'great effect in forcing you to consider what really matters, or what you already do know if you think, or what you want to get to know when you can'.[29]

Evidently practical criticism was not simply practical in wartime but downright pragmatic. But what is quite striking about Empson's and Watt's post-war careers is how little interested either critic was in making the case for reading 'the text in itself'—or, for that matter, how unconvinced they were that any such thing existed. In his invaluable biography of Empson, John Haffenden writes that it is 'surprising, and ironic' that Empson has been characterized so often as 'the founding father' of New Criticism.[30] Empson could hardly have been more dismissive of its best-known principles, as when, in his published response to a 1976 questionnaire from the influential poetry journal *Agenda*, he decried 'the absurd veto' on considering the intentions of the author.[31] I have already quoted from one of his denunciations of what he saw as

26. John Haffenden, *William Empson*, i. *Among the Mandarins* (Oxford: Oxford University Press, 2009), 280.
27. William Empson, 'Teaching English in the Far East and England', in Empson, *The Strengths of Shakespeare's Shrew*, 211.
28. William Empson, 'A Chinese University', in Empson, *The Strengths of Shakespeare's Shrew*, 190.
29. Empson, 'Teaching English in the Far East and England', 212.
30. Haffenden, *William Empson*, i. 2.
31. William Empson, 'On Criticism: Questionnaire', *Agenda*, 14/3 (Autumn 1976), 24.

the preciousness of New Critical procedures: 'To say that you won't be bothered with anything but the words on the page...strikes me as petulant,' he wrote in a 1955 review essay. 'If you cared enough you would. For one thing, you might want to know whether the author has really had the experience he describes.'[32]

Empson's most substantial statement on the matter came not long after the war in 'The Verbal Analysis' (1950), which went further than merely defending, as he always did, the interest of authors' aims and circumstances. Here, historical contexts are not the extrinsic points of reference that they typically were for contemporary formalists but already immanent in the bare words on the page:

> I should think indeed that a profound enough criticism could extract an entire cultural history from a simple lyric, rather like Lancelot Andrewes and his fellow preachers, 'dividing the Word of God', who were in the habit of extracting all Protestant theology from a single text. A critic obviously does not need to do this kind of thing often, if at all; it is not really a convenient way to teach cultural history. But it is not my fault, or the fault of any other analytic critic, that our equipment threatens to make us become bores; it is wonderful how many ways there are to be a bore, and almost any line of intellectual effort, however true and useful, presents this threat.[33]

None other than Raymond Williams spotted a similarly reconstructive quality in Empson's notoriously demanding *The Structure of Complex Words* (1952), which he reviewed as 'an example of that kind of literary criticism which, beginning from analysis of language, proceeds not only to specific judgements on works, but also to generalizing judgements in the history of language and of society'.[34] Williams had some misgivings about Empson's method: 'a combination of close and vigorous analysis with the retailing of a considerable amount of miscellaneous information'.[35] In the hands of Empson or Watt, so-called close reading proved to be historically capacious and inclusive reading.

Close reading in its canonized mid-century forms spoke to neither of them. When Watt was asked in 1959 to deliver a lecture on textual explication to an audience of non-university teachers of English, he began with an account of the institutional modes of close analysis then available. First, he discounted the traditional French model of

32. Empson, 'Still the Strange Necessity', 125.
33. William Empson, 'The Verbal Analysis', *Kenyon Review*, 12/4 (Autumn 1950), 599.
34. Raymond Williams, 'The Structure of Complex Words', *English*, 9/49 (March 1952), 27.
35. Williams, 'The Structure of Complex Words', 27.

'explication de texte' with an arrestingly macabre comic analogy: 'a sort of bayonet drill in which the exposed body of literature is riddled with etymologies and dates before being despatched in a harrowingly insensitive résumé'.[36] Meanwhile, he found that the main effect of reading linguistic criticism 'was to deprive [him] of the innocent pleasure that comes from imagining you know the names of things'.[37] More soberly and at greater length, he discussed the Cambridge model of practical criticism in which he had been educated. He considered it 'a technique of supreme value for teaching and examining students', but it nonetheless had three main drawbacks: first, it aspires to a bogus objectivity; second, it is of little use for speaking about novels; and, third, 'its exclusion of historical factors seems to authorize a more general antihistoricism'.[38]

The one mode of uniting the textual with the historical that he recalled in this lecture was that of Leo Spitzer and Erich Auerbach. 'I yield to no one in my admiration,' Watt wrote, but theirs was 'not so much a Method as a small group of isolated, though spectacular, individual triumphs': 'If I am tempted to emulate the *bravura* with which they take off from the word on the page to leap into the farthest empyreans of *Kulturgeschichte*, I soon discover that the Cambridge east winds have condemned me to less giddy modes of critical transport.'[39] This was an obviously self-deprecating way of insisting that there are important calling points—for example, national, economic, and social—on the journey from the words on the page to the whole history of civilization. In practice, Watt was never averse to extrapolating a historical world view from a stylistic detail, as when we learn in an elegant discussion of the eighteenth-century development of the periodic sentence that this 'is the extreme example of the sentence as the intellectual imposition of order upon the items of experience'; as with its poetic counterpart, the closed or heroic couplet, 'the effort is for the speaker or writer to contain or stabilize order, in some way impose a pattern, on the miscellaneous multifariousness of experience and individual attitudes'.[40]

36. Ian Watt, 'The First Paragraph of *The Ambassadors*: An Explication', in Watt, *The Literal Imagination*, 194.
37. Watt, 'The First Paragraph of *The Ambassadors*', 197.
38. Watt, 'The First Paragraph of *The Ambassadors*', 195.
39. Watt, 'The First Paragraph of *The Ambassadors*', 196.
40. Ian Watt, 'The Ironic Voice', in Watt, *The Literal Imagination*, 44.

Empson's and Watt's understanding of textual analysis as a way of accessing cultural history anticipates the kind of analysis that Edward Said praised in 'The Return to Philology', one of the late lectures collected as *Humanism and Democratic Criticism* (2004). For Said, 'a true philological reading is active; it involves getting inside the process of language already going on in words and making it disclose what may be hidden or incomplete or masked or distorted in any text we may have before us'.[41] On the face of it 'about the least with-it, least sexy, and most unmodern of any of the branches of learning associated with humanism', philology means undertaking 'acts of reading and interpretation grounded in the shapes of words as bearers of reality, a reality hidden, misleading, resistant, and difficult'; it moves outwards from 'detailed, patient scrutiny' of the words on the page 'to the often obscure or invisible frameworks in which they exist, to their historical situations and the way in which certain structures of attitude, feeling, and rhetoric get entangled with some currents, some historical and social formulations of their context'.[42] Textual analysis is not an end in itself, but a way of accessing through the close reading of the textual fragment worlds that are otherwise irretrievably lost. Or, as Tzvetan Todorov described Watt's mode, making him sound a little like Williams' version of Empson: 'patient commentary, the restitution of the meaning of words and syntactic constructions, a search for information of all sorts'.[43]

Literary language, then, is an archive. Writing about the 'total war' historical background of interwar fiction, Paul Saint-Amour has brilliantly unpacked the connections between interwar apprehensions of absolute disaster and encyclopedic modes of writing. [44] As a mode of reading, philology might be seen as a critical counterpart to the war-anxious literary encyclopedism that Saint-Amour describes, a salvage job to replenish a depleted world. This is certainly what Said seems to suggest when he summarizes Auerbach's wartime *Mimesis* as 'an attempt to rescue sense and meanings from the fragments of modernity with which, from his Turkish exile, Auerbach saw the downfall of Europe'.[45] Famously, each chapter of *Mimesis* consists of a short

41. Edward Said, *Humanism and Democratic Criticism* (New York: Columbia University Press, 2004), 59.
42. Said, *Humanism and Democratic Criticism*, 57, 58, 61.
43. Todorov, *Literature and its Theorists*, 107.
44. Paul Saint-Amour, *Tense Future: Modernism, Total War, Encyclopedic Form* (New York: Oxford University Press, 2015).
45. Said, *Humanism and Democratic Criticism*, 115.

passage of a primary text followed by chapter-length explication of its meaning as a phase in literary, social, and intellectual history, from Homer and scripture all the way up to the interwar period.

In the same lecture series, Said names Watt in passing as an example of 'humanistic heroism' for how far he went beyond his Cambridge education under the charismatic figures of Richards and Leavis.[46] Although he does not mention the book here, Said's praise for a patient attention to language that yields up a lost historical world is obvious in a work he had admired decades earlier, Watt's *Conrad in the Nineteenth Century* (1979)—'worldly in the best sense of that term'[47]—in which we find a chapter on *Heart of Darkness* that is, as Herbert Lindenberger has pointed out, 'about twice as long as the novella itself'.[48] Said's laudatory review had noted Watt's 'encyclopedic approach', but it was with some unease as well as admiration that Samuel Hynes marvelled at the book's exegetical detail when he also reviewed it on its first appearance: 'But what sort of historicism is Watt demonstrating, that takes nothing for granted, but chooses to reconstruct the whole historical background, as though modern criticism were a city or a state that had suffered some terrible calamity—a war or a natural disaster—and had to be built again from the ruins?'[49] Hynes intended only to suggest that *Conrad in the Nineteenth Century* was symptomatic of a newly problematic phase of literary criticism in the age of theory, with an older critic like Watt seeming unsure what kind of historical knowledge could now be taken for granted. By chance, though, he found a startlingly apt way of evoking the limit-case deprivation that had helped to form Watt's intellectual orientation all those years earlier. Conrad's whole lost world has been reassembled in Watt's book: it has been 'built again from the ruins'.

Creative Writing on the River Kwai

Decades earlier on the Burma–Thailand Railway, Watt and his friends and students in the prison-camp university had tried to leave traces

46. Said, *Humanism and Democratic Criticism*, 68.
47. Said, 'Conrad in the Nineteenth Century', 23.
48. Herbert Lindenberger, 'The Singular Career of Ian Watt', *Stanford Humanities Review*, 8/1 (2000), 6.
49. Said, 'Conrad in the Nineteenth Century', 23. Samuel Hynes, '*Conrad in the Nineteenth Century*, by Ian Watt', *Nineteenth-Century Fiction*, 35/4 (March 1981), 536.

of their own precarious way of life as they buried comrades in the all-encompassing, all-concealing jungles. Introducing his wartime drawings for publication decades later, Ronald Searle explained what these illicit sketches had meant to him at the time:

> These drawings were not a means of catharsis. Circumstances were too basic for that. But they did at times act as a mental life-belt. Now, with the perspective and detachment that a gap of forty years or so can achieve, they can be looked on as the *graffiti* of a condemned man, intending to leave rough witness of his passing through, but who found himself—to his surprise and delight—among the reprieved.[50]

Watching men exactly like them dying around them every day, prisoners could not expect to survive to bring their writings and drawings home. Ian Denys Peek remembers asking himself, 'what records concerning us prisoners will survive to tell the world what has happened to us?'[51] Their documents—Searle's 'graffiti'—were almost posthumous in spirit for many prisoners, ways of registering after their likely deaths in captivity what had happened to them in their final months. This was the 'need to record and testify' that Watt saw as the main lesson for the humanities of those who had risked their already vulnerable lives in order to keep writing in the face of the Japanese prohibition.

And so it is revealing that Watt's prison-camp English department was a place not only of academic literary study, but also where creative writing was produced and workshopped. When Watt, Moir, Alexander, and Durnford found themselves together again at the Tamuang and then Kanchanaburi camps after the building of the Burma–Thailand Railway, they revived their former literary studies with new recruits from among Alexander's injured friends (one of them injured by Watt himself, an amused Alexander specified, because Watt had dropped a rail on his foot on a forced working party).[52] By then, there was no doubt that intellectual activities had to be conducted in secret—pencils or paper were still strictly forbidden, and even movement among huts was intermittently prohibited—because the downturn in Japan's military fortunes had made guards, in Alexander's words, 'ever more explosive and brutal'.[53] 'People wrote poems and stories on surreptitious bits of paper,' Watt mentions in passing in 'The Liberty

50. Searle, *To the Kwai—and Back*, 10.
51. Peek, *One Fourteenth*, 377.
52. Alexander, *Sweet Kwai*, 170.
53. Alexander, *Sweet Kwai*, 188.

of the Prison'.[54] What he does not say is that he himself was guiding these activities.

'In his dry way he was a patient inspiration to us,' Alexander writes of Watt's literature teaching, but he was 'such a stern critic of our verse that we challenged him to show us a poem of his own'.[55] The poem that he showed them survives. The typescript is dated 'Chung'kai 1943' and is titled 'P. O. W. Song':

> O the amazing elegance,
> And the painted faces,
> The surrealist extravagance
> Of prewar places.
>
> From our escalator time
> We glimpsed Edwardian graces,
> But now the garden suburbs
> Vanish from our gazes.
>
> What doctrinaire ascetics,
> Will mould our future phases
> With streamlined economics
> Exterminate the lazy?
>
> I don't much like the present,
> And I can't believe the past,
> At the grimaces of the future
> Idler, stand aghast.[56]

'P. O. W. Song' is an almost perverse poem for a forced labourer to write: a witty, deflationary poem about laziness and the awful prospect of being made to work on his homecoming.

Watt's eschewal of sentimentality and self-dramatization was very much a public position, not to mention a brave one. On prisoner Terence Charley's poem about the beauty of Thailand, for example, Alexander tells us that 'Ian doubted if it would do much for Terence's post-war image as a tortured hero of the Burma–Siam railway'.[57] Durnford writes of his own poetic contributions ('no technical purity and too much feeling') as an embarrassment to the others in their copiousness and effusion.[58] In fact, Watt kept copies of some of them, albeit alongside a satirical poem by an unnamed member of the group

54. Watt, 'The Liberty of the Prison', 526.
55. Alexander, *Sweet Kwai*, 169, 172.
56. Ian Watt, 'POW Song', Stanford University Special Collections, SC401-ACCN 1994–106, Box 22, Folder 'Jap. Stuff Misc'.
57. Alexander, *Sweet Kwai*, 175.
58. Durnford, *Branch Line to Burma*, 162.

teasing Durnford's productivity: 'No war deters our poetaster | The mills of John turn ever faster.' More soberly, Watt recalled that the psychological riskiness of expressing real emotion ('the inner private world that was still full of nameless fears') 'set very strict limits to what we could accomplish. I can certainly remember no poem or story which got to grips with what our life was really like.'[59] His efforts with the creative writers seem to have been focused on steering his students away from using poetry to express what were liable to be unmanageably painful feelings.

But here in the middle of the war, in a prison camp in Thailand, was the embryonic model for the kind of English department—with its historicizing literature seminar and the creative writing workshop—that found institutional expression only much later in the new universities of the 1960s. To institutionalize a subject is a matter of mode as well as content, and one democratic innovation that Watt introduced at UEA was the break with the old tutorial-and-exam system in favour of a degree course consisting half of assessed seminars; prior to the opening of UEA, he had described the undergraduate seminar as 'the most satisfactory method of teaching that I have ever encountered' (by then he had encountered it formally at Berkeley as well as by necessity in Thailand).[60] The main problem that Watt identified with the seminar—'It can more easily produce the egalitarian form than its substance'—would become notorious thanks to a scholar and novelist appointed a year after Watt's departure.[61] In Malcolm Bradbury's memorable caricature of the 1960s universities in *The History Man* (1975), the seminar is a mere pseudo-democracy where radical sociologist Howard Kirk can bully his students. This is where

> an apparently casual remark about one's schoolboy stamp collection, or a literary reference to the metaphoric significance of colour, will lead to a sudden psychic foray from a teacher who will dive down into your unconscious with three shrewd enquiries and come up clutching something in you called 'bourgeois materialism' or 'racism'. Howard's classes are especially famous for being punitive in this way.'[62]

59. Watt, 'The Liberty of the Prison', 527.
60. Watt, 'The Idea of an English School', 43.
61. Ian Watt, 'The Seminar', *Universities Quarterly*, 18 (1964), 377.
62. Malcolm Bradbury, *The History Man* (London: Picador, 2000), 137.

As a distinguished Americanist, a prolific comic novelist, and an academic critic of modern literature at a time when some British universities were still struggling with (in Watt's sardonic phrase) 'the giddy modernity of Thomas Hardy', Bradbury is undoubtedly an important figure in UEA's first half-century.[63] But Watt deserves a good deal of the credit for introducing creative writing into British universities via UEA. Michelene Wandor's history of British writing programmes recounts the conventional story when she writes that in 1970 Bradbury introduced creative writing from the United States. Along with colleague Angus Wilson, Bradbury established Britain's first creative writing MA in 1970 because he 'had regularly visited and taught in American universities': 'the immediate influence of the US' was 'explicitly evident in the MA at UEA'.[64] But, as Kathryn Holeywell has been the first to point out, creative writing at UEA has a 'longer, more complex, and more organic history' than this.[65] Watt was already back in California by the time Bradbury arrived in 1965, but everything hinged on Watt's earliest personnel choices when, before the university even opened, he courted and appointed Wilson, then approaching the height of his reputation: this was the first time a creative writer had been hired *as* a creative writer into a British department of English.[66] Holeywell attributes Wilson's appointment to the fact that *Watt* had spent years in the United States, where writers in residence were already fixtures of university campuses. In this respect, her argument is continuous with those crediting Bradbury: that it was simply an American import.

But Watt had been conducting creative writing workshops—and writing fiction and poetry himself—both back in the Thai camps and soon after demobilization, years before he set foot on American soil, and twenty years before he arrived at UEA. Creative writing at the University of East Anglia had been on Watt's mind from the start. Aside even from his appointment of Wilson, there is additional evidence in the university's first undergraduate prospectus. Under the entry for the School of English Studies that Watt alone authored, we find that 'the

63. Watt, 'The University of East Anglia', 247.
64. Michelene Wandor, *The Author is Not Dead, Merely Somewhere Else: Creative Writing Reconceived* (Basingstoke: Palgrave Macmillan, 2008), 8, 81.
65. Kathryn Holeywell, 'The Origins of a Creative Writing Programme at the University of East Anglia, 1963–66', *New Writing: The International Journal for the Practice and Theory of Creative Writing*, 6/1 (2009), 16.
66. Holeywell, 'The Origins of a Creative Writing Programme', 17. On Watt's appointment of Wilson, see Drabble, *Angus Wilson*, 312–15.

examiners may take into account any writings such as poems or novels which the candidate may wish to submit'.[67]

The Uses of Literature

In the moving memorial resolution that his colleagues at Stanford drafted on Watt's death, we learn that 'Watt once said, insisting that he was being hard-headed, not sentimental, that he was sure that, in his World-War II internment, it was the fact that works of literature existed and could still touch him—and his awareness of what that fact said about humanity—that enabled him to survive'.[68] It is impossible to generalize about what the humanities meant in the camps of the Second World War because, while we would expect almost everything to depend on people's physical state and the conditions under which they were living, even these can be an unreliable guide to the conclusions that individual prisoners drew.

For example, to take two men I have already discussed together because their wartime hardships seem comparably atrocious—Jean Améry and 'my barracks mate Primo Levi', as he designates him in an essay on the very topic of the humanist in Auschwitz—we find discussions of literature in their memoirs that point in diametrically opposite directions.[69] A whole chapter of Levi's *If This Is a Man* is devoted to (the chapter's title) 'The Canto of Ulysses', canto 26 of Dante's *Inferno*. This is an expressively disjointed chapter, its pages a choppy patchwork of quoted lines interspersed with the fragmentary story of Levi's struggle to remember the poem for a French friend who does not know it. Levi's desperation is such that he would 'give today's soup' to connect the lines.[70] 'For a moment I forget who I am and where I am,' Levi writes.[71] But then there is Améry, for whom in Auschwitz 'the intellect very abruptly lost its basic quality: its transcendence'.[72]

67. 'University of East Anglia Prospectus, 1963–4', University of East Anglia Special Collections, 'UEA Collection'.

68. 'Memorial Resolution: Ian Watt', *Stanford Report*, 8 March 2000, <http://news.stanford.edu/news/2000/march8/memwatt-38.html> (accessed 21 August 2017).

69. Améry, *At the Mind's Limits*, 3.

70. Levi, *Survival in Auschwitz*, 114.

71. Levi, *Survival in Auschwitz*, 113.

72. Améry, *At the Mind's Limits*, 7.

> I recall a winter evening when after work we were dragging ourselves, out of step, from the IG-Farben site back into the camp to the accompaniment of the Kapo's unnerving 'left, two, three, four', when—for God-knows-what reason—a flag waving in front of a half-finished building caught my eye. 'The walls stand speechless and cold, the flags clank in the wind,' I muttered to myself in mechanical association. Then I repeated the stanza somewhat louder, listened to the words sound, tried to track the rhythm, and expected that the emotional and mental response that for years this Hölderlin poem had awakened in me would emerge. But nothing happened. The poem no longer transcended reality. There it was and all that remained was objective statement: such and such, and the Kapo roars 'left', and the soup was watery, and the flags are clanking in the wind.[73]

Améry wonders if the problem was that there was no one he could share the poem with, for he no longer knew anyone whom aesthetic experience could even potentially touch. In this, as in many other respects, British prisoners of war of the Japanese had the advantage of their common language and culture, although there are obviously many other reasons why it would be hard to conceive of a 'university' at Auschwitz.

What did literature do on the Burma–Thailand Railway? Watt is not an illuminating reporter about how his teaching in the prison camps might have helped him or others. Even in chatty private references to the prison-camp English department, his default mode is self-deprecating comedy, as when he and Brigadier Toosey corresponded about a common acquaintance from Watt's Shakespeare seminar: 'I well remember how, at the very end of the course, he purloined the notebook of Colonel Hingston. He had apparently only thought worthy of note the information "Shakespeare, William. 37 plays. Perhaps 39".'[74] Watt tells the story as if it were a joke as much against his own tutorial failings as the academic deficiencies of Colonel Hingston.

Shakespeare also makes a comic appearance in Alexander's memoir, when we learn that Japanese guards took exception to some of the prisoners' plays, and 'did not warm to Ian Watt's assertion that "gentlemen in England now a-bed shall think themselves accurs'd they were not here"', a darkly funny gloss on the disparity between the prisoners' unromantic situation and the heroisms called up in Henry V's legendary

73. Améry, *At the Mind's Limits*, 7.
74. Letter to Brigadier Philip Toosey dated 9 August 1967, Stanford University Special Collections, SC401-ACCN 1994-106, Box 24, Folder 1.

peroration.[75] A half-French, Shakespeare-teaching prisoner of war might also have recalled a less celebrated aspect of Henry V's conduct at Agincourt, his massacre of the French soldiers whom his troops took prisoner there. Obviously Watt could not have known of the iconic propaganda use to which Laurence Olivier was putting *Henry V* back in Britain in the same years. He may have known of *This Sceptred Isle*, though, the patriotic Shakespeare revue that G. Wilson Knight performed from the summer of 1940 through to a culminating week in London a year later: heavy on the best-known passages of the history plays, it inevitably included the speech from which Watt mockingly quoted.[76] In any case, Watt certainly knew that there was a Shakespeare more appropriate to the camps than the military virtues conjured up by Henry V, or even by disarmed warriors such as Coriolanus and Othello ('Othello with his occupation gone' is Hynes's summary of the prisoner of war)—or, to take one of the truly eccentric uses of Shakespeare in the Second World War, the improbably 'heroic, masculine, and American', 'virtuous and soldierly', uniformed Hamlet of the famous morale-building production that Maurice Evans staged for GIs in Hawaii in 1944.[77] Instead, it was from *Measure for Measure* that Watt took the title of the first piece of writing that he published about the camps, 'The Liberty of the Prison'. This was an especially relevant play to recall in the context of prison camps, given Vivian Thomas's summary of the problem plays as texts about 'the relationship between human behaviour and institutions'; they are 'concerned with authority, hierarchy, decision-making and the consequence of these decisions for the society as a whole and for particular individuals'.[78]

'The Liberty of the Prison' never names *Measure for Measure*, but Watt nonetheless mentions his reading of Shakespeare as a prisoner:

Below a certain level no intellectual interests can survive. In the camp where I had come down with malaria, I had lain with my head on pack in a kind of coma, only getting up to collect my rice, hardly talking and hardly thinking.

75. Alexander, *Sweet Kwai*, 186.
76. The early text was published as G. Wilson Knight, *This Sceptred Isle: Shakespeare's Message for England at War* (Oxford: Basil Blackwell, 1940); the programme from the final week at the Westminster Theatre, London, is published as an appendix to G. Wilson Knight, *Collected Works*, vi. *Shakespearian Production* (London: Routledge, 2002), 314.
77. Hynes, *The Soldiers' Tale*, 234. Anne Russell, 'Maurice Evans' *G. I. Hamlet*', in Irena R. Makaryk and Marissa McHugh (eds), *Shakespeare and the Second World War: Memory, Culture, Identity* (Toronto: University of Toronto Press, 2012), 235, 238.
78. Vivian Thomas, *The Moral Universe of Shakespeare's Problem Plays* (London: Routledge, 1991), 15.

But one day I had suddenly realized that inside my pack I had the works of Shakespeare: and for a week I read them all through with enormous pleasure, and had gone through half way again before relapsing into my previous apathy. It wasn't till many months later that I understood what had happened: the same battalion doctor rejoined me in one of the base camps, and explained that my brief spurt of intellectual energy had begun and ended with a small supply of vitamin B which had come into the camp, and which I'd taken for the few days it had lasted.[79]

This battalion doctor appears earlier in the essay diagnosing the malaria that had left Watt 'for about two months in a state of dull insensibility'.[80] Watt's references to the mind-killing effects of sickness and malnutrition suggest that there is something even more complex and troubling going on in this essay than its declared argument about the difficulties of ceasing to be a prisoner and having to make choices again. After all, choicelessness as a consequence of catatonic indifference to your own fate sounds very little like meaningful liberation. Put back in its original context, the paradoxical phrase 'the liberty of the prison' tells this much darker story.

The phrase appears in *Measure for Measure* when the Duke, incognito, asks about the prisoner Barnadine, who has been condemned to death:

> DUKE. Hath he borne himself penitently in prison? How seems he to be touched?
>
> PROVOST. A man that apprehends death no more dreadfully but as a drunken sleep: careless, reckless, and fearless of what's past, present, or to come: insensible of mortality and desperately mortal.
>
> DUKE. He wants advice.
>
> PROVOST. He will hear none. He hath evermore had the liberty of the prison: give him leave to escape hence, he would not. Drunk many times a day, if not many days entirely drunk. We have very oft awaked him, as if to carry him to execution, and showed him a seeming warrant for it. It hath not moved him at all.[81]

'We have very oft awaked him, as if to carry him to execution, and showed him a seeming warrant for it': the criminal Barnadine is actually

79. Watt, 'The Liberty of the Prison', 525.
80. Watt, 'The Liberty of the Prison', 522.
81. William Shakespeare, *The New Cambridge Shakespeare: Measure for Measure*, ed. Brian Gibbons (Cambridge: Cambridge University Press, 2006), 166 (4. 2. 123–34).

intended to die, but mock execution is an established form of torture precisely because of the psychological agony it is meant to inflict—and, in most cases, surely does. Yet imprisonment has left Barnadine so unreachably far gone that not even the prospect of his imminent death can touch him. We remember Watt's references to his own 'state of dull insensibility' and 'a kind of coma... hardly talking and hardly thinking'. The obvious contrast to Barnadine's indifference ('careless, reckless, and fearless of what's past, present, or to come') is in the play's previous act, when the condemned Claudio pleads with his sister, Isabella, to sleep with the corrupt regent Angelo in order to save his life. Claudio's courage completely fails him as he confronts his own execution: 'The weariest and most loathèd worldly life | That age, ache, penury, and imprisonment | Can lay on nature, is a paradise | To what we fear of death.'[82] Claudio's moral collapse in consequence of his fear of dying is altogether human whereas Barnadine's numbed, stupefied fearlessness is terrible in a completely different way.

Watt's thinking when he took his title from this moment in *Measure for Measure* is hard to reconstruct. Perhaps he thought that 'the liberty of the prison' was an appropriately contradictory phrase in its own right and either forgot its origin or supposed that the reader would—it hardly supports the essay's ostensible argument about how much easier it is to be imprisoned than free. Or perhaps Watt understood that the reader would catch the reference; he would certainly have known that the most intuitive way to approach what is so obviously a quotation is to restore its original context. Either way, the allusion tells an unbearably painful story about knowing how close you came to losing yourself and never coming back. I think Watt recognized this a decade later when he wrote about a return he had made to Thailand in the late 1960s: 'I'd sometimes thought of our life here as the liberty of the prison; at least we'd been freed of the burden of choosing our own lives. But day after day, just keeping away from our own fear must have blunted our capacity to feel. We hadn't noticed these slow lobotomies at the time, but they'd happened; and afterwards, whatever it was that made you able to live freely couldn't be put back.'[83]

Finally, Watt's interest in the continuities and discontinuities of a life story encourages us to ask who came back at all after this kind of

82. Shakespeare, *Measure for Measure*, 143 (3. 1. 129–32).
83. Watt, 'Reunion on the Kwai', 711.

imprisonment. Whereas the postmodernist Ballard found a shape to his post-war life that allowed him a faintly paranoid but pleasing illusion of necessity ('assignments run through all our lives; there are no coincidences'), the realist Watt stressed the ways in which we are, like characters in eighteenth-century novels, hostages to contingency. 'Looking back on our lives it seems inconceivable that things could possibly have been otherwise, or that they should actually have been mainly determined by accident or momentary convenience; and yet such is often, perhaps usually, the case,' or so he wrote of the painful ruptures of Conrad's biography (*C.* 15). But the imagined lives that we were never allowed to live always shadow in our minds the one that we actually lived, Watt suggests, when he writes that 'to be pleasantly surprised at what we have become does not efface the imprint of what was not to be' (*C.* 24).

Eric Lomax wrote that his time as a prisoner 'had put a huge distance between me and my previous life, yet I behaved—was expected to behave—as though I were the same person. In the legal and civil senses I suppose I was, but that was about all.'[84] Watt likewise believed that the war had changed him; but he also knew that one ironic effect of the change was that by definition it could never be quantified. In an unpublished poem titled 'Kanburi 1945', he cast his years of imprisonment as already an ending:

> The man I was stopped being
> so many years ago
> that what and who I was before
> the man I am can't know.[85]

All Watt's major criticism is about subjectivity in history, and the contingent shape of an individual life in time. I hope to have shown in this book that his own war experience helped to give him an unusual perspective on this topic, exorbitant though its price clearly was. And as the author of those seemingly self-cancelling terms 'formal realism' and 'realism of assessment', Watt would know better than anyone that to speak of 'perspective' is to identify not only someone's personal vantage point, which may be accidental, but also the quality of his or her perception, which is probably not.

84. Lomax, *The Railway Man*, 207.
85. Ian Watt, 'Kanburi 1945', Stanford University Special Collections, SC401-ACCN 1994-106, Box 22, Folder 'Jap. Stuff Misc'.

Bibliography

ARCHIVES

Stanford University Special Collections

Fowler, H. W., and Watt, I. P., 'Japanese—Prisoner of War Language', SC401-ACCN 1994-106, Box 24, Folder 4.

Watt, Ian, 'A Chap in Dark Glasses', SC401-ACCN 1990-131, Box 56, Folder 'POW Stuff'.

Watt, Ian, 'Concrete or Abstract?', Forces Educational Broadcast, 1951, SC401-ACCN 1990-131, Box 41, Folder 'BBC: Past'.

Watt, Ian, 'Dover, November 1945', SC401-ACCN 1994-106, Box 23, Folder 1.

Watt, Ian, 'Dying in the Summer: Chung'Kai 1943', SC401-ACCN 1994-106, Box 22, Folder 'Jap. Stuff Misc'.

Watt, Ian, 'Every Word Has a Meaning', SC401-ACCN 1990-131, Box 41, Folder 'BBC: Past'.

Watt, Ian, 'The Japanese', SC401-ACCN 1990-131, Box 56, Folder, 'The Gahanese Character').

Watt, Ian, 'Kanburi 1945', SC401-ACCN 1994-106, Box 22, Folder 'Jap. Stuff Misc'.

Watt, Ian, 'Kings, Rats, and Opticians', SC401-ACCN 1994-106, Box 23, Folder 9.

Watt, Ian, 'POW Song', SC401-ACCN 1994-106, Box 22, Folder 'Jap. Stuff Misc'.

Watt, Ian, 'Shakespeare's Wisdom: An Approach', SC401-ACCN 1994-106, Box 23, Folder 3.

Watt, Ian, 'The Strangest Thing', SC401-ACCN 1990-131, Box 56, Folder 'The Strangest Thing').

Watt, Ian, 'Too Much Foresight', SC401-ACCN 1994-106, Box 22, Folder 'POW Stuff'.

Watt, Ian, 'The Ways of Guilt', SC401-ACCN 1990-131, Box 56, Folder 'Revenge of Mercy'.

The National Archives

War Office: Directorate of Military Intelligence: Liberated Prisoner of War Interrogation Questionnaires, WO 344/407.

University of East Anglia Archives

Annual Report of the Vice-Chancellor, 1963–4, University of East Anglia Special Collections.

'University of East Anglia Prospectus, 1963–4', University of East Anglia Special Collections, 'UEA Collection'.

Washington University Archives

Watt, Ian, 'Jane Austen and the Tradition of Comic Aggression', Fall Honors Lecture, Washington University in St Louis, 22 September 1982, Office of Public Affairs, Assembly Series Administrative Records, University Archives, Department of Special Collections.

PUBLISHED WORKS

Agamben, Georgio, *Homo Sacer: Sovereign Power and Bare Life*, trans. Daniel Heller-Roazen (Stanford: Stanford University Press, 1998).

Agamben, Georgio, *Remnants of Auschwitz: The Witness and the Archive*, trans. Daniel Heller-Roazen (New York: Zone, 2002).

Alexander, Stephen, *Sweet Kwai Run Softly* (Bristol: Merriots, 1996).

Allport, Alan, *Demobbed: Coming Home after the Second World War* (New Haven: Yale University Press, 2009).

Alter, Robert, *Rogue's Progress: Studies in the Picaresque Novel* (Cambridge, MA: Harvard University Press, 1965).

Alter, Robert, *Fielding and the Nature of the Novel* (Cambridge, MA: Harvard University Press, 1968).

Améry, Jean, *At the Mind's Limits: Contemplations by a Survivor on Auschwitz and its Realities*, trans. Sidney Rosenfeld and Stella P. Rosenfeld (Bloomington: Indiana University Press, 1980).

Anderson, Amanda, *Bleak Liberalism* (Chicago: University of Chicago Press, 2016).

Arendt, Hannah, *Eichmann in Jerusalem: A Report on the Banality of Evil* (London: Penguin, 1994).

Arendt, Hannah, *The Origins of Totalitarianism* (Orlando, FL: Harcourt, 1979).

Armstrong, Nancy, *Desire and Domestic Fiction: A Political History of the Novel* (Oxford: Oxford University Press, 1987).

Armstrong, Nancy, *How Novels Think: The Limits of Individualism from 1719–1900* (New York: Columbia University Press, 2005).

Austen, Jane, *Northanger Abbey* (London: Penguin, 2003).

Azim, Firdous, *The Colonial Rise of the Novel* (London: Routledge, 1993).

Bailey, James, '"Repetition, Boredom, Despair": Muriel Spark and the Eichmann Trial', *Holocaust Studies*, 17/2–3 (Autumn–Winter 2011), 185–206.

Baldick, Chris, *The Social Mission of English Criticism, 1848–1932* (Oxford: Clarendon Press, 1987).

Ballard, J. G., *The Atrocity Exhibition: New Revised Edition* (San Francisco: Re/Search, 1990).
Ballard, J. G., *The Kindness of Women* (New York: Picador, 1991).
Ballard, J. G., *Concrete Island* (New York: Picador, 2001).
Ballard, J. G., *Empire of the Sun* (New York: Simon & Schuster, 2005).
Ballard, J. G., *Miracles of Life: Shanghai to Shepperton: An Autobiography* (London: Harper Perennial, 2008).
Ballard, J. G., 'The Dead Time', in *The Complete Stories of J. G. Ballard* (New York: Norton, 2009), 925–39.
Ballard, J. G., '1986: Solveig Nordlund. Future Now', in *Extreme Metaphors: Interviews with J. G. Ballard 1967–2008*, ed. Simon Sellars and Dan O'Hara (London: Fourth Estate, 2012), 224–30.
Ballard, J. G., *Extreme Metaphors: Interviews with J. G. Ballard 1967–2008*, ed. Simon Sellars and Dan O'Hara (London: Fourth Estate, 2012).
Ballard, J. G., *The Drowned World* (London: Fourth Estate, 2014).
Ballaster, Ros, *Seductive Forms: Women's Amatory Fiction from 1684 to 1740* (Oxford: Clarendon Press, 1992).
Barth, John, *The Floating Opera and The End of the Road* (New York: Anchor, 1988).
Beaumont, Joan, *Gull Force: Survival and Leadership in Captivity, 1941–1945* (Sydney: Allen & Unwin, 1988).
Bender, John, *Imagining the Penitentiary: Fiction and the Architecture of Mind in Eighteenth-Century England* (Chicago: University of Chicago Press, 1987).
Bergonzi, Bernard, *The Situation of the Novel* (London: Macmillan, 1970).
Bergonzi, Bernard, *Wartime and Aftermath: English Literature and its Background, 1939–1960* (Oxford: Oxford University Press, 1993).
Bevis, Matthew (ed.), *Some Versions of Empson* (Oxford: Clarendon Press, 2007).
Biess, Frank, *Homecomings: Returning POWs and the Legacies of Defeat in Postwar Germany* (Princeton: Princeton University Press, 2006).
Blackater, C. F., *Gods without Reason* (London: Eyre & Spottiswoode, 1948).
Booth, Wayne C., *The Rhetoric of Fiction* (Penguin: Harmondsworth, 1991).
Borowski, Tadeusz, *This Way for the Gas, Ladies and Gentlemen*, trans. Barbara Vedder (London: Penguin, 1976).
Bourke, Roger, *Prisoners of the Japanese: Literary Imagination and the Prisoner-of-War Experience* (St Lucia, Queensland: University of Queensland Press, 2006).
Bowden, Tim, *Changi Photographer: George Aspinall's Record of Captivity* (Sydney: ABC Books, 1993).
Bradbury, Malcolm, *The Modern British Novel* (London: Penguin, 1993).
Bradbury, Malcolm, *The History Man* (London: Picador, 2000).
Braddon, Russell, *End of a Hate* (London: Cassell, 1958).
Braddon, Russell, *The Naked Island* (Edinburgh: Birlinn, 2005).
Brecht, Bertolt, *Mother Courage and her Children: A Chronicle of the Thirty Years' War*, trans. Eric Bentley (New York: Grove, 1991).

Brenkman, John, *The Cultural Contradictions of Democracy: Political Thought since September 11* (Princeton: Princeton University Press, 2007).

Brown, Homer Obed, *Institutions of the English Novel: From Defoe to Scott* (Philadelphia: University of Pennsylvania Press, 1997).

Brownlow, Kevin, 'The Making of David Lean's Film of *The Bridge on the River Kwai*', *Cineaste*, 22/2 (1996), 10–16.

Burgess, Anthony, *A Clockwork Orange* (London: Heinemann, 1962).

Calvocoressi, Peter, Guy Wint, and John Pritchard, *The Penguin History of the Second World War* (London: Penguin, 1999).

Cameron, Deborah, '"The Virtues of Good Prose": Verbal Hygiene and the Movement', in Zachary Leader (ed.), *The Movement Reconsidered: Essays on Larkin, Amis, Gunn, Davie, and their Contemporaries* (Oxford: Oxford University Press, 2009), 139–54.

Campbell, Jill, *Natural Masques: Gender and Identity in Fielding's Plays and Novels* (Stanford: Stanford University Press, 1995).

Camus, Albert, *The Fall*, trans. Justin O'Brien (New York: Vintage, 1991).

Camus, Albert, *The Plague*, trans. Stuart Gilbert (New York: Vintage, 1991).

Carnell, Rachel, *Partisan Politics, Narrative Realism, and the Rise of the British Novel* (Basingstoke: Palgrave, 2006).

Carnochan, W. B. 'The Literature of Confinement', in Norval Morris and David J. Rothman (eds), *The Oxford History of the Prison: The Practice of Punishment in Western Society* (Oxford: Oxford University Press, 1995), 427–55.

Carnochan, W. B., '"A Matter *Discutable*": *The Rise of the Novel*', *Eighteenth-Century Fiction*, 12/2 (2000), 167–84.

Carnochan, W. B., 'The Persistence of *The Rise of the Novel*', *Stanford Humanities Review*, 8/1 (2000), 86–93.

Carter, Alan, *Survival of the Fittest: A Young Englishman's Struggle as a Prisoner of War in Java and Japan* (Great Britain: Paul T. Carter, 2013).

Caruth, Cathy, *Unclaimed Experience: Trauma, Narrative, and History* (Baltimore: Johns Hopkins University Press, 1996).

Cervantes, Miguel de, *Exemplary Stories*, trans. Lesley Lipson (Oxford: Oxford University Press, 2008).

Chalker, Jack, *Burma Railway: Images of War: The Original War Drawings of Japanese POW Jack Chalker* (Shepton Mallet: Mercer Books, 2007).

Churchill, Winston, *The Second World War*, iv. *The Hinge of Fate* (New York: Mariner, 1986).

Clavell, James, *King Rat* (New York: Delta, 1999).

Coast, John, *Railroad of Death* (Newcastle: Myrmidon, 2014).

Collingham, Lizzie, *The Taste of War: World War II and the Battle for Food* (London: Penguin, 2011).

Collini, Stefan, *Absent Minds: Intellectuals in Britain* (Oxford: Oxford University Press, 2006).

Connolly, Cyril, *Enemies of Promise* (Chicago: University of Chicago Press, 2008).

Conrad, Joseph, *Almayer's Folly* (London: Penguin, 1976).
Conrad, Joseph, *Lord Jim* (Oxford: Oxford University Press, 2002).
Conrad, Joseph, *Heart of Darkness and the Congo Diary* (London: Penguin, 2007).
Conrad, Joseph, *The Nigger of the 'Narcissus' and Other Stories* (London: Penguin, 2007).
Conrad, Joseph, *Chance* (Oxford: Oxford University Press, 2008).
Crews, Frederick, 'Foreword', in Ian Watt, *The Literal Imagination: Selected Essays*, ed. Bruce Thompson (Palo Alto: Society for the Promotion of Science and Scholarship and the Stanford Humanities Center, 2002), ix–xiii.
Davidson, Cathy, *Revolution and the Word: The Rise of the Novel in America* (New York: Oxford University Press, 1986).
Davie, Donald, *Purity of Diction in English Verse* (London: Chatto & Windus, 1952).
Davis, Lennard J., *Factual Fictions: The Origins of the English Novel* (New York: Columbia University Press, 1983).
Davis, Lennard J., 'Who Put the "The" in "the Novel"? Identity Politics and Disability in Novel Studies', *NOVEL: A Forum on Fiction*, 31/3 (Summer 1998), 317–34.
Daws, Gavan, *Prisoners of the Japanese: POWs of World War II in the Pacific* (New York: William Morrow, 1994).
Defoe, Daniel, *Roxana* (Oxford: Oxford University Press, 1998).
Defoe, Daniel, *A Journal of the Plague Year* (London: Penguin, 2003).
Defoe, Daniel, *Robinson Crusoe* (London: Penguin, 2003).
Defoe, Daniel, *Moll Flanders* (Oxford: Oxford University Press, 2009).
Defoe, Daniel, *The True-Born Englishman and Other Writings*, ed. P. N. Furbank and W. R. Owens (London: Penguin, 2011).
De Somogyi, Nick, *Shakespeare's Theatre of War* (Aldershot: Ashgate, 1998).
Des Pres, Terrence, *The Survivor: An Anatomy of Life in the Death Camps* (Oxford: Oxford University Press, 1980).
Dickens, Charles, *A Tale of Two Cities* (London: Penguin, 2003).
Donovan, Josephine, *Women and the Rise of the Novel, 1405–1726* (Basingstoke: Macmillan, 1999).
Doody, Margaret Anne, *The True Story of the Novel* (New Brunswick: Rutgers University Press, 1996).
Dower, John W., *War without Mercy: Race and Power in the Pacific War* (London: Faber, 1986).
Dowling, Christopher, 'Introduction', in Robert Hardie, *The Burma–Siam Railway: The Secret Diary of Dr Robert Hardie 1942–45* (London: Imperial War Museum, 1983), 8–10.
Doyle, Sir Francis Hastings, 'The Private of the Buffs', in Sir Francis Hastings Doyle, *The Return of the Guards and Other Poems* (London: Macmillan, 1866), 105–7.

Doyle, Laura, *Freedom's Empire: Race and the Rise of the Novel in Atlantic Modernity* (Durham, NC: Duke University Press, 2008).

Drabble, Margaret, *Angus Wilson: A Biography* (London: Secker & Warburg, 1995).

Durnford, John, *Branch Line to Burma* (London: Macdonald, 1958).

During, Simon, *Against Democracy: Literary Experience in the Era of Emancipations* (New York: Fordham University Press, 2012).

Empson, William, *Seven Types of Ambiguity* (2nd edn.; London: Chatto & Windus, 1947).

Empson, William, 'The Verbal Analysis', *Kenyon Review*, 12/4 (Autumn 1950), 594–601.

Empson, William, 'Tom Jones', *Kenyon Review*, 20/2 (Spring 1958), 217–49.

Empson, William, 'On Criticism: Questionnaire', *Agenda*, 14/3 (Autumn 1976), 23–5.

Empson, William, 'Autumn on Nan-Yüeh', in William Empson, *Collected Poems* (London: Hogarth, 1984), 72–80.

Empson, William, *Using Biography* (London: Chatto & Windus and the Hogarth Press, 1984).

Empson, William, 'The Hammer's Ring', in William Empson, *Argufying: Essays on Literature and Culture*, ed. John Haffenden (London: Hogarth, 1988), 216–24.

Empson, William, *Selected Letters*, ed. John Haffenden (Oxford: Oxford University Press, 2006).

Empson, William, 'A Chinese University', in William Empson, *The Strengths of Shakespeare's Shrew: Essays, Memoirs and Reviews*, ed. John Haffenden (London: Bloomsbury, 2015), 190–4.

Empson, William, 'Basic and Communication', in William Empson, *The Strengths of Shakespeare's Shrew: Essays, Memoirs and Reviews*, ed. John Haffenden (London: Bloomsbury, 2015), 161–9.

Empson, William, 'Basic English and the Modern World', in William Empson, *The Strengths of Shakespeare's Shrew: Essays, Memoirs and Reviews*, ed. John Haffenden (London: Bloomsbury, 2015), 170–5.

Empson, William, 'Still the Strange Necessity', in William Empson, *Argufying: Essays on Literature and Culture*, ed. John Haffenden (London: Hogarth, 1988), 120–8.

Empson, William, 'Teaching English in the Far East and England', in William Empson, *The Strengths of Shakespeare's Shrew: Essays, Memoirs and Reviews*, ed. John Haffenden (London: Bloomsbury, 2015), 201–19.

Far East, 1/1 (February 1944).

Far East, 1/2 (March 1944).

Felman, Shoshana, *The Juridical Unconscious: Trials and Traumas in the Twentieth Century* (Cambridge, MA: Harvard University Press, 2002).

Felman, Shoshana, and Dori Laub, *Testimony: Crises of Witnessing in Literature, Psychoanalysis, and History* (New York: Routledge, 1992).

Ferguson, Frances, 'Rape and the Rise of the Novel', *Representations*, 20 (Autumn 1988), 88–112.

Fiedler, Leslie, 'Afterthoughts on the Rosenbergs', in *The Collected Essays of Leslie Fiedler*, i (New York: Stein & Day, 1971), 25–45.
Fiedler, Leslie, 'Introduction: No! in Thunder', in *The Collected Essays of Leslie Fiedler*, i (New York: Stein & Day, 1971), 221–38.
Fiedler, Leslie, 'Introduction to the Second Edition of *An End of Innocence*', in *The Collected Essays of Leslie Fiedler*, i (New York: Stein & Day, 1971), xvii–xix.
Fiedler, Leslie, 'Looking Backward: America from Europe', in *The Collected Essays of Leslie Fiedler*, i (New York: Stein & Day, 1971), 124–8.
Fielding, Henry, *The Journal of a Voyage to Lisbon* (London: Chiswick Press, 1892).
Fielding, Henry, *Amelia*, ed. Martin C. Battestin (Oxford: Clarendon Press, 1983).
Fielding, Henry, *Tom Jones* (Oxford: Oxford University Press, 1996).
Fielding, Henry, *Joseph Andrews and Shamela* (London: Penguin, 1999).
Fielding, Henry, *Jonathan Wild* (Oxford: Oxford University Press, 2008).
Flower, Sibylla Jane, 'Captors and Captives on the Burma–Thailand Railway', in Bob Moore and Kent Fedorowich (eds), *Prisoners of War and their Captors in World War II* (Oxford: Berg, 1996), 227–52.
Flower, Sybilla Jane, 'Memory and the Prisoner of War Experience: The United Kingdom', in Kevin Blackburn and Karl Hack (eds), *Forgotten Captives in Japanese-Occupied Asia: National Memories and Forgotten Captivities* (Abingdon: Routledge, 2008), 57–72.
Forster, E. M., *Aspects of the Novel* (San Diego: Harcourt, 1955).
Forster, E. M., 'George Orwell', in E. M. Forster, *Two Cheers for Democracy* (San Diego: Harcourt Brace, 1967), 60–3.
Frank, Joseph, 'Foreword', *Stanford Humanities Review*, 8/1 (2000), ix–xii.
Frank, Joseph, 'The Consequence of Ian Watt: A Call for Papers on Diminished Reputations', *Common Knowledge*, 13/2–3 (2007), 497–511.
Freud, Sigmund, *Beyond the Pleasure Principle*, trans. James Strachey (New York: Norton, 1961).
Freud, Sigmund, *Civilization and its Discontents*, trans. James Strachey (New York: Norton, 1961).
Frye, Northrop, *Anatomy of Criticism: Four Essays* (Princeton: Princeton University Press, 1990).
Fuller, Randall, *Emerson's Ghosts: Literature, Politics, and the Making of Americanists* (New York: Oxford University Press, 2007).
Fussell, Paul, *The Rhetorical World of Augustan Humanism: Ethics and Imagery from Swift to Burke* (Oxford: Clarendon Press, 1965).
Fussell, Paul, *The Great War and Modern Memory* (New York: Oxford University Press, 1975).
Gallagher, Catherine, *Nobody's Story: The Vanishing Acts of Women Writers in the Marketplace, 1670–1820* (Berkeley and Los Angeles: University of California Press, 1994).
Gillies, Midge, *The Barbed-Wire University: The Real Lives of Allied Prisoners of War in the Second World War* (London: Aurum, 2012).

Golding, William, *Lord of the Flies* (New York: Perigee, 1954).

Golding, William, *Pincher Martin* (London: Faber, 1956).

Gombrich, E. H., *A Little History of the World*, trans. Caroline Mustill (New Haven: Yale University Press, 2005).

Gombrich, E. H., *The Story of Art* (London: Phaidon, 2006).

Goody, Jack, 'Watt, War, and Writing', *Stanford Humanities Review*, 8/1 (2000), 223–5.

Goody, Jack, and Ian Watt, 'The Consequences of Literacy', *Comparative Studies in Society and History*, 5/3 (April 1963), 304–45.

Gordon, Ernest, *Miracle on the River Kwai* (London: Collins, 1963).

Gordon, Ernest, 'No Hatred in My Heart', in Guthrie Moir (ed.), *Beyond Hatred* (Philadelphia: Fortress Press, 1970), 11–21.

Graff, Gerald, *Clueless in Academe: How Schooling Obscures the Life of the Mind* (New Haven: Yale University Press, 2003).

Green, Henry, *Back* (Champaign, IL: Dalkey Archive Press, 2009).

Greenblatt, Stephen, 'The Survivor: Life in the Death Camps', *San Francisco Review of Books*, 2 (May 1976), 3, 16.

Greene, Graham, 'The Portrait of a Lady', in Graham Greene, *Collected Essays* (London: Vintage, 2014), 44–50.

Greener, Leslie, *No Time to Look Back* (London: Gollancz, 1951).

Greif, Mark, *The Age of the Crisis of Man: Thought and Fiction in America, 1933–1973* (Princeton: Princeton University Press, 2015).

Haffenden, John, *William Empson*, i. *Among the Mandarins* (Oxford: Oxford University Press, 2009).

Hamilton, Patrick, *Impromptu in Moribundia* (London: Constable, 1939).

Hamilton, Patrick *Mr Stimpson and Mr Gorse*, in Patrick Hamilton, *The Gorse Trilogy* (London: Black Spring, 2007), 245–507.

Hamilton, Patrick, *The Slaves of Solitude* (New York: New York Review of Books, 2007).

Hardie, Robert, *The Burma–Siam Railway* (London: Imperial War Museum, 1983).

Hare, R. M., 'A Philosophical Autobiography', *Utilitas*, 14/3 (November 2002), 269–305.

Hastain, Ronald, *White Coolie* (London: Hodder & Stoughton, 1947).

Havers, R. P. W., *Reassessing the Japanese Prisoner of War Experience: The Changi Camp, Singapore, 1942–5* (London: RoutledgeCurzon, 2003).

Hepburn, Allan, 'Trials and Errors: *The Heat of the Day* and Post-War Culpability', in Kristin Bluemel (ed.), *Intermodernism: Literary Culture in Mid-Twentieth-Century Britain* (Edinburgh: Edinburgh University Press, 2009), 131–49.

Herman, Judith Lewis, *Trauma and Recovery: From Domestic Abuse to Political Terror* (London: Pandora, 1992).

Herman, Peter C. (ed.), *Historicizing Theory* (Albany, NY: State University of New York Press, 2004).

Hilliard, Christopher, *English as a Vocation: The* Scrutiny *Movement* (Oxford: Oxford University Press, 2012).

Hirsch, David H., 'The Reality of Ian Watt', *Critical Quarterly*, 2/2 (Summer 1969), 164–79.
Hitchens, Christopher, *Hitch-22* (London: Atlantic Books, 2010).
Hoggart, Richard, *The Uses of Literacy* (London: Penguin, 1990).
Holderness, Clifford G., and Jeffrey Pontiff, 'Hierarchies and the Survival of Prisoners of War during World War II', *Management Science*, 58/10 (October 2012), 1873–86.
Holeywell, Kathryn, 'The Origins of a Creative Writing Programme at the University of East Anglia, 1963–66', *New Writing: The International Journal for the Practice and Theory of Creative Writing*, 6/1 (2009), 15–24.
Hough, Graham, *Image and Experience: Studies in a Literary Revolution* (London: Duckworth, 1960).
Hough, Graham, 'Prisoners', *London Review of Books*, 8 May 1986, 8–9.
Howe, Irving, 'Criticism at its Best', *Partisan Review*, 25 (1958), 145–50.
Howe, Irving, *Politics and the Novel* (New York: Horizon Press, 1960).
Hunter, J. Paul, *Before Novels: The Cultural Contexts of Eighteenth-Century Fiction* (New York: Norton, 1990).
Hynes, Samuel, '*Conrad in the Nineteenth Century*, by Ian Watt', *Nineteenth-Century Fiction*, 35/4 (March 1981), 535–40.
Hynes, Samuel, *Flights of Passage: Recollections of a World War II Aviator* (New York: Penguin, 2003).
Hynes, Samuel, *The Soldiers' Tale: Bearing Witness to Modern War* (London: Penguin, 1997).
Inglis, Fred, *Raymond Williams* (London: Routledge, 1995).
Isherwood, Christopher, *The Berlin Novels* (London: Vintage, 1999).
Jackson, Daphne, *Java Nightmare* (Padstow: Tabb House, 1979).
Johnson, Samuel, 'The New Realistic Novel', in Samuel Johnson, *The Major Works*, ed. Donald Greene (Oxford: Oxford University Press, 2008), 175–9.
Jordan, John O., 'The Critic as Host: On Ian Watt's "Oral Dickens"', *Stanford Humanities Review*, 8/1 (2000), 197–205.
Joyaux, Georges, '*The Bridge over the River Kwai*: From the Novel to the Movie', *Literature/Film Quarterly*, 2 (1974), 174–82.
Judt, Tony, *Postwar: A History of Europe since 1945* (New York: Penguin, 2005).
Kemball Price, R., 'R. A. P. W. I.: An Impression', *British Medical Journal*, 1/4451, 27 April 1946, 647.
Kermode, Frank, 'Foreword', in Ian Watt, *Essays on Conrad*, ed. Frank Kermode (Cambridge: Cambridge University Press, 2000), vii–xi.
Keymer, Tom, *Richardson's* Clarissa *and the Eighteenth-Century Reader* (Cambridge: Cambridge University Press, 1992).
Kinvig, Clifford, 'Allied POW's and the Burma–Thailand Railway', in Philip Towle, Margaret Kosuge, and Yoichi Kibata (eds), *Japanese Prisoners of War* (London: Hambledon and London, 2000), 37–58.
Kinvig, Clifford, *River Kwai Railway: The Story of the Burma–Siam Railroad* (London: Brassey's, 1992).
Kirsch, Adam, *Why Trilling Matters* (New Haven: Yale University Press, 2011).

Knights, L. C., 'The University Teaching of English and History: A Plea for Correlation' (1939), in L. C. Knights, *Explorations: Essays in Criticism Mainly on the Literature of the Seventeenth Century* (London: Chatto & Windus, 1946), 186–99.

Koestler, Arthur, *The Invisible Writing: The Second Volume of an Autobiography: 1932–40* (London: Vintage, 2005).

Kundera, Milan, *The Curtain: An Essay in Seven Parts*, trans. Linda Asher (New York: HarperCollins, 2008).

Lamb, Jonathan, *The Rhetoric of Suffering: Reading the Book of Job in the Eighteenth Century* (Oxford: Clarendon Press, 1995).

Leavis, F. R., *Education and the University: A Sketch for an 'English School'* (London: Chatto & Windus, 1943).

Leavis, F. R., *The Great Tradition: George Eliot, Henry James, Joseph Conrad* (London: Penguin, 1983).

Leavis, Q. D., *Fiction and the Reading Public* (London: Chatto & Windus, 1939).

Leavis, Q. D., 'Letters: The Leavises on Dickens', *Listener*, 8 April 1971.

Levi, Primo, *The Drowned and the Saved*, trans. Raymond Rosenthal (New York: Vintage, 1989).

Levi, Primo, *The Reawakening*, trans. Stuart Woolf (New York: Simon & Schuster, 1995).

Levi, Primo, *Survival in Auschwitz: The Nazi Assault on Humanity*, trans. Stuart Woolf (New York: Simon & Schuster, 1996).

Levi, Primo, 'Germaine Greer Talks to Primo Levi', in Primo Levi, *The Voice of Memory: Interviews 1961–87*, ed. Marco Belpoliti and Robert Gordon, trans. Robert Gordon (Cambridge: Polity, 2001), 3–12.

Lewis, C. S., *The Abolition of Man* (Las Vegas: Lits, 2010).

Leys, Ruth, *Trauma: A Genealogy* (Chicago: University of Chicago Press, 2000).

Lindenberger, Herbert, 'The Singular Career of Ian Watt', *Stanford Humanities Review*, 8/1 (2000): 3–9.

Lomax, Eric, *The Railway Man* (New York: Norton, 1995).

Luckhurst, Roger, 'Petition, Repetition, and "Autobiography"', *Contemporary Literature*, 35/4 (Winter 1994), 688–708.

Lynch, Deidre Shauna, *The Economy of Character: Novels, Market Culture, and the Business of Inner Meaning* (Chicago: University of Chicago Press, 1998).

MacArthur, Brian, *Surviving the Sword: Prisoners of the Japanese in the Far East, 1942–45* (New York: Random House, 2005).

McCormack, Gavan, and Hank Nelson (eds), *The Burma–Thailand Railway* (Chiang Mai: Silkworm Press, 1993).

McDougall, William H., *By Eastern Windows: The Story of a Battle of Souls and Minds in the Prison Camps of Sumatra* (London: Arthur Barker, 1951).

McGinn, Colin, 'Philosophy and Literature in the 1950s: The Rise of the "Ordinary Bloke"', in Zachary Leader (ed.), *The Movement Reconsidered: Essays on Larkin, Amis, Gunn, Davie, and their Contemporaries* (Oxford: Oxford University Press, 2009), 123–38.

McGowran, Tom, *Beyond the Bamboo Screen: Scottish Prisoners of War under the Japanese* (Dunfermline: Cualann Press, 1999).
MacKenzie, S. P., 'The Treatment of Prisoners of War in World War II', *Journal of Modern History*, 66/3 (September 1994), 487–520.
McKeon, Michael, *Origins of the English Novel, 1600–1740* (Baltimore: Johns Hopkins University Press, 1987).
McKillop, A. D., *The Early Masters of English Fiction* (Lawrence, KS: University of Kansas Press, 1956).
McKillop, Alan D., '*The Rise of the Novel: Studies in Defoe, Richardson, and Fielding*, by Ian Watt', *Modern Philology*, 55/3 (February 1958), 208–9.
MacKillop, Ian, *F. R. Leavis: A Life in Criticism* (London: Penguin, 1995).
Macpherson, Sandra, *Harm's Way: Tragic Responsibility and the Novel Form* (Baltimore: Johns Hopkins University Press, 2010).
Mepham, John, 'Varieties of Modernism, Varieties of Incomprehension: Patrick Hamilton and Elizabeth Bowen', in Marina MacKay and Lyndsey Stonebridge (eds), *British Fiction after Modernism: The Novel at Mid-Century* (Basingstoke: Palgrave, 2007), 59–76.
Miller, D. A., *The Novel and the Police* (Berkeley and Los Angeles: University of California Press, 1988).
Morgan, Charlotte E., *The Rise of the Novel of Manners: A Study of English Prose Fiction between 1600 and 1740* (New York: Columbia University Press, 1911).
Moser, Thomas C., 'Some Reminiscences', *Stanford Humanities Review*, 8/1 (2000), 33–41.
Mowry, Melissa, 'Women, Work, Rearguard Politics, and Defoe's Moll Flanders', *Eighteenth Century*, 49/2 (Summer 2008), 97–116.
Murdoch, Iris, *Under the Net* (London: Penguin, 1982).
Norris, Margot, *Writing War in the Twentieth Century* (Charlottesville, VA: University Press of Virginia, 2000).
North, Joseph, *Literary Criticism: A Concise Political History* (Cambridge, MA: Harvard University Press, 2017).
Noszlopy, Laura, 'Railroad of Death: An Introduction', in John Coast, *Railroad of Death* (Newcastle: Myrmidon, 2014), xiv–xxxv.
Novak, Maximillian E., *Daniel Defoe: Master of Fictions* (Oxford: Oxford University Press, 2001).
Orwell, George, *Nineteen Eighty-Four* (New York: Signet, 1977).
Orwell, George, 'Politics and the English Language', in *The Complete Works of George Orwell*, xvii, ed. Peter Davison assisted by Ian Angus and Sheila Davison (London: Secker & Warburg, 1998), 421–32.
Orwell, George, 'Why I Write', in *The Complete Works of George Orwell*, xviii, ed. Peter Davison assisted by Ian Angus and Sheila Davison (London: Secker & Warburg, 1998), 316–21.
Owtram, Cary, *1000 Days on the River Kwai* (Barnsley: Pen & Sword, 2017).
Parkes, Meg, 'Tins, Tubes and Tenacity: Inventive Medicine in Camps in the Far East', in Gilly Carr and Harold Mytum (eds), *Cultural Heritage and*

Prisoners of War: Creativity behind Barbed Wire (New York: Routledge, 2012), 51–65.

Parkes, Meg, and Geoff Gill, *Captive Memories: Starvation, Disease, Survival* (Lancaster: Palatine Books, 2015).

Parkin, Ray, *Into the Smother: A Journal of the Burma–Siam Railway* (London: Hogarth, 1963).

Parrinder, Patrick, *Nation and Novel: The English Novel from its Origins to the Present Day* (Oxford: Oxford University Press, 2006).

Paulson, Ronald, *The Life of Henry Fielding* (Oxford: Blackwell, 2000).

Peek, Ian Denys, *One Fourteenth of an Elephant: A Memoir of Life and Death on the Burma–Thailand Railway* (London: Bantam, 2005).

Piette, Adam, *Imagination at War: British Fiction and Poetry 1939–1945* (London: Papermac, 1995).

Piper, David, *I Am Well, Who Are You? Writings of a Japanese Prisoner of War* (Exeter: Anne Piper, 1998).

Ponge, Francis, *Le Parti pris des choses* (Paris: Gallimard, 1942).

Powell, Anthony, *Temporary Kings*, in Anthony Powell, *A Dance to the Music of Time, Fourth Movement* (Chicago: University of Chicago Press, 1995).

Price, Leah, *The Anthology and the Rise of the Novel* (Cambridge: Cambridge University Press, 2000).

Raber, Karen, 'Michel Foucault and the Specter of War', in Peter C. Herman (ed.), *Historicizing Theory* (Albany, NY: State University of New York Press, 2004), 49–67.

Radcliffe, Ann, *The Mysteries of Udolpho* (Oxford: Oxford University Press, 1998).

Radford, R. A., 'The Economic Organisation of a P. O. W. Camp', *Economica*, 12/48 (November 1945), 189–201.

Ransom, John Crowe, 'Criticism as Pure Speculation', in Donald A. Stauffer (ed.), *The Intent of the Critic* (Princeton: Princeton University Press, 1941), 91–124.

Rawicz, Piotr, *Blood from the Sky*, trans. Peter Wiles (New Haven: Yale University Press, 2003).

Rawlings, Leo, *And the Dawn Came up like Thunder* (Newcastle upon Tyne: Myrmidon, 2015).

Rawson, C. J., *Henry Fielding* (London: Routledge & Kegan Paul, 1968).

Read, Rupert, 'Wittgenstein's *Philosophical Investigations* as a War Book', *New Literary History*, 41/3 (Summer 2010), 593–612.

Reeve, Clara, *The Progress of Romance*, ii (New York: Facsimile Text Society, 1930).

Richards, I. A., *Practical Criticism: A Study of Literary Judgment* (San Diego: Harcourt Brace Jovanovich, 1929).

Richardson, Samuel, *Pamela* (Oxford: Oxford University Press, 2001).

Richardson, Samuel, *Clarissa* (Penguin: London, 2004).

Richetti, John, 'Defoe as Narrative Innovator', in John Richetti (ed.), *The Cambridge Companion to Daniel Defoe* (Cambridge: Cambridge University Press, 2008), 121–38.

Richetti, John, 'The Legacy of Ian Watt's *The Rise of the Novel*', in Leo Damrosch (ed.), *The Profession of Eighteenth-Century Literature: Reflections on an Institution* (Madison: University of Wisconsin Press, 1992), 95–112.

Richetti, John, *The English Novel in History, 1700–1780* (London: Routledge, 1999).

Richetti, John, *The Life of Daniel Defoe* (Malden, MA: Blackwell, 2005).

Rivett, Rohan D., *Behind Bamboo: An Inside Story of the Japanese Prison Camps* (Sydney: Angus & Robertson, 1946).

Robson, D., E. Welch, N. J. Beeching, and G. V. Gill, 'Consequences of Captivity: Health Effects of Far East Imprisonment in World War II', *QJM: An International Journal of Medicine*, 102/2 (2009), 87–96.

Rodden, John, *Lionel Trilling and the Critics* (Lincoln, NE: University of Nebraska Press, 1999).

Roland, Charles G., 'Stripping away the Veneer: P. O. W. Survival in the Far East as an Index of Cultural Atavism', *Journal of Military History*, 53/1 (January 1989), 79–94.

Russell, Anne, 'Maurice Evans' *G. I. Hamlet*', in Irena R. Makaryk and Marissa McHugh (eds), *Shakespeare and the Second World War: Memory, Culture, Identity* (Toronto: University of Toronto Press, 2012), 233–51.

Russell, Lord Russell of Liverpool, *The Knights of Bushido* (Bath: Chivers Press, 1985).

Sage, Lorna, 'Obituary: Professor Nicholas Brooke', *Independent*, 10 November 1998.

Said, Edward W., 'Conrad in the Nineteenth Century', *New York Times*, 9 March 1980.

Said, Edward, *Humanism and Democratic Criticism* (New York: Columbia University Press, 2004).

Saint-Amour, Paul, *Tense Future: Modernism, Total War, Encyclopedic Form* (New York: Oxford University Press, 2015).

Sanderson, Michael, *The History of the University of East Anglia, Norwich* (London: Hambledon & London, 2000).

Sanyal, Debarati, 'A Soccer Match in Auschwitz: Passing Culpability in Holocaust Criticism', *Representations*, 79/1 (Summer 2002), 1–27.

Sartre, Jean-Paul, *What Is Literature? and Other Essays* (Cambridge, MA: Harvard University Press, 1988).

Schwartz, Daniel R., 'The Importance of Ian Watt's *The Rise of the Novel*', *Journal of Narrative Technique*, 13/2 (Spring 1983), 59–73.

Seager, Nicholas, *The Rise of the Novel* (Basingstoke: Macmillan, 2012).

Searle, Ronald, *To the Kwai—and Back: War Drawings 1939–1945* (London: Souvenir Press, 2006).

Shakespeare, William, *The New Cambridge Shakespeare: Measure for Measure*, ed. Brian Gibbons (Cambridge: Cambridge University Press, 2006).

Shephard, Ben, *A War of Nerves* (London: Jonathan Cape, 2000).

Siebers, Tobin, *Cold War Criticism and the Politics of Skepticism* (New York: Oxford University Press, 1993).

Sillitoe, Alan, 'The Disgrace of Jim Scarfedale', in Alan Sillitoe, *The Loneliness of the Long Distance Runner* (New York: Vintage, 1987), 139–55.
Slaughter, Joseph, *Human Rights, Inc: The World Novel, Narrative Form, and International Law* (New York: Fordham University Press, 2007).
Smith, Donald, *And All the Trumpets* (London: Geoffrey Bles, 1954).
Solzhenitsyn, Alexsandr, *One Day in the Life of Ivan Denisovich*, trans. H. T. Willetts (New York: Farrar, Straus & Giroux, 2005).
Solzhenitsyn, Aleksandr, *In the First Circle*, trans. Harry Willets (New York: HarperCollins, 2009).
Spanos, William V., *In the Neighborhood of Zero: A World War II Memoir* (Lincoln, NE: University of Nebraska Press, 2010).
Spark, Muriel, *The Ballad of Peckham Rye* (New York: New Directions, 1999).
Spark, Muriel, 'Daughter of the Soil', in Muriel Spark, *The Golden Fleece: Essays*, ed. Penelope Jardine (Manchester: Carcanet, 2014), 151–4.
Spark, Muriel, *The Girls of Slender Means* (New York: New Directions, 1998).
Spencer, Jane, *The Rise of the Woman Novelist* (Oxford: Oxford University Press, 1986).
Sprat, Thomas, *History of the Royal Society* (Whitefish, MT: Kessinger, 2003).
Stark, Ryan J., 'Language Reform in the Late Seventeenth Century', in Tina Skouen and Ryan J. Stark (eds), *Rhetoric and the Early Royal Society: A Sourcebook* (Leiden: Brill, 2015), 94–127.
Stonebridge, Lyndsey, *The Judicial Imagination: Writing after Nuremberg* (Edinburgh: Edinburgh University Press, 2011).
Swaminathan, Srividhya, 'Defoe's Alternative Conduct Manual: Survival Strategies and Female Networks in *Moll Flanders*', *Eighteenth-Century Fiction*, 15/2 (January 2003), 185–206.
Tawney, R. H., *Social History and Literature* (London: Cambridge University Press for the National Book League, 1950).
Thirkell, Angela, *Miss Bunting* (Wakefield, RI: Moyer Bell, 1996).
Thistlethwaite, Frank, *Origins: A Personal Reminiscence of UEA's Foundation* (Cambridge: Frank Thistlethwaite, 2000).
Thomas, Vivian, *The Moral Universe of Shakespeare's Problem Plays* (London: Routledge, 1991).
Todorov, Tzetan, *Literature and its Theorists: A Personal View of Twentieth-Century Criticism*, trans. Catherine Porter (Ithaca, NY: Cornell University Press, 1987).
Twigg, Reg, *Survivor on the River Kwai: The Incredible Story of Life on the Burma Railway* (London: Penguin, 2013).
Urquhart, Alistair, *The Forgotten Highlander: My Incredible Story of Survival during the War in the Far East* (Abacus: London, 2011).
Velmans, Loet, *Long Way back to the River Kwai: Memories of World War II* (New York: Arcade, 2003).
Vickers, Brian, 'The Royal Society and English Prose Style: A Reassessment', in Brian Vickers and Nancy S. Streuver, *Rhetoric and the Pursuit of Truth:*

Language Change in the Seventeenth and Eighteenth Centuries (Los Angeles: William Andrews Clark Memorial Library, 1985), 1–76.

Wandor, Michelene, *The Author is not Dead, Merely Somewhere Else: Creative Writing Reconceived* (Basingstoke: Palgrave Macmillan, 2008).

War Office, *A Handbook for the Information of Relatives and Friends of Prisoners of War* (London: HMSO, 1943).

Warner, William Beatty, *Reading 'Clarissa': The Struggles of Interpretation* (New Haven: Yale University Press, 1979).

Warner, William Beatty, *Licensing Entertainment: The Elevation of Novel Reading in Britain, 1684–1750* (Berkeley and Los Angeles: University of California Press, 1998).

Waterford, Van, *Prisoners of the Japanese in World War II* (Jefferson, NC: McFarland, 1994).

Watson, George, *Never Ones for Theory? England and the War of Ideas* (Cambridge: Lutterworth Press, 2000).

Watt, Ian, '*Robinson Crusoe* as a Myth', *Essays in Criticism*, 1/2 (April 1951), 95–119.

Watt, Ian, 'Should Criticism be Humanist?', *Listener*, 4 September 1952.

Watt, Ian, 'The Liberty of the Prison: Reflections of a Prisoner of War', *Yale Review*, 44 (1956), 514–32.

Watt, Ian, '*The Early Masters of English Fiction*, by Alan Dugald McKillop', *Modern Philology*, 55/2 (November 1957), 132–4.

Watt, Ian, 'Bridges over the Kwai', *Listener*, 6 August 1959.

Watt, Ian, 'Dr. Samuel Johnson after 250 Years', *Listener*, 24 September 1959.

Watt, Ian, 'The Idea of an English School: English at Norwich', *Critical Survey*, 1 (Autumn 1962), 42–6.

Watt, Ian, 'The Seminar', *Universities Quarterly*, 18 (1964), 369–89.

Watt, Ian, 'The University of East Anglia: Some Notes on Progress', *Critical Survey*, 1/4 (Summer 1964), 246–53.

Watt, Ian, 'Samuel Richardson', in Ian Watt et al., *The Novelist as Innovator* (London: British Broadcasting Corporation, 1965), 1–15.

Watt, Ian, 'The Recent Critical Fortunes of Moll Flanders', *Eighteenth-Century Studies*, 1/1 (Autumn 1967), 109–26.

Watt, Ian, 'Reunion on the Kwai', *Southern Review*, 5 (1969), 704–26.

Watt, Ian, 'Writing about Literature', *Glosses*, 1/1 (1970), 2–4.

Watt, Ian, 'The Leavises on Dickens', *Listener*, 11 March 1971.

Watt, Ian, 'On not Attempting to Be a Piano', *Profession* (1978), 13–15.

Watt, Ian, *Conrad in the Nineteenth Century* (Berkeley and Los Angeles: University of California Press, 1979).

Watt, Ian, *Joseph Conrad: Nostromo* (Cambridge: Cambridge University Press, 1988).

Watt, Ian, *Myths of Modern Individualism: Faust, Don Quixote, Don Juan, Robinson Crusoe* (Cambridge: Cambridge University Press, 1996).

Watt, Ian, 'Around Conrad's Grave in the Canterbury Cemetery—A Retrospect', in Ian Watt, *Essays on Conrad*, ed. Frank Kermode (Cambridge: Cambridge University Press, 2000), 186–91.

Watt, Ian, 'Conrad Criticism and *The Nigger of the "Narcissus"*', in Ian Watt, *Essays on Conrad*, ed. Frank Kermode (Cambridge: Cambridge University Press, 2000), 64–84.

Watt, Ian, 'Flat-Footed and Fly-Blown: The Realities of Realism', *Stanford Humanities Review*, 8/1 (2000), 53–69.

Watt, Ian, 'Joseph Conrad: Alienation and Commitment', in Ian Watt, *Essays on Conrad*, ed. Frank Kermode (Cambridge: Cambridge University Press, 2000), 1–19.

Watt, Ian, 'Oral Dickens', *Stanford Humanities Review*, 8/1 (2000), 206–22.

Watt, Ian, 'Realism and Modern Criticism of the Novel', *Stanford Humanities Review*, 8/1 (2000), 70–85.

Watt, Ian, '*The Bridge over the River Kwai* as Myth', in Ian Watt, *Essays on Conrad*, ed. Frank Kermode (Cambridge: Cambridge University Press, 2000), 192–207.

Watt, Ian, *The Rise of the Novel: Studies in Defoe, Richardson and Fielding* (Berkeley and Los Angeles: University of California Press, 2001).

Watt, Ian, 'The Augustan Age', in Ian Watt, *The Literal Imagination: Selected Essays*, ed. Bruce Thompson (Palo Alto: Society for the Promotion of Science and Scholarship and the Stanford Humanities Center, 2002), 20–36.

Watt, Ian, 'The First Paragraph of *The Ambassadors*: An Explication', in Ian Watt, *The Literal Imagination: Selected Essays*, ed. Bruce Thompson (Palo Alto: Society for the Promotion of Science and Scholarship and the Stanford Humanities Center, 2002), 194–215.

Watt, Ian, 'The Humanities on the River Kwai', in Ian Watt, *The Literal Imagination: Selected Essays*, ed. Bruce Thompson (Palo Alto: Society for the Promotion of Science and Scholarship and the Stanford Humanities Center, 2002), 229–52.

Watt, Ian, 'The Ironic Voice', in Ian Watt, *The Literal Imagination: Selected Essays*, ed. Bruce Thompson (Palo Alto: Society for the Promotion of Science and Scholarship and the Stanford Humanities Center, 2002), 37–50.

Watt, Ian, 'On Reading *Joseph Andrews*', in Ian Watt, *The Literal Imagination: Selected Essays*, ed. Bruce Thompson (Palo Alto: Society for the Promotion of Science and Scholarship and the Stanford Humanities Center, 2002), 117–25.

Watt, Ian, 'Serious Reflections on *The Rise of the Novel*', in Ian Watt, *The Literal Imagination: Selected Essays*, ed. Bruce Thompson (Palo Alto: Society for the Promotion of Science and Scholarship and the Stanford Humanities Center, 2002), 1–19.

Watt, Ian, 'Winston Smith: The Last Humanist', in Ian Watt, *The Literal Imagination: Selected Essays*, ed. Bruce Thompson (Palo Alto: Society for the Promotion of Science and Scholarship and the Stanford Humanities Center, 2002), 216–28.

West, Rebecca, *The Meaning of Treason* (London: Reprint Society, 1952).

West, Rebecca, *A Train of Powder: Six Reports on the Problem of Guilt and Punishment in our Time* (Chicago: Ivan R. Dee, 2000).

Whitecross, Roy, *Slaves of the Son of Heaven: A Personal Account of an Australian POW, 1942–1945* (East Roseville, New South Wales: Kangaroo Press, 2000).
Williams, Raymond, 'The Structure of Complex Words', *English*, 9/49 (March 1952), 27–8.
Williams, Raymond, *Keywords: A Vocabulary of Culture and Society* (London: Fontana, 1976).
Williams, Raymond, *Politics and Letters: Interviews with New Left Review* (London: New Left Books, 1979).
Williams, Raymond, *The Long Revolution* (Peterborough, Ontario: Broadview Press, 2001).
Wilson Knight, G., *This Sceptred Isle: Shakespeare's Message for England at War* (Oxford: Basil Blackwell, 1940).
Wilson Knight, G., *Collected Works*, vi. *Shakespearian Production* (London: Routledge, 2002).
Wood, Michael, *On Empson* (Princeton: Princeton University Press, 2017).
Woolf, Virginia, *The Common Reader, First Series* (Orlando, FL: Harcourt, 1984).
Wright, Pattie, *Men of the Line: Stories of the Thai–Burma Railway Survivors* (Carlton, Victoria: Miegunyah Press/Melbourne University Publishing, 2008).
Yeats, W. B. (ed.), *The Oxford Book of Modern Verse, 1892–1935* (Oxford: Oxford University Press, 1936).

[illegible] Has Everything[illegible]

[illegible]

Index